Your
10 Keys to
Happiness

Chicken Soup for the Soul: Your 10 Keys to Happiness
101 Real-Life Stories that Will Show You How to Improve Your Life
Amy Newmark

Published by Chicken Soup for the Soul, LLC www.chickensoup.com

Front cover photo courtesy of iStockphoto.com/RichVintage (©RichVintage)
Back cover and interior photo courtesy of iStockphoto.com/Sergnester (©Sergnester)
Photo of Amy Newmark courtesy of Susan Morrow at SwickPix

Cover and Interior by Daniel Zaccari

Distributed to the booktrade by Simon & Schuster. SAN: 200-2442

Publisher's Cataloging-In-Publication Data
(Prepared by The Donohue Group, Inc.)

Names: Newmark, Amy, compiler.
Title: Chicken soup for the soul : your 10 keys to happiness : 101 real-
    life stories that will show you how to improve your life / [compiled
    by] Amy Newmark.
Other Titles: Your 10 keys to happiness : 101 real-life stories that will
    show you how to improve your life | Your ten keys to happiness : 101
    real-life stories that will show you how to improve your life
Description: [Cos Cob, Connecticut] : Chicken Soup for the Soul, LLC,
    [2022]
Identifiers: ISBN 9781611590913 (print) | ISBN 9781611593303 (ebook)
Subjects: LCSH: Happiness--Literary collections. | Happiness--Anecdotes. |
    Self-actualization (Psychology)--Literary collections. | Self-
    actualization (Psychology)--Anecdotes. | Conduct of life--Literary
    collections. | Conduct of life--Anecdotes. | LCGFT: Anecdotes.
Classification: LCC BF575.H27 .C45 2022 (print) | LCC BF575.H27 (ebook) |
    DDC 158.1--dc23

Library of Congress Control Number: 2022933739

PRINTED IN THE UNITED STATES OF AMERICA
on acid∞free paper

28 27 26 25 24 23 22   01 02 03 04 05 06 07 08 09 10 11

Your
10 Keys to
Happiness

101 Real-Life Stories that Will Show You How to Improve Your Life

Amy Newmark

Chicken Soup for the Soul, LLC
Cos Cob, CT

Changing your life one story at a time®
www.chickensoup.com

Table of Contents

❸

~Help Someone Else~

❹

~Have Less Stuff~

5

~Think Positive~

6

~Make Me Time~

7

~Step Outside Your Comfort Zone~

8

~Be Yourself~

9

~Pursue Your Passion~

⑩

~Get Outside in Nature~

Introduction

've been the publisher and editor-in-chief of Chicken Soup for the Soul since 2008, and I've been privileged to publish 182 of our books during that time, comprising almost 18,000 stories. I've also read about 15,000 stories that were published in the *Chicken Soup for the Soul* books that predated me. And then there are the tens of thousands of stories that I've read that were submitted to us but not used in our books.

It's a lot of reading, but more importantly, it's a lot of exposure to the personal, revealing, introspective stories that our writers have shared with us. I've noticed certain recurring themes, and they all revolve around finding a path to happiness. Over these fourteen years, I've developed an understanding of what makes people tick and what helps the most in that quest.

So, this new collection of Chicken Soup for the Soul stories presents to you the ten most important keys to happiness based on my analysis of those tens of thousands of stories. I've tried out these ten keys to happiness in my own life and I can report that I am a happier, more grateful, more grounded, and more relaxed person as a result.

The wonderful thing is that you already have all the necessary tools to find your happiness — you just need to learn how to use them. And I chose these 101 inspirational, true stories from Chicken Soup for the Soul's library as great examples for you — so that you can figure out how you will use these ten keys to happiness in your own life. You don't have to implement all ten keys, by the way. Even one will make a huge difference!

You'll find the stories organized into the following chapters, one for each key:

1. Count Your Blessings
2. Free Yourself with Forgiveness
3. Help Someone Else
4. Have Less Stuff
5. Think Positive
6. Make Me Time
7. Step Outside Your Comfort Zone
8. Be Yourself
9. Pursue Your Passion
10. Get Outside in Nature

I'll meet you at the beginning of each chapter with an introduction that will serve as a guide to what you'll be reading. See you inside...

— Amy Newmark —

Count Your Blessings

What You'll Find in This Chapter

Grateful people are more fun. No one likes a complainer, and everyone loves an upbeat, optimistic person. Perhaps that's why scientific studies have proven that people who practice gratitude in their daily lives are happier, healthier, and more successful in their work and their relationships.

The wonderful thing about counting your blessings and practicing gratitude is that you don't have to be *born* that way. You can *learn* how to be a thankful person and enjoy the benefits of gratitude. It only takes a little practice to make it a regular part of your outlook—a habit.

Jennifer Quasha learned how to do that, as you'll read in her story, "The Happy Book," about how she overcame a fairly negative attitude toward life. Every night she wrote down one good thing that had happened that day—just one thing—and before she knew it, she had turned herself into an optimist instead of a pessimist.

"We can only be said to be alive in those moments when our hearts are conscious of our treasures," said the American playwright and novelist Thornton Wilder. That's what counting your blessings does—it keeps you energized and participating in the world with vim and vigor. And the great thing is that it's something you can easily do, just by *deciding*.

Another way that our contributors developed their "attitude of gratitude" was by saying thank you—a lot. Just the act of giving thanks is a way to focus on what's good in your life and how blessed you are to have the people in your circle. In Allison Hermann Craigie's story,

"The Gratitude Party," you'll read about how she and her children went through a terrible period after a divorce and two family deaths. One day, they were discussing how they had made a comeback from that challenging time. They decided to hold a gratitude party for the people who had helped them over the prior year, and it became an annual tradition, motivating them to practice gratitude every day as they identified who should be on the guest list for their next party.

Some of us learn to use the power of gratitude early in our lives, and for some it even comes naturally. We each have different traits that are stronger in us. For me, gratitude is one of the strong ones. I almost always feel lucky and privileged and thankful for what I have. And that makes my days much brighter. Counting my blessings is my constant state of being.

In this chapter you will read stories about how to find your gratitude, whether it's by making lists, reaching out to thank people, or just approaching each day with a positive attitude. You'll read about families who have gone back to basics and are so much happier with their new focus on what really matters. You'll read inspirational tales of people who have overcome great challenges and the lessons they've learned. We also have some "wow" stories about silver linings, good fortune, and lucky coincidences that happened to people in the middle of their struggles.

I don't think you can be truly happy without incorporating gratitude into your life. That's why I've put this chapter first. It's the most important key to happiness that I know.

The Happy Book

Every day may not be good, but there's
something good in every day.
~Author Unknown

've spent a lot of my life unhappy. Looking back there were times that it was okay to feel that way, for example when my parents got divorced, when I was mugged at gunpoint during a vacation, when two friends died in a car accident when I was in high school, and when I was brutally assaulted in my early twenties.

But there were the other times, too. In middle school I didn't think that I was as smart as everyone else; I didn't have cool enough clothes; my mother dropped me off at school in a beat-up car. Junior high was the same. I wasn't as tall and thin as all the other girls; my baby teeth hadn't fallen out yet; and where were my boobs? Fast forward to high school. Still the boys had eyes for others; still everyone was smarter; still everyone dressed better. Yes, my boobs had finally arrived, but somehow that paled in comparison to everything else. In my first job out of college I wasn't making as much money as my friends; my apartment wasn't as nice; when I looked around there was always something to feel miserable about.

I come from a long line of people who have suffered from diagnosable depression. When I was single, I assumed that was just who I was — it was the genes I had been dealt.

When I was twenty-four I met my husband. We got married three years later, and three years after that I had my first child.

Once we had kids, my excuse of "it's-in-the-genes" didn't work so well for me anymore because that meant my kids were going to be depressed. And although I realize that that still might be the case, I began looking at my unhappiness in a new way.

It was something I had to work on myself.

Over the years many things have helped me fight depression: healthy eating, exercise, fresh air, friends, volunteering, church, therapy and medicine. It all helps.

But I have a little secret, too.

It's an exercise that I do every night before bed. By the side of my bed I have a small datebook. It covers January to December, but it's small — every day only has enough space to write one line.

Every night I ask myself this question: "What made me the happiest today?"

Because I don't have space to write very much it seems easy, and it only takes me a few seconds. But in those seconds I replay my day and decide on its happiest moment. Some days I come up with answers I expect, and other days I find myself surprised.

> *Every night I ask myself this question: "What made me the happiest today?"*

Some days it's: "my husband came home early," "reading before bed with the kids," "laughing with a friend on the phone," "getting a parking space when I was late... right in front!"

And some days aren't as easy and it's: "finally getting to get into bed," "being able to stay calm during a fight with my daughter," "not having to cook dinner — again."

But the spin on my life has changed. I actively seek the positive. Every day.

And sometimes, if I have a sour day, I look back through the book, read, and remember those happy moments in the past.

In fact, I wish I had started my happy book back in middle

school. Entries might have been: "I don't need braces like everyone else," "I caught Charlie S. looking at me today," and "I didn't trip when I went up on stage to receive my Most Improved Player award."

—Jennifer Quasha—

Doing Dishes

*When all the dust is settled and all the crowds
are gone, the things that matter are faith,
family, and friends.*
~Barbara Bush

I survey the pile of dirty dishes filling the sink, trailing across the counter, spilling onto the stove, seeming to reproduce exponentially. With no working dishwasher other than my two hands, the task is daunting. Thank goodness we'd had leftovers the night before. No big pots and pans to scrub, just plates, glasses and silverware... tons of silverware. How can nine people, three of them children, use every knife, fork and spoon I own?

While I wait for hot water to fill the sink, I pick up a glass jammed into one corner of the counter. I study it. My eight-year-old grandson beamed last night when I handed it to him, milk sloshing over the rim. Shaped like a football, that glass has become his special glass every time he visits. I smile at his smile.

Still grumbling, though now somewhat subdued, I think back to how I was left with this mountain of dishes. This was what my family calls a "Birthday Weekend." We observe birthdays as long and as hard as we can. It's pure luck my birthday falls during the holiday season, wedged equidistant between Thanksgiving and Christmas. Sometimes, birthday "weekends" can last a full seven or eight days. Friday night was a birthday party for me, which included hosting thirteen people — nine family and four friends. My friends brought mounds of mashed sweet potatoes and a ham casserole, while my two daughters brought homemade rolls and a pot of delicious pinto beans. I supplied grilled chicken, gravy, and mincemeat pie.

My family returned last night, Saturday, to enjoy a leftover feast. Instead of cooking something new, we simply reheated — for the nine of us.

After dinner and with darkness threatening, the out-of-town daughter and son-in-law announced they had to leave. "Sorry about the dishes, Mom, but we've got a long drive ahead and, you know, the kids… school… work…" There was a hug with a whispered birthday wish for me. *Okay,* I thought. *Maybe I won't be left all alone.* I turned to my other daughter, who, with amazingly perfect timing, announced, "Didn't realize the time. Tomorrow's an early day. Gotta go." I think I heard a mumbled "Sorry" trailing after her. *Next time I see her, I'd better get a nice, long hug.* The door closed, and she and her husband drove off before I could hand her a dishtowel.

My husband, no stranger to hot water and dirty dishes, is recovering from slicing his hands while repairing a water heater. He reminds me his doctor gave strict instructions to "keep your hands dry." And besides, he shrugs, no gloves fit his big, bandaged hand.

Which left… me.

Now with the water nice and frothy and up to the brim, I plunge my hands into the warmth and bring up a tiny spoon, still encrusted with applesauce. I smile as I recall the eleven-month-old eating it with wild abandon.

I pick up a plate. Remnants of grilled chicken cling to the rim. The fragrance lingers. I smile. My husband cooked the chicken using one of those big-as-a-small-house grills, one he even polishes on occasion. He took great pride in doing the chicken just right.

A bowl with bits of lettuce stuck like glue to the side reminds me that my younger daughter's trying to eat healthy. It's a battle she wins at times, but when the craving for pasta at Olive Garden takes over, she succumbs. We've had countless discussions about food, weight and desires. I wash away the lettuce and piece of cabbage and wish she still lived at home. Even though she's set up her own house across town, I miss her.

My older daughter lives in the south-central part of the state, over sixty miles away, so I don't see her all that often. Busy with three active boys, her life is one of naps, diapers, homework and cooking. I remember her struggling to cut meat for the four-year-old, pick up the sippy cup thrown by the baby for the hundredth time, and correct the eight-year-old's table manners while attempting to eat her own supper.

Then it hits me. Standing with a spoon in my hand, tears run down my cheeks. Every dish, spoon and glass bring back memories. Good memories. My two daughters, now grown, get along better than they ever did as children. Their discussions range from current fashions to the best way to freeze blueberries to efficient vacuuming techniques. My sons-in-law now engage in long discussions over politics, educational reform and gaming strategies. They've become friends over the years. And the three grandsons seem to be perfectly at ease here in our house. The two oldest, as usual, wanted their bikes brought out of the garage to ride in last night's waning light. They whined when their dad nixed the idea. The baby, having taken his first steps mere days before, delighted us when he erupted with bursts of giggles at the feel of soft carpet under his foot instead of the usual hard vinyl.

It all floods back to me. My husband and I did the same thing at this same table not too many years ago — pick up sippy cups, correct table manners, listen to tiny, excited voices talk about Christmas. I sniff back a tear and pick up another fork, another memory.

Before I know it, the dishes are done, and the counter, stove and sink are empty once more.

Empty. But I'm not empty. My life isn't empty. It's full of happy, healthy adult children and blossoming grandchildren. My life is full.

And I thank the dishes for reminding me.

— Melody S. Groves —

The Blessings Box

Life's challenges are not supposed to paralyze you,
they're supposed to help you discover who you are.
~Bernice Johnson Reagon

The house seemed huge and empty. There was no talking, laughing, crying, stomping, thumping, music playing, television blaring. It was all gone.

My children, who were now nineteen and twenty years old, had both left for college at the same time. They moved too far away for quick visits and I found myself alone, struggling with this depressing change in my life. I had devoted my life to raising my children and although I worked, it was either at their school or from home where I would see them every day.

As the days turned to weeks and weeks to months I found that my loneliness and anxiety was only getting worse. I found a part-time job that got me out of the house. My husband tried to be around more and we worked on our marriage, but still, I felt like I was in mourning, dealing with the loss of my children, the family we once had. I suddenly had no purpose, no reason to get out of bed in the morning, no motivation to do anything.

My son Eric lived hours away in Virginia now and was active in ROTC and school. My daughter Emma lived even farther away from our Maryland home, in Vermont, and kept busy with school, her church and a job. She also fell in love with a young man she met at church. My kids were doing what I always prayed they would do — grow up and become respectful, serving adults — but I missed them terribly.

Of course, Emma's time was preoccupied with school and her new love. We adored him as well and when he asked if he could surprise Emma at Christmas by driving down from Vermont we were all thrilled. Suddenly the entire family was going to be together to celebrate Christmas. As excited as I was, I could not help but dwell on the fact that this time would go by quickly and in a matter of a few weeks, I would be back again in my empty, cold house. As hard as I tried to enjoy life with all the holiday festivities and kids home, I dared not let myself get too happy because I knew that once they left and the holidays were over I would be more depressed than ever.

After Kyle surprised Emma we all gathered in the living room to exchange some gifts. I smiled at all the happy faces and the love that filled the room. The house echoed with Christmas music, laughter and talk; a fire crackled and popped and sent a warm glow throughout the room. Having my kids at home was the best Christmas present ever. And then Emma handed me a wrapped gift. I slowly unwrapped it and held it in my hands. It was a wooden box.

"I made the box from old barn wood," Kyle said, smiling. And I knew immediately how special that was because Kyle was a carpenter and tore down old barns for the beams and timber.

"And I did the wood burning," Emma followed up.

I ran my fingers over the intricate scrolls and curves of the word "Blessings" and the flowers and vines Emma had burned into the wood. On the underside she had burned: "Merry Christmas, Love Emma and Kyle."

"It's a blessings box," Emma said. "You write down things you are thankful for and put them in the box. Then you can read them later when you're feeling down or sad and remind yourself of all the good things in your life."

That night, while the family was all there and the house seemed full of love and joy, I cleared a spot on my nightstand for the box. I wrote down the first thing I was thankful for and dated the paper: "Blessed to remember that no matter how far away my kids are they will always be my kids." I folded it up and tucked it into the box.

The next night I did the same thing. "Thankful for my husband and all he does for me."

And the next night, before bed, I wrote: "Thankful for the big house that can accommodate the family when they come to visit."

And the nights after that: "Blessed that I have a job to go to each day." "Thankful that I'm in good health." "Thankful for my parents."

I wrote down my blessings and prayers and things I was thankful for, no matter how big or small, for each night until the kids left. The holiday decorations came down and the house was once again empty, cold and lonely. My husband worked each day and I did too, but when I came home I felt like I was being swallowed up in the cold and loneliness of the house. As I changed into my pajamas one day after work, I spied the blessing box sitting under a pile of books and I quickly pulled it out. I ran my fingers over the box and the dovetail woodworking that was so carefully and thoughtfully done. I ran my fingers over the words and flowers and smiled, remembering the two special people who had made this gift for me.

One by one I pulled out each piece of paper, unfolded it, and read. I read them out loud so I could hear clearly what I had written.

"Thankful for the big house that can accommodate the family when they come to visit!"

I breathed in deeply as if trying to suck in the chill in the air, and the silence. I remembered the holiday season when the kids were home and thought about future visits. I thought about how not even distance can take my kids away — they will always be my children, and our home will always be their home. With each note I tucked in that box, I was reminded of all the good things in my life, all that I had to be thankful for.

As each week passed, and I wrote a note for the box nearly every night, it helped me to stay focused on the positive. And when I needed a lift or a reminder, there was always a word of encouragement in the Blessings Box.

Now I write notes weekly and re-read my notes of thankfulness often. It has helped me cope with depression and anxiety and has given me a new outlook on life. I'm learning to embrace the quiet times and even the big, old, empty house that has blessed us with so many memories and promises of more to come.

I am blessed and forever thankful for a daughter who recognized a need in her mother and helped her to cope and adjust with a simple idea, a precious gift that has changed everything—a blessings box.

—Jennifer Reed—

Being Happy Is Enough

*The happiest people don't necessarily have the best of
everything. They just make the best of everything.*
~Author Unknown

Someone on Facebook had shared pictures of her vacation in Europe. The delivery truck had dropped off a gargantuan entertainment system at my neighbor's house. And the kids came home from school raving about the new video game their friends had just gotten.

Meanwhile, we were living in a house furnished mostly with freebies and dressing our kids in secondhand clothes. And even when we and the kids had to go in three different directions at night, we didn't eat out. Ever.

I like to cook, and I'm good at it. But sometimes, you just want to be spared the hassle and the cleanup!

My poor mother-in-law, in town for a visit, got to hear the whole tirade that night. "I feel so resentful sometimes," I told her, as we cleared the table after dinner. "I know we're doing the right thing, living frugally, saving money, but it feels so hard. There are so many things I'd like to have, so many things I'd like to do, and we just can't."

She hummed once or twice, nodding as she folded a cloth napkin in silence. Then she turned to me. "You know," she said, "when you compare yourself to others, it's easy to focus on what you don't have. But there's one thing you two do that we don't see too much of in other married couples. You two make a priority of going out together and

> *"When you compare yourself to others, it's easy to focus on what you don't have."*

taking time to focus on your marriage. And that's a very important thing. You two have such a great marriage."

I stopped wiping the table and pondered that for a minute. I thought of the movie my husband and I had seen a week earlier, and the English country-dance we'd attended a few weeks before that. I remembered the bike rides and the concerts, the hikes and the picnics. Most of all, I thought of how happy we were together, even after twenty years. How many people can say that?

I looked around my home with new eyes. Our refrigerator is almost too small for a family of six, but it's always filled with food that is both nourishing and delicious. Our kitchen décor is cobbled together, but it comes to us from our grandmothers' homes after they passed away. And our deck overlooks a sycamore grove where our family cooks s'mores in the fire pit every few weeks.

Even without the big TV and the European vacations and the new wardrobe every season, we are… well… happy.

And you know what? That's enough.

— Kathleen M. Basi —

Every Day Is a Good Day

If you don't think every day is a good day,
just try missing one.
~Cavett Robert

"That's it. This is my last Christmas season working a retail job!" Those were the words I had uttered almost a year ago.

But here I was again, looking at aisles stocked with Christmas merchandise that we'd been receiving for the last four months. Our extended holiday hours would start the next week. I was still working retail, despite the pronouncement I'd made at the end of the last Christmas season.

I couldn't quit. I was in the midst of extensive dental work that would take another three months to complete. I needed the dental insurance and I needed the paychecks.

So here I was, locked into another holiday sales cycle, with the long hours, the demanding work, a new manager who pushed-pushed-pushed, and a store filled with stressed and irritable shoppers.

Our co-manager — the nice one, so I'll call him Angel — had a pet phrase he often used. It was his attempt to inspire us and remind us that we were in charge of our attitudes. "Every day's a good day!" he'd bellow as he unlocked the doors to let us in. "Welcome to where happy people come to work. Where every day's a good day."

Most of us, in our pre-caffeinated, still bleary-eyed state, mumbled a greeting in return. It was usually along the lines of "yeah, yeah" or "right," said as sarcastically as possible. We didn't appreciate Angel's "every day's a good day" line one bit.

And then one day I left work even more frustrated, aggravated, and angry than usual. It was one of those days when I would have given my notice in an instant. Except I couldn't. Not yet. I felt trapped.

For the first few minutes in the car I screamed at the top of my lungs. I shrieked. I yelled words that I typically don't use. I would be hoarse for the next two days.

That's when I knew that something had to change. I started listening to the words I told myself: "I'm too old for this. I'm too tired for this. I'll never make it through Christmas. I can't keep going like this. I don't have the energy to deal with this." I realized how negative the words I spoke to myself were.

The first change I made was in response to Angel's morning greeting. He'd say, "Every day's a good day!" Instead of scoffing, laughing or coming back with a smart aleck response, I'd answer, "Yes! Yes it is." Whether I agreed with the statement or not, I starting replying with positive words.

Next, I made a list of affirmations — positive statements to read aloud before I went to work each day:

- *I am flying through this Christmas season with ease.*
- *My energy levels are higher than ever.*
- *I enjoy my job and am thankful for the benefits I receive from it.*
- *I complete my tasks easily and quickly.*
- *I am drawn to foods that keep me healthy and give me energy.*
- *This is the easiest holiday season I've ever worked through.*

I started looking for other positive methods. I didn't want to merely survive these frantic months. I wanted to maintain a peaceful demeanor and have the energy to enjoy a happy home life after the work hours ended.

A CD with peaceful, meditative music caught my eye in the store. It turned out to be one of the best purchases I ever made. I listened to it on the way to work, to gear up for a good day. I listened to it on the way home, to calm down after a long, busy day.

One change that made the largest impact in my life was consciously developing an "Attitude of Gratitude." When I found myself reverting back to my negative, grumbling ways, I would deliberately shift my mind to an attitude of gratitude state. I would remind myself of all the good things:

- *I'm thankful that I have a car to get me here.*
- *I'm thankful that all my limbs are working.*
- *I'm thankful I can walk into work without assistance.*
- *I'm thankful to have a job and an income.*
- *I'm thankful I have eyes to see.*
- *I'm thankful I have the intelligence to do the math I need to properly do my job.*
- *I'm thankful I have a warm, dry house to go home to.*
- *I'm thankful for my children and grandchildren's health.*
- *I'm thankful the car is paid off.*
- *I'm thankful there's gas in the car.*
- *I'm thankful there are groceries in the house.*

As I started listing the multitude of reasons I had to be thankful, the list kept expanding. And as the list grew, the minor aggravations of my job seemed to shrink in comparison.

Another lesson I learned was to go easy on myself. If I had a bad day, one when I slipped back into negativity, instead of berating myself, I needed to accept my own imperfection. We all have bad days, and we move on from them.

Before I knew it, with consistent conscious thought, every day *was* a good day. One by one, they passed, and soon the Christmas season was behind us.

I not only survived, I thrived. And now I can join Angel and proudly proclaim: "Every day's a good day!"

— Trisha Faye —

The Gratitude Party

*Gratitude makes sense of our past, brings peace
for today, and creates a vision for tomorrow.*
~Melody Beattie

took a moment to step back and look around my patio. I smiled, because there, mingling in the glow of Tiki torches and citronella candles, were forty people who had earned a very special place in our hearts that year. I was struck by the perfect blend of delicious food, upbeat music and lively conversation.

I have always considered myself to be a grateful person. I was raised to thank people each time I received something as simple as a compliment and I was very conscious of this etiquette, so they knew I did not take them or their kindness for granted. In turn, I raised my children with the same values. Presents could be unwrapped but not played with until they had written a thank-you note. During dinner, we played the "Good News" game and shared the best things that happened that day. We live in a society of instant gratification and entitlement, so I wanted to slow my children down to appreciate what they had, irrespective of amount, magnitude or value.

I have been fortunate to enjoy a good life, albeit not always an easy one. I have two children who make me very happy, but each has issues that have required a good portion of my time and attention. I was divorced and living away from my family but enjoyed a network of wonderfully supportive friends. I always had a full-time job and spent countless additional hours working with my kids and volunteering.

To some, when I remarried, I lived a fairy tale. Life as we knew it changed dramatically and we happily moved near my family. It was the kind of life most only dreamt about, filled with vacations, private schools, household help, and effusive love bursting through the joints of the beautifully grand home we shared. It was perfect.

However, nothing is truly perfect, and in 2010 we were woken from our dream by a chain of events that unraveled our world in an excruciating manner with alarming speed. It began with the death of my devoted dad, whom I had been caring for over the last year. Losing the parent who was the heart of my support system and had guided me through some very difficult situations was my worst experience to date. We struggled to navigate life without his warmth, spot-on advice, and spirited wit.

While we mourned, we simultaneously took care of my mom, seeing her through chemotherapy as she bravely battled terminal cancer. In the midst of this, my husband abruptly left and filed for divorce. The shock of his departure and the numerous issues I now faced alone continued my slide into depression. The next few months brought the passing of my favorite aunt and then my favorite uncle. I felt lost when my kids visited their father, but in hindsight it gave me precious alone time with my mom, which was filled with long talks and laughter as our sarcastic nature deflected the pain of our circumstances.

My dream skidded into a living nightmare when shortly thereafter, my mom succumbed to her cancer and I became an overwhelmed, single, orphaned mom of two special needs kids. She was my best friend, confidante and cheerleader and her loss seemed insurmountable.

I don't remember many details from that year except that I was instantly humbled, knowing there were people smirking at my fall from grace. I have no recollection of house hunting, moving, enrolling my kids in a new school, or flying back and forth to meet with my siblings to manage the details of my parents' deaths.

I hid from the world, shopping at late hours and staying away from places frequented by people I knew. I couldn't wrap my head around all that had happened and I felt horribly alone. I had turned my kids' lives upside down, couldn't get an interview, let alone a job, and was in a house I soon wouldn't be able to afford, filled with possessions from my marriages that constantly reminded me of my failure.

I vacillated between wanting to live and hoping to die, believing my kids were better off without me. It was a daily battle with a deep depression where I struggled to get out of bed. I expressed my wish to die, be cremated and placed in the casket with my mother, where I could rest peacefully next to the one who understood and loved me unconditionally.

It was fortuitous that I had saved all of mom's voicemails from that last year and I listened to them often. At other times, I heard my mom's lilting voice in my head reminding me who I was at my core. "You were always a plugger" and "you're made of steel" she would tell me. Finally, I listened to her classic adage — "when you're done licking your wounds, you've got to pick yourself up by the bootstraps" — and I did just that. I went to a therapist, got medication, and many applications later, landed a job. Gratitude returned to my vernacular.

One day, my kids and I were discussing the positive path our lives were now on. With increasing fervor, we talked about all the people who had helped us through those dark days when nothing seemed possible. How could we ever thank them enough? Did they know just how much impact they had on our lives? Did they realize that watching the dog, meeting us for dinner, having a workout partner, hiring me for temporary work, providing oft-needed rides, a place to stay, a text to check in, a shoulder to cry on… that they had saved our lives? It was then that our annual Gratitude Party was conceived.

So, as I looked around the patio of the house I was now able to afford, during our third annual Gratitude Party, I was reminded of how far we had come. Every year we invite the people who had a positive impact on our lives in the previous year. They may have helped us in ways that seemed insignificant to them but were powerful to us. One year we read poems we had written about each person expressing why we were grateful. Another year, they wore custom-made badges that contained cryptic maxims like "I give Allison a reason to get up every morning" and the other guests had to guess why.

Although the Gratitude Party is a summation of the prior year, it is the daily practice of gratitude that keeps me moving forward. I take nothing for granted and continue to encourage my kids, now with renewed purpose, to be selfless, recall the good events of every day, and pay it forward. We maintain perspective and are thankful for the little things. We know very well that the little things are sometimes all we have and are quite often worthier than the big things.

> *It is the daily practice of gratitude that keeps me moving forward.*

—Allison Hermann Craigie—

The Journal

For each new morning with its light,
For rest and shelter of the night,
For health and food, for love and friends,
For everything Thy goodness sends.
~Ralph Waldo Emerson

t was almost Christmas in 1997. After going through a sad divorce I was happily remarried and enjoying life once again. My wonderful husband Joe and I went to work each morning to jobs we loved. On the weekends we went dancing at the local country western roadhouse. All of our children were doing well and were happy for our happiness. We were in a very good place and grateful for all that we had found in each other's love.

While I was Christmas shopping for my sisters at the local bookstore, I saw a display of gratitude journals. I decided to buy four of them, one for me and three for my sisters. My plan was that beginning on January 1st, we would write five things every day that we were grateful for in our lives. I looked forward to sharing my good life with my journal.

Starting the journal was fun, and I found five things to be grateful for every day without any problem at all. With my life sailing along so joyfully, it was easy to be grateful. I enjoyed the simple pleasure of sitting at my vanity every evening and writing my five entries. I entered the names of new friends we met and the musicals we saw together, the new restaurants we tried, the touching things my husband said to me, the exciting things my sons were doing, and the encouraging comments from the parents at work. On and on the words spilled from my pen.

But my life changed quickly and unexpectedly. On a Wednesday afternoon in early February there was a knock on my door that changed my life forever. When I opened the door, two men who worked with Joe stood in front of me with distraught expressions on their faces. They told me that Joe had been found on the floor in his office and taken to the hospital. They came to take me to see him. I climbed into the company car with shock. It was an icy day and the ride to the hospital was painfully slow. With the pinging sound of ice hitting the roof, I prayed to and bargained with God for Joe's life during the entire ride. But, it was too late. My husband had already died.

Keeping my gratitude journal wasn't so easy after that. Through February and March the pages of my journal stayed empty. I was too filled with fear and sorrow to make room for gratitude and optimism. But as the weeks went by, I began to realize that it is during the hard times that we most need to find and acknowledge the good things in our lives. I remembered learning at church that we are to be thankful in all circumstances. We're not expected to be thankful for all circumstances, but we are to be thankful in all circumstances.

I didn't want to be the kind of person who gave up on life. I decided to take on the challenge of being thankful and positive in the midst of my grief. Once again I sat down at the end of the day and tried to find five things that I was grateful for and write them in my journal. What had been so easy before my husband's death became a nightly struggle.

My first new entries into my journal were like those beginning steps that a little one takes on her first birthday. They were wobbly but determined, and often ended with a fall. One evening I remember crying and writing "I'm glad that this day is over" five times. But I stuck with it and slowly my gratefulness for life returned. By making myself write something every day, I forced my soul to see and feel the good mixed within my pain. The sun still rose, the flowering dogwood tree bloomed, the toddlers at the center still reached their arms out to me, the robins came back, and I could laugh at a corny joke once again!

Instead of trying to figure out the answers to all of my problems by myself, I asked God to send the right people into my life to help me. Again and again He did. A real estate friend found the perfect small house for me, and my family and friends helped me move into it on a warm day in May. Some family members and close friends donated money to help me out, and co-workers covered for me on days when I was clearly struggling. My sons knew when to comfort me and when to make me laugh. My best friend and her husband met me every Friday night for dinner and never once made me feel like the proverbial third wheel. Blessings just gushed into my life, and every night I listed them in my journal.

I still cried into my pillow some nights, but I began to understand that I was lucky to have memories so good they were worth crying about. It wasn't easy, but I began to feel powerful and strong enough to handle my life with grace and a sense of humor. I became the person I was meant to be.

I remarried three years ago, and despite many bumps along the way, my positive outlook continues to bring joy and contentment into my life. Even though my pessimistic husband Tom teases me about being a Pollyanna, I know that life looks better through the lenses of gratitude and positivity. Life is going well for me now, but I am wise enough to realize that I will face more difficult times. I know that I will be sad again, but I also know that with time a thankful optimism will replace my tears and carry me through. The twelve-dollar cost of that journal I bought so many years ago was such a small price for the lesson of a lifetime!

— Audrey Smith McLaughlin —

The Onion Room

Instead of complaining that the rosebush is full of thorns,
be happy that the thorn bush has roses.
~Proverb

I would have quit if I weren't the boss. It started when my first patient arrived thirty minutes late but demanded she still be seen. "It wasn't my fault — traffic was terrible."

The next patient screamed at my secretary for trying to collect a co-pay. After smoothing my receptionist's ruffled feathers, I entered the next exam room only to be handed a massive pile of forms needing completion — by tomorrow. Stir in the twenty minutes on hold with an insurance company, a patient hostile about her forty-minute wait, and a man who fainted when his blood was drawn, and my day became as enjoyable as a balloon ride in a tornado.

The final straw? Mrs. Smith informed me she had stopped her blood pressure medication a month ago and had replaced it with an herbal remedy she learned about online. The website claimed the 100 percent all-natural herb had "miraculous powers" to lower blood pressure.

"I'm just more comfortable going organic," she insisted. "According to the Internet, the blood pressure pills you prescribed are a synthetic poison." She glared at me as though I'd prescribed arsenic.

By stopping her "synthetic poison," her blood pressure registered a dangerous 220/110. In short, her all-natural, organic herb was nothing more than an expensive placebo — she might as well have swallowed a fistful of crabgrass. But try telling her that!

I exited her exam room a full hour behind schedule. My head pounded like a kettledrum and my neck muscles felt tighter than a banjo string. I rolled my neck, relaxed my jaw, and inhaled several deep breaths. The charts on my desk resembled the Leaning Tower of Pisa. I flopped into my chair for a two-minute respite and tackled the medication refills.

What had possessed me to hang a medical shingle? My mental image of *Marcus Welby, M.D.* shared little in common with the modern internist's life — insurance hassles, paperwork, and patients who believe the Internet over their physician.

I scribbled my signature on the last chart, lugged the unwieldy heap to my medical assistant's desk, and braced myself for the next disaster. Malpractice lawsuit? Cardiac arrest? Power outage? Employee catfight? Today, they all seemed possible.

I bustled into the next exam room and greeted Marge Moreland, a pleasant forty-year-old, who gazed up at me with red, puffy eyes. She looked as though she'd cried non-stop for a month.

Not surprisingly, she'd made the appointment to investigate what could be done for her irritated eyes. One by one I eliminated all the usual culprits: crying jags due to stress or depression, new mascara, pink eye, allergens such as ragweed, mold, dust, or animal dander. I scratched my head, perplexed. She then commented, "I think it's my workplace."

I nodded. "I get it. You work in one of those 'sick buildings' we hear about and now you and your co-workers all walk around with red, swollen eyes."

"No, none of the others are affected, just me."

I glanced up from writing in her chart. "So why do you think it's your job if none of your co-workers are affected?"

"Cause they aren't in the onion room."

"The onion room?"

"They have me peeling and slicing onions eight hours a day."

"You slice onions eight hours a day?" I couldn't imagine! No wonder her eyes were red.

"Yes, and the room is small and unventilated."

Surely torturing an employee in a non-ventilated onion room for eight hours a day must violate OSHA safety laws. Rage welled up in me like a geyser.

I exited the exam room, stomped to my office, and rang up the local OSHA officer, ready to demand he investigate and improve her work conditions. Imagine my amazement when he informed me he had already investigated the room and no laws were violated. There was nothing legally he could do. "Since onions are just a type of food and are not a toxin or poison, my hands are tied."

"But her work environment is intolerable. How would you like to chop onions all day?"

"I can hardly stand to walk into the room, let alone inspect it—the odor is overwhelming. Trust me, I get a call at least monthly on that position. The turnover is unreal."

I returned to her exam room and broke the bad news. I shook my head in disgust. "How long have you been stuck in the onion room?"

"Three months. My boss says I've lasted longer than any previous employee," she boasted.

I crossed my arms. "Why do you stay?"

"I'm hoping to be promoted to cabbages."

"Cabbages?" I bit the inside of my cheek to keep from laughing.

"The slaw room. It's the next step up in the company and it comes with a fifty cents an hour raise."

I stared at her in awe, chagrined at my own bad attitude and petty complaints. Here I'd sputtered all morning about a few insurance hassles, an overzealous Internet reader, and a heap of paperwork, while this poor woman endured the noxious odor and irritation of chopping onions for eight long hours a day—all for minimum wage. Yet somehow, she looked forward to a promotion to cabbages?

Now, whenever I'm having one of those days and I'm tempted to whine, I remind myself it could be worse. Much worse. I could be chopping onions.

—Sally Willard Burbank—

Thanksgiving x 100

Gratitude turns what we have into enough, and more.
~Melody Beattie

Thanksgiving, to me, used to mean a long weekend, turkey and football. Now, however, it has become my favorite holiday because of a tradition at my church that has taught me to literally count my blessings.

For years, I had suffered from bouts of depression. One thing that fed the depression was an attitude of discontentment. I never seemed to be happy with my life, especially when I would compare it to someone else's. Everybody always appeared to be more successful than I was, and I would frequently feel I was not measuring up to either my own potential or the world's expectations.

Then, in 2008, I started attending Cherry Hills Church in Springfield, Illinois. Every year, they have an evening service on the Sunday before Thanksgiving. Two things happen every time — the food drive and The List.

The week before the Thanksgiving service, every chair in the church has a paper bag underneath it for people to take to a grocery store and fill with food items to be donated to local ministries. Then, at the evening Thanksgiving service, a team of volunteers places all the filled bags of food at the front of the church. The bags of food completely cover all of the steps up to the stage, which is more than fifty feet across. It is quite a sight!

Included in the church bulletin is a sheet with blanks numbered

1 to 100 on the front and back. At the top, it says, "Lord, I thank you for..." The first time I saw this at a Thanksgiving service, I wondered how I would ever be able to think of 100 things I was thankful for.

The pastor allowed a few minutes at the end of the service for us to start filling in our 100 blanks. He said we didn't have to necessarily complete it just then. Rather, this was an exercise to help us focus on gratitude. I looked at my blank list and was somewhat intimidated. I figured I could probably do ten or twelve, but 100?

Then I heard some kids next to me challenge each other to a race to see who could fill in all 100 the fastest. My competitive nature kicked in. I was not about to be shown up by a bunch of kids. So I started filling in blanks with anything I could think of — big things, little things, serious things and silly ones. I tried to think of any situation in my life where I had ever said, "Thank God for..." Something. Anything. To my own astonishment, I completely filled in the list in four minutes. Then I stuck it back in my bulletin and promptly forgot about it because the service was about to end. What I didn't know was that the real "service" was just beginning.

There were well over a thousand bags of food sitting at the altar, but every item in every one of those bags needed to be sorted and loaded on a truck. While we had been in the Worship Center hearing a message, singing songs, and filling in our lists, the same group of volunteers that had brought all the bags of food to the altar was setting up tables in the lobby for sorting. There were a dozen or so categories of food items, and two or three volunteers manned each table.

As soon as service was dismissed, many of the 600-plus people in attendance came forward to grab a bag of groceries, and the sorting began. The lobby at Cherry Hills became a roiling sea of humanity, bags, boxes, and cans. In just about an hour, thousands of food items were sorted, counted, boxed and loaded. By 8:30, anyone could have walked into the lobby unaware that anything had taken place there. What a night!

One day not long afterward, I was feeling particularly sorry for myself for no good reason. I found myself sinking into my familiar emotional chasm when I remembered the list.

I took it out and read through it. Obviously, I had filled it out in a rush, but now that I stopped to really think about the 100 entries on the list, my perspective began to change. I found myself laughing and crying at the same time. I started to realize that not only did I have a lot to be thankful for but that the things I had written on that list defined me as a person. They brought out my talents, hobbies, passions, faith, people who had a great impact on me, and so much more.

When one is straining to think of 100 things, the list contains some really random items. For example, #11 on my list was hot sauce. I love hot sauce. I put it on almost everything. But when I think about being thankful for it? Well, then I think back to the food drive that we did the night I made the list. That food was going to people who didn't have any food of their own on which to put hot sauce. People who didn't have a place to live. People who didn't have a job and would have loved to have a boss they couldn't get along with just to be able to have a paycheck to buy some of that food on which to put their hot sauce.

So, as it turns out, it's really not a stretch to think of 100 things to be thankful for. I carry my list with me every day in my planner. I do this so that wherever I am, if I am having a bad day, I can pull out my list, circle the next number, and take a few minutes to thank God for it.

Choosing to have an attitude of gratitude has made me more than happy. It has filled me with joy. We use those words interchangeably in our culture, but they mean something different. Happiness is a feeling that comes and goes, but joy is an attitude that can be cultivated. It's like gas in the tank of my soul. When I give thanks, I feel stronger because I know that there is a power greater than I am who provides me with everything on my list, and so much more.

And knowing that, I can be content and continue to choose joy.

— M. Scott Coffman —

10

Worst Day Ever

I am happy because I'm grateful. I choose to be grateful.
That gratitude allows me to be happy.
~Will Arnett

t was the worst day ever. In fact, that's what we named it, all caps: WORST DAY EVER. The exact date was March 19, 2007, and I'll never forget it.

The day began as usual, with my husband, Alan, entering his office in our home to catch up on paperwork and participate in conference calls. He had worked his way up the corporate ladder and now managed multiple stores for a national restaurant chain. From my spot in the kitchen, I could hear him speaking on the phone to his boss. Suddenly, I overheard words that seemed unusual, some downright alarming. They were words like "turn in my laptop" and "severance pay."

When he exited his office moments later, my fears were confirmed. Alan's position had been eliminated. Downsizing, they said. Nothing personal; thanks for everything; you're no longer needed. I hugged my sweet husband as my heart sank, and my mind raced. What were we going to do? Would we lose our house if we couldn't afford to pay our mortgage?

"We'll be fine," he said.

"I know," I responded.

But, frankly, neither one of us was very convincing.

I wanted to crawl back in bed and pull the covers over my head, but I had to get to my own job. So, I quickly showered, dressed, and made my way to work. I was a few hours into my shift when I received a call from the surgeon's office. I had been noticing some strange lumps in my neck and underarms, and he'd been in the process of performing several tests to figure out the cause. The surgeon had removed one of the lumps from under my arm and was calling with the biopsy results.

"It's lymphoma. You have cancer," he stated, way too matter-of-factly. I distinctly remember my precise response: "What?" I must have misheard. It sounded like he said I had cancer, but that was completely ridiculous. I was a healthy, salad-eating, forty-two-year-old runner.

Cancer was out of the question. Wasn't it? The surgeon repeated those terrible words. It was true: Cancer was in my body. *My body.* He went on discussing future treatment plans and appointments, I think. I really wasn't listening anymore.

As I drove home, I thought about how wonderful things had been up until this day. Alan and I had enjoyed a happy life in a lovely suburban home in Orlando, Florida. We loved our jobs and the traveling and fancy dinners they afforded us. *It was all too good to last,* I thought. *Now it's time to pay back for all those amazing years.* I imagined hospital beds, chemo bags, my bald head, and worse. I prepared myself for a future of coping, or no future at all.

Alan scooped me into his arms when I arrived home, and I cried as he held me tight. "Someday in the future, we're going to write about today," he whispered in my ear, "and we'll call it Worst Day Ever."

We both got right to work. Alan began calling everyone he could think of with possible connections in the restaurant industry. He tirelessly applied and interviewed for dozens of positions. We were able to find a brilliant oncologist who immediately began to perform intensive scans and other tests to determine the stage and severity of my cancer. Time dragged on. Our anxiety was high, but we kept our heads up and always looked forward.

It eventually paid off.

Within several months, Alan was offered a new position at a thriving restaurant chain, with excellent pay and terrific benefits. My oncologist completed her tests, and the results were more than encouraging. She explained that my cancer was "indolent," a word completely foreign to me. "It's lazy," she replied, "not aggressive like other forms. This is manageable. You will most likely survive this." After I stopped crying, I gave her an enormous hug.

As the one-year anniversary of Worst Day Ever approached, I asked Alan how he'd like to commemorate it. I didn't really like remembering such an awful day, but I had another idea. "Let's celebrate it!" I suggested. "Let's take back control of March 19th, celebrate that we prevailed, and have a blast!" That's exactly what we did. We purchased tickets to Las Vegas that very afternoon and spent the day of March 19, 2008, reveling in our survival. Take that, Worst Day Ever.

In fact, Alan and I celebrate March 19th every year. In addition to Las Vegas, we've been to Savannah, Destin, and even Dublin, Ireland on the ten-year anniversary! Each year, we raise a glass and toast that awful day and all the days since, which we survived solely because of a bounty of blessings. And sure, there've been plenty of bad days mixed in, like when I finally did have to start chemo, and recently when Alan once again found himself without a position due to downsizing and COVID quarantines. Guess what? We prevailed. The only difference was that, this time, we absolutely knew we could. We survived March 19, 2007, didn't we?

And the greatest blessing of all? Worst Day Ever itself. It stripped away all the trivial stuff and shone a bright spotlight on all the important things, like faith, family, perseverance, love, and health. Alan and I were blessed with an abundance of these things. We'll never, ever take them for granted again. Worst Day Ever taught us how to cherish each one, on a much deeper, more profound level. Aren't we lucky?

—Joan Donnelly-Emery—

11

The Grocery Store

There is a calmness to a life lived
in gratitude, a quiet joy.
~Ralph H. Blum

Grocery shopping was the chore I hated most. I could always find plenty to complain about on any shopping trip. What did I forget to put on the list? Why did they have to keep moving things around? Who ever thought that self-checkouts were a good idea? And how come these plastic bags last 500 years in a landfill, but won't make it to my car without breaking?

On the worst grocery-shopping day of the entire year, the day before Thanksgiving, I stood with a full cart waiting to check out. I counted eleven carts ahead of mine as I stood in a line that backed down the frozen food aisle. Every line was filled with grumpy shoppers in a big hurry. And I was no exception. My in-laws were coming for Thanksgiving and everything had to be perfect. Every moment I was captive in the store put my schedule in jeopardy. There were pies to make, dressing to assemble, and my cranberry–Jell-O salad, which absolutely had to be made the night before.

As I stood there feeling sorry for myself, the ladies in front of me began talking.

"I feel almost guilty standing here in all this abundance," one said. I don't know who she was talking about, but she went on to say, "You wouldn't believe how poor they are. They labor all week, and the food they can buy with their wages fits in their two hands."

The ladies moved on to other topics but I started thinking. I'd never spent a week's wages on groceries. I only used a fraction of our weekly income even when I planned a feast like Thanksgiving. I bought treats routinely and splurged on luxuries whenever I wanted. Also, I couldn't possibly carry all of the groceries I bought every week. The store gave us shopping carts to push around because we were buying so much. And then there were even employees to bag our groceries and help put them in our cars if we bought more than we could handle alone.

How had I never noticed all this before? The shelves were jammed with food from around the world. Anything we wanted was trucked in or even flown in for us. The store was comfortable, safe and well lit. The food was monitored for freshness and inspected. If I didn't have time to cook, I could buy my whole Thanksgiving dinner pre-made, and there was a bank, a pharmacy and a flower shop in the store, too, just to make life even more convenient.

Everywhere I looked — amazing. By the time I got to the register, I was about to burst. How wonderful my life was! The cashier was frazzled, so I told her she was doing a great job and she relaxed a little. I thanked her and the bagger, telling them what a pleasure it was to have their help. I wished them a happy Thanksgiving. People stared at me, and then I heard others doing the same thing. On my way out, I told the store manager how efficient his employees were and how much I appreciated his store. He smiled and stood straighter, thanking me for saying that. He'd probably heard a lot of complaints that day.

In the parking lot, tears of gratitude stung my face in the November cold as I loaded my car. I rode to my comfortable, warm house and cooked a fine dinner that night. Compliments abounded from my family the next day, and I responded that it was my pleasure.

Going to the grocery store is no longer a chore. Ever since that day, I have seen it as a gift that many people in the world don't have. Whenever I enter a store, I'm reminded of all I have to be thankful for in my life. Gratitude — it's contagious. I caught it from a couple of ladies standing in front of me at the grocery store.

— Susan Boltz —

Chapter 2

Free Yourself with Forgiveness

What You'll Find in This Chapter

I n my opinion, the second most important key to happiness is forgiveness. It's one of the best tools we have at our disposal to create a better life for ourselves. It's an amazing tool, too, because it can transform your life in just one second! The person you were angry at doesn't even need to know that you've exercised your right to forgive them.

In this chapter, I share some of my favorite stories about how our contributors used forgiveness to repair relationships, reduce stress, shed the weight of resentments, and find a way forward to happiness and joy.

Why is forgiveness so important? It's because of the emotional weight we carry when we *don't* forgive.

I always think of those resentments and disappointments that we carry in our hearts as if they were sewn onto a heavy cloak. Imagine that cloak is covered with your collection of bad experiences, and you feel it pressing down on your shoulders as you try to move through life.

Now imagine that you've shrugged it off. That cloak is lying on the ground behind you, with all those bad things attached to it. And you're light and free, walking forward. You've left the past *in the past* — where it belongs — and you have a bright, warm, welcoming road ahead of you.

Lynn Sunday describes that process in her story, "You Take Him with You." She was so angry with her ex-husband that her blood pressure rose every time she thought about him, which was frequently. She talked about him all the time, too. Finally, her best friend said,

"You might as well still be married to the man. You take him with you wherever you go."

That's when Lynn realized that the only person she was hurting was herself. She was living in a prison of her own making, and the man she resented was happily living his new life.

That happens all the time; we realize that we hurt only ourselves through holding on to resentment and anger. The other party—the person we think is in the wrong—is blissfully unaware of the whole situation!

When Lynn forgave the father of her sons, she says, "I felt light and buoyant, as though an emotional weight had been lifted off me."

In "There for Each Other" Lauren Magliaro describes how her father and his younger brother were estranged for many years, not even talking to each other at family functions. But when Lauren's father was hospitalized, his brother showed up to help, and whatever had transpired between them was put in the past. Lauren's father recovered, and the two brothers enjoyed twenty more years together, which was not only life-changing for them but for their families.

It's astounding how many of the contributors to this book talk about the freedom they feel after forgiving someone. They hadn't realized how much they were limiting their lives by holding on to resentment, plotting revenge, and staying angry.

12

You Take Him with You

If we forgave for as long as we hold grudges,
the world would be a healthier and happier place.
~Charmaine J. Forde

I was so angry with my ex-husband that I felt my blood pressure shoot up every time I thought about him. Years ago, we said "I do" and "I love you," but whatever we meant by that wore thin in nearly twelve years and came to an abrupt end. But we'd had two sons together and, like it or not, by the rules of our separation agreement, I saw him on a regular basis when he picked up the kids. And, let's rub salt into the wound, he took them to the new home he'd made with his live-in girlfriend.

Seeing him walk into what used to be our home made me mad all over again. Only a deep desire to protect the boys from more angst and confusion kept me marginally civil during our brief interactions.

And when my ex-husband wasn't around, I still went on and on about him, not only to my friends but to anyone who'd listen — including our local librarian and my hairdresser. He'd been a liar! A cheater! I'd been hurt to the core when I'd learned the truth. My family and friends were kind and patient. Sometimes, though, when I began ranting about "the betrayal," and "what an insensitive jerk he was," and "how life's just plain not fair," they let me know by the glazed look in their eyes that they'd heard my story at least once too often.

"You may want to let go of some of that anger," my best friend Pat said one day over lunch. "You might as well still be married to the

> **"You take him with you wherever you go."**

man. You take him with you wherever you go."

Her words resonated in me. *She's right,* I thought. *I do take him with me wherever I go. My anger's a prison, and my ex-husband and I are locked in it together. I've recited my story of betrayal and outrage so often that even I'm bored with hearing it. And by doing so, I keep the anger fresh and alive inside me like a dark, toxic cloud.*

That was the moment I decided to forgive him. I'd lived with my anger long enough. It was time to move on.

I forgave my ex-husband — although that did not mean we became friends. Too many disappointments had passed between us for that. But he's the father of my sons. They love him, no matter what, and are entitled to the best relationship they can work out together. Frankly, I still don't like the guy — but after I forgave him by letting go of my anger, I felt light and buoyant, as though an emotional weight had been lifted off me.

How strange. Nothing changed. We're still divorced. I'm still a single mom, doing the work of two people. Nothing really changed except me, but that seems to have made a world of difference in my life.

— Lynn Sunday —

13

My Fifth Grade Bully

*Throughout life people will make you mad,
disrespect you and treat you bad. Let God
deal with the things they do, cause hate
in your heart will consume you too.*
~Will Smith

When I was in the fifth grade, there was a boy in my class named Kyle. At the time, he was the meanest person I had ever met. For the first couple days of school, Kyle and I sat across from each other. He would stealthily reach his legs across the table and slam his shoe down on mine, causing a rapid rush of pain. Eventually, I told a teacher, and my seat was moved. But Kyle's abuse didn't stop. He continued to call me names, such as "stupid" and "freak." His words were quite distressing to an eleven-year-old girl. He also continued to physically hurt me. In "morning meeting" he once stepped on my foot so hard that I burst into tears. This continued for most of the school year.

Kyle also bullied my friend Megan. At one point she ran out of the classroom because he mimicked her nonstop. Both of us were absolutely miserable. And despite meetings with teachers and guidance counselors, nothing changed. We had a large class of rowdy boys, and the teacher had a hard time keeping order.

The climax of the Kyle saga occurred in mid-May. Kyle had elbowed me into a wall and insulted my brother (who has special needs), calling him a "retarded freak." I lost it. With my teacher standing behind me, I

Free Yourself with Forgiveness | 45

told Kyle exactly how much he had hurt Megan and me — both physically and emotionally. I had tears streaming down my face and probably looked ridiculous, but I didn't care. I had been waiting for the opportunity to tell Kyle how much I hated him for months. At the end of our confrontation, I glowed inside as Kyle quietly apologized. I felt as if I had conquered Mt. Everest, I was that happy.

Kyle's teasing didn't completely end, but it definitely subsided. He never physically hurt me again, and the final month of school went by fairly smoothly. Kyle was going to a private school the next year; I wouldn't have to worry about him. Summer came and went, as did sixth grade, and seventh grade. I had only seen Kyle once, at a movie theater. We did not speak, instead preferring to look at the floor and pretend we didn't see each other.

It was only in eighth grade that I really thought about fifth grade again. It was late at night as I remembered the abuse Kyle had put me through. I waited for the pang of anger I'd always felt when thinking or talking about Kyle. But no anger came. I tried again, thinking about the marks he'd left so many times on the tops of my feet, the words, the pain… but I felt no hate for him. Instead, I felt a small beating of pity inside my heart. This boy, who had ruined a great portion of my fifth grade experience, had probably been going through his own issues back then. He was obviously mad at the world and maybe, I reasoned, he was simply taking that anger out on my friend and me. It was no excuse for what he did, but it was a reason.

I felt as if I'd had an epiphany. Being angry with Kyle for what he had done was — as Buddha puts it — like drinking poison and expecting him to die. By holding my hatred for Kyle inside of me, I was only hurting myself. That night, I chose to let old wounds heal, and I forgave my fifth grade bully.

In letting go of that pain, I felt free. I wasn't letting a three-year-old incident bother me. In that way, I guess forgiveness is the most important tool humans have been blessed with. Because, with it, we can let go of unnecessary burdens and truly own our lives.

Who knew an eleven-year-old boy could teach me that?

— Kathryn Malnight —

14

He's My Brother

Life is too short to hold a grudge, also too long.
~Robert Brault

Like the Christmas before, we didn't send Christmas cards; we called my family in Canada. Ginny and I talked to my mom. We spoke to my uncles and aunts. I hadn't seen any of them in seven years and Ginny hadn't met them yet, but she hoped to one day.

Those calls were completed, but I couldn't relax. I still had one more call to make, and I was afraid. I paced the house. I wasted time at my computer. I needed to call but I couldn't.

Five years before, I had received an e-mail from my brother. At the time, I had been out of work for several months. My life was very stressful. My brother's e-mail was nothing terrible but it made me angry.

I wrote back. As I typed, my anger grew. Months of frustration flowed into my nasty response. I said things that were not nice, but I hit send anyway. More thoughts occurred to me. I wrote a second nasty e-mail.

I basically told my brother to go to hell. I didn't care if I ever heard from him again.

The next day I received another e-mail from him. I didn't read it. I just deleted it, and then I blocked his e-mail address.

For five years, he tried to get through to me but I ignored him. I had lived with this terrible guilt. I thought about contacting him, but was ashamed of myself for what I'd said.

It was time to fix it. I picked up the phone and stepped outside. I wanted privacy. Ginny didn't know I was calling my brother. I took a deep breath, blew out a cloud of my breath into the cold December air, and dialed his number. Even after five years, I still knew it by heart. A phone rang 3,700 miles away in Nova Scotia.

There was no answer. I left a message. "Bob, it's Mike." I paused to take another breath. My hand holding the phone shook. "Bob, I guess I'll start by saying I'm sorry. I said some things I regret. I want to wish you and Delores a Merry Christmas and hope all is well with you. I realize you may not want to talk to me, but I thought I would try. I want to make it right again. If you want to talk…" I left my number.

I walked back into the house and looked at Ginny. "I did it."

She looked puzzled. "You did what?"

"I called Bob."

"Oh, honey!" She walked up to me and put her arms around my neck. "I'm glad. You needed to do it. It's family Mike and it's been too long." She kissed me. "You did right, hun."

Christmas came and went. I waited for the call that never came. I prayed for his forgiveness. The phone didn't ring. Then a week after I called, I received an e-mail. My brother left me a message on my Facebook page. He said he listened to my voice message over and over and knew I was sincere. In the weeks to follow, we e-mailed back and forth. The healing began.

Why had I let five years of my brother's life slip through my fingers? Why was I too proud to call and say I was sorry?

> *Why had I let five years of my brother's life slip through my fingers?*

If I had the answers, it would never have happened in the first place, but I knew I don't want it to happen again. I had wrecked my relationship with my brother. Like a jigsaw puzzle that has been dropped, the pieces had scattered everywhere. It was time to gather them up and try to put them back together.

Since then, we have grown close again. Even though I haven't been able to afford the trip home, we are still family.

I swallowed my pride. I did it. Five years was too long. After all, he's my brother.

— Michael T. Smith —

Heavenly Forgiveness

You know you really love someone, when you
can't hate them for breaking your heart...
~Author Unknown

My older brother, Paul, had a very troubled life. We moved around a lot as children, partly because my parents were always trying to get him away from what they called a "bad element." After moving fifteen times, they reluctantly admitted that he was the bad element. When he couldn't find trouble in a new location he created it.

There were some whoppers. Like the day he came home with soot on his hands and told my parents it was only dirt. Later they saw an article in the local paper about a mysterious fire in the back yard of an abandoned house down the street. There were constant reports of school fights and disruptive behavior in class. Paul's black eyes actually overlapped. He always had a fresh one while the last one was yellowing.

I was shy and grew accustomed to my parents giving more attention to Paul because of his bad behavior.

My brother and I played together a lot as young children, but around the time that he became a teenager, he started using alcohol and marijuana and changed drastically. The brother I knew, who had always protected me from bullies, began to bully me severely. I didn't understand what was happening to him.

Many people scoff at the idea that marijuana is a gateway drug, but in my brother's case it was absolutely true. When he was sixteen,

I was skateboarding with friends when one said to me, "Isn't that your brother?" I saw Paul across the street, skipping along the sidewalk and singing, clearly high as a kite. He saw me and came over. Nothing he said made any sense. He was like a different person. I was terrified. He was my brother but not my brother.

Eventually, he started using heroin and spent a total of eight years in jail for drug-related offenses, including burglary of a pharmacy. He was shot in the ankle during that arrest. The officer was either a bad shot or merciful.

I wasn't perfect but I avoided drugs, mainly as a result of seeing Paul's life deteriorate. I also didn't want to add to our parents' pain.

One night in a supermarket parking lot I heard a familiar voice behind me and turned to see Paul shaking down an elderly man for change. As drug addicts often do, he had become a panhandler, struggling to get enough money for a fix. The only thing that saved him then was my parents' support. They let him live with them, fearing he would die on the street if they didn't. When he finally moved out, they paid his rent for many more years. It was all for naught, however, because he died of a heroin overdose at the age of thirty-seven. It was the grand finale of a lifetime of mayhem and misery.

I had grown increasingly resentful of him over the years. It started with the bullying as children and grew as a teenager when my parents and I visited him in prison. I couldn't believe he was dragging us through that dark world with him. With every tear my mother shed, my resentment and anger grew. The only thing that kept our bond from breaking completely was my memory of the brother who played with me in the sun as kids, who consoled me when I cried, and with whom I shared an identical sense of humor. In fact, our ability to laugh together was the last connection we had in his most troubled years. There were moments between bullying sessions when he was a lot of fun to be with and we laughed ourselves sick. He was the only sibling I had, so I was always eager to connect with him.

When we got older, I spent countless hours talking with him, struggling to find the right words to divert him from the destructive path he was on. He always hugged and thanked me, but he never changed.

During the last year of his life, I stopped talking to him completely. It hurt me to abandon him, but I was desperate and thought I would try "tough love" for a change. I had already tried everything else.

When he died, I felt guilty for two reasons — I never forgave him for the pain he caused my parents and me, and I couldn't forgive myself for not being there for him at the end. I couldn't stop thinking that abandoning him added to his pain and made him more careless, or that I might have been able to save him somehow if I had been accessible to him. For months after he died, I buried my grief under anger. When it finally subsided, I prayed for his soul and asked him to forgive me, hoping he could hear me somehow.

He never talked about it, but he had become a Christian in prison. I only knew this because of a journal I found in his apartment after he died in which he had written, "I can't win this fight. I'm laying it all down at the foot of the old rugged cross," referencing an old hymn. On another page, he had written about feeling guilty for not being a better brother to me. He ended this passage with, "Despite it all, I love Mark and I know he loves me, too." I tore that page out and carry it in my wallet to this day, fifteen years later. There were also many rambling entries about his past and present problems.

A month or so after he died, I took the journal to his grave and burned it page by page, hoping the smoke would reach him in heaven, and praying to him to let go of all the pain and confusion those pages represented.

I have always imagined heaven as a place where our pain-filled bodies fall away like worn-out clothes, where sadness is washed away, and where we forgive others and ourselves for our mistakes in life. I can't imagine we bring all our mortal pettiness with us or heaven would be as full of misery as earth is. As Colossians 1:13-14 says, "For he has rescued us from the dominion of darkness and brought us into the kingdom of the Son he loves, in whom we have redemption, the forgiveness of sins."

One night, I had a dream that Paul and I were on a beach where we had spent many happy days as children. In life, he was heavily tattooed from his time in prison and had lost most of his teeth from drug use, but in my dream he looked pristine and healthy. He said, "Mark, stop torturing yourself. Of course I forgive you. You didn't do anything wrong. I made the mistakes, not you. You were just trying to save me."

I hugged him and cried. I told him I forgave him too, and begged him to let me take him to my parents because they needed him back so desperately. He said, "I can't. I have a new home now." I asked where. He smiled and looked up. It was a smile filled with the peace he was never able to find in mortal life. I just kept hugging him and crying, afraid if I let him go he would be gone again. I woke up heartbroken that it was only a dream, but with a heart lighter than it had been since he died. I felt like I had just seen him again.

The psychologist Sigmund Freud said one of the main purposes of dreams is wish fulfillment. Since there is no greater wish than to see our lost loved ones just one more time and make peace with them, I know there may be no supernatural reason for this dream. Nevertheless, I choose to believe that my brother came to me that night to ease my pain, and perhaps his own.

In the years since, as I have meditated about that dream, I have often thought about the many times he and I argued, and how we had always forgiven each other afterward no matter how upset we had become. Why wouldn't he forgive me from his "new home" as I had forgiven him? As his journal entry said, despite it all, he always knew I loved him. No matter how messy life gets, in the end, love is all that matters, and all we take with us. There is no need to beg those we have lost for forgiveness. It comes naturally in heaven.

— Mark Rickerby —

The Clean Record

Forgiveness is the key to action and freedom.
~Hannah Arendt

"Love doesn't keep a record of wrongs," the teacher said, and continued through the end of the Bible passage. I heard only the first words, and those words echoed in my head like a song on repeat. It was a Wednesday night Bible class, and we were studying the "fruit of the Spirit." We were on a familiar subject — love. I had thought that I knew about love, but that one sentence hit me like a battering ram.

A record of wrongs? I went through the rest of the class with a sick feeling in my stomach, the words playing over and over. But I couldn't put my finger on why they disturbed me.

We left class to go to the weekly devotional, and as we sat down, my husband turned to me. "Are you okay?"

"I'm fine," I said, ignoring the bustle about us as everyone found a seat. "Why?"

"You just seem really quiet."

"I'm fine."

And that was true — in part. But the verse kept playing in my head as I listened with half an ear to the devotional. I couldn't put my heart in it. Once the final prayer was said, I figured it out, as if I needed some quiet to sort everything out properly.

I was keeping a record of wrongs.

And not just wrongs, but perceived wrongs, too. Could I claim I loved her? The sick feeling in my stomach returned as we pulled out of the parking lot. "No."

I didn't grow up in Ohio. I'd only been there once before I got married and moved there to be with my husband. I'd only met my mother-in-law that one time.

She did a lot of things that bothered me during our first year of marriage. But the most painful one was assuming that I wouldn't be in the family pictures at my brother-in-law's wedding.

She told me to get my husband's place card while he was busy taking pictures. I remember staring sadly at my own card. It wasn't that she was trying to be mean; it really hadn't occurred to her that I'd be in the family pictures.

"Love doesn't keep a record of wrongs."

But surely I am justified in being hurt, I told myself as we pulled into the Toys "R" Us parking lot. I grabbed my purse and followed my husband inside. I barely saw the toys as I told myself again, *Surely, I have that right.*

Yes, the rational part of me said, *you can be upset. But you don't have to keep a record to hold over her head. That's worse than any of the things you think she's done — and how many of those are because you don't talk to her, either? How many are just ignorance you haven't corrected? It's not her fault she has no idea how you feel.*

The guilt pricked at me in the store and over the next few days. What could I do about it? I knew it was unfair and wrong. But my feelings had festered over the course of the year. I wanted her to understand the pain — even if she hadn't meant to cause it. But I knew it wasn't fair, and so I decided to act.

It took me a few days before I thought of something to try. I wasn't sure if it would work or even help. And even though I had a plan and had committed to following it through, it took me several more days to sit down and put my fingers on my keyboard.

I was going to write out the record of wrongs I had been carrying around in my head and heart.

It took days to scour my brain for every single thing that had bothered me — I wasn't going to miss one. Once my list was complete, it took me another week to get up the courage to do what I knew I needed to do next. But, finally, I sat down and pulled up her record.

I highlighted the item at the bottom of the list, said a fervent prayer asking God to help me, and pressed Delete.

I'd written down her record, and now I had to wipe it clean. Keeping it wasn't right or fair, and a lot of it was my perception, not her fault.

I moved on to the next one, highlighted it, and pressed Delete.

I had to stop a few times to pray and breathe. It was hard releasing all of the things I had held onto for so long.

But my hurt was just as much my fault as it was hers. It wouldn't hurt as much if I hadn't kept holding on to it. I prayed that as I deleted each item on the list, God would help me erase it from my memory.

I moved up the list. Highlight, delete, highlight, delete. After half an hour, I reached the top of the list.

Her blank record stared at me, clear of everything I had held against her.

Nothing changed right away except that my heart felt lighter. But over the next few months, the changes in myself became more obvious. I found that I was no longer looking for reasons to be upset with her, and I could think of things that I appreciated about her.

Her parenting style would not have worked for me, and there's nothing wrong with that because my husband wouldn't be the kind of man that I need him to be if it did. She provided the only thing that made the move worthwhile. And that makes her one of the best moms ever.

And her record? It's still blank.

— L. Y. Levand —

17

New Year's Eve Party

*Forgiveness is not a feeling; it is a commitment.
It is a choice to show mercy, not to hold the
offense up against the offender. Forgiveness
is an expression of love.*
~Gary Chapman

'm still not sure how I got talked into it, but one year I agreed to throw a couples' New Year's Eve party. It took me days to prep, especially with cleaning up after our toddlers.

Then there were the lists to be made and shopping to be done. I scurried through the supermarket, keeping the cart moving with one hand and funneling Cheerios into four open toddler hands with the other.

I would make lasagna, bread, salad, and cheesecake—the baking could be done while the kids napped. I quite enjoyed the baking. The smells of yeasty bread and tomato sauce lifted my mood until I glanced around the kitchen and realized I should have waited to clean until after I cooked.

The night before, my husband helped me set up tables. After the tablecloths were on, it looked like one long table extending from the kitchen island across the family room to the fireplace. I felt a growing sense of excitement. Even though I didn't like hosting parties, this could be fun.

The morning of the party, I woke to the sun shining. Everything was ready. It was going to be a lovely evening.

At 4:00 p.m., my mom arrived to pick up the babies. My husband would be home in an hour. I puttered around wiping up nonexistent spills.

At 5:00 p.m., I texted my husband. "Are you on your way?"

"I'm going to be held up here for a few minutes. Sorry."

"Oh. Okay. Everyone will be here in an hour."

"I know. I should be there, no problem."

At 5:30, I texted him again.

At 5:45, I called him.

"They will be here in fifteen minutes. If you leave now, you won't even have time to change."

"So sorry, honey. I'm still tied up. I'll be there as soon as I can."

The conversation that followed wasn't one of my finest moments. He was trying to get off the phone so he could get home sooner. I wanted a pound of flesh. This was my greatest fear — hostessing alone. I worried I'd be standing there with a room full of people not knowing what to say and wishing the ground would open up and swallow me alive. I hadn't even wanted to have the party and now I had to handle it by myself. It ended with me bursting into tears and slamming down the phone as the doorbell rang.

The first guests were early.

I wiped my face and threw open the door with a cheery smile, thankful the guests ignored the telltale signs of tears.

I kept texting my husband as guests arrived and time passed.

I tried to hide the panic and frustration from my guests at my plans going haywire. I felt awkward and unsure of how to proceed. By 7:30, stomachs were growling. His texts promised he would be home before dinner was done. So we all sat, with one empty chair beside me. Everyone said the food was amazing. I didn't notice. I tried to make conversation while I was terribly embarrassed by the empty seat beside me.

At 9:30, I hid in the bathroom. "This night was a disaster," I ranted to myself. In the other room, though, I heard laughter as the group set up *Taboo*. It was time to play as couples. And I was the only one without the rest of my couple — at my own party.

Then my husband called. "Honey, I never imagined this could have happened. I know how uncomfortable you are being there alone. I am doing my absolute best. Please forgive me. I know it's not what you want to hear, but I'll be there by midnight — for sure."

By midnight? He was going to miss the entire party?

My husband continued to explain, "I know it won't help, but I promise I'd be there if I could. This is the first second I've had to call. Things are crazy here. The final numbers for year-end inventory must be in by midnight. Some imbecile wrote random numbers on boxes and boxes of parts instead of counting them. Now we have to recount them all. Everyone is mad at me because they have to stay instead of being at home with their families."

I realized what the night had been like for my husband. Up until that point, I'd been far too worked up to see his side. All I knew was that he wasn't home. But he was taking a lot of heat at work. He wanted to be at the party. And the icing on the cake was a wife who was being Host-zilla.

"Will you forgive me?" he asked again.

In that moment, I made a choice. I chose forgiveness. I also realized much of my crash-and-burn night had been in my control. While I couldn't control the circumstances, I could control my reactions. "Yes." I took a breath. "I'm sorry for being so impatient. Take your time. I'll see you when you get here. Happy New Year."

I washed my teary face, turned off my phone, and joined the game. The next two hours flew by as we yelled out answers and laughed until our bellies hurt. I almost forgot about my husband until I heard the garage door open. I looked at the time: 11:38.

A few minutes later, we watched the ball drop on TV, and my husband leaned over and kissed me. "Happy New Year."

"Happy New Year." As I said the words, I was thankful for a new year. New beginnings. I resolved to be more patient, understanding and forgiving in the coming year.

— Nancy Beach —

18

Happiness Through Forgiveness

Forgiveness does not change the past,
but it does enlarge the future.
~Paul Boese

t was raining the day I found out. Not just a light sprinkle, but a heavy, foggy, cold February downpour. I had spent a lazy day at Color-Me-Mine painting a teddy bear with my friends. I was twelve years old. I was starting to fit in at school. I was happy. But little did I know that was all about to change.

I came home to my ten-year-old brother watching TV and playing a video game. Just past the television was a sliding glass door leading to our patio. My dad was standing outside on the phone with his back turned towards us.

"Dad's mad," my brother said, not even bothering to look up from his Game Boy. I was in such a good mood from spending the day with friends that I didn't even care to know why. I went into my bedroom and sat down at my computer, ready to spend the rest of my Saturday online. Not even two minutes later, my dad walked into the bedroom my brother and I shared, sat down, and said, "Nicole, we need to have a family meeting." He called for my brother to come into the bedroom, and as we waited for him, my mind raced, trying to think of anything I might have done to get in trouble. It was never a good sign when he called me Nicole. My brother finally shuffled in and sat down on the bed next to my father.

Without any warning at all, he looked at me and said, "Your mom's gone." I didn't understand what he meant. I didn't want to. Everything went silent. I could hear only my own breath echoing in my ears like a bad horror movie, and I watched my dad and my brother hold each other and cry.

"You're lying," I said, starting to laugh. Why was I laughing? I knew they weren't lying. My father was sitting in front of me bawling his eyes out—a grown man crying like a toddler. But I couldn't believe him. My mother was my best friend. He handed me his cell phone and told me to call my grandmother, and that she would tell me everything I wanted to know.

I ran outside and I stood in the rain and I listened as my grandma cried and told me that my mother, my role model, my favorite person in the world, had killed herself. I was devastated. I wanted to cry, but the tears just wouldn't come. They built themselves up in my chest forming a heavy anchor, but they would not come. I hung up the phone and walked inside. My brother was back at the television; my father was outside on the phone again. Everything looked normal. It didn't appear as if the world had just rolled over on its back. I returned to my bedroom, and did what any twelve-year-old girl would do in a situation like this: I updated my AIM status—"RIP Mom."

And finally, the next day, I woke up crying. I cried for two weeks straight. I didn't eat or go to school. I left the house once: for the funeral. I was guilty. I felt like I should have been a better daughter, gotten her a better birthday gift, done more chores around the house. I couldn't stand to look at myself. Suddenly, every little thing I used to do seemed like another cause of her suicide. She killed herself because I never did what she asked. She did it because I wasn't who she wanted me to be.

I beat myself up until there was nothing left to beat. I broke myself down so far that I could think of nothing else to do but hate myself. And that led to hating her. I hated her for leaving me. For making me feel worthless. For leaving me to take on the role of mother, of woman of the house. I was twelve years old. I needed her. How did she expect me to be raised by just my dad? Every girl needs her mother! She couldn't just leave when things got hard! Isn't the point of having children to be completely selfless and only think of them? I had endless thoughts, endless questions.

After two weeks, my father made me go back to school and promised me that everything would be fine. But he was wrong. Everyone knew what had happened. My friends could barely look at me. People I didn't even know pointed at me when I walked through the halls. I couldn't deal with the pain of everyone staring, asking questions I didn't know how to answer. So I turned away from my friends and spent all of my time alone. I was miserable.

My mother had gone from being my best friend to my worst enemy. This was all her fault. I hated her and I hated myself.

But the problem with hatred is that it eats you up. It burrows inside every little pore in your body. It drains you of all your energy. Living with hatred is an incredibly difficult thing to do. So I started working at forgiving. Because when it comes to forgiveness, sometimes it helps you more than the person you are forgiving. My mom will never know that I forgave her. I will never be able to go up to her, look her in the eye, and say, "I forgive you." But now, I can look myself in the mirror, and know that sometimes people are selfish. People are stupid and act without thinking. People are people and we all do things we regret, but if we are never forgiven and never forgive, we will never be able to move on in our own lives.

> *The problem with hatred is that it eats you up.*

I took all the anger that I was feeling and I channeled it into forgiveness and understanding. Everyone deserves a second chance no matter how hard they have hurt you. I may never know the reason why she hurt me the way she did, but I don't need to. I have forgiven her, and because of that, I can be happy.

— Nicole Guiltinan —

19

Moving Forward

The foolish man seeks happiness in the distance;
the wise grows it under his feet.
~James Oppenheim

The story that changed my life is called "Dancing in the Rain" by Jeannie Lancaster and appeared in the book *Chicken Soup for the Soul: Think Positive*. I read the entire book cover to cover. There were many stories that resonated with me but that story in particular made me smile and I keep going back to it.

The key phrase that captured me was "Life isn't about waiting for the storm to pass. It's about learning to dance in the rain." The story talked about how the author discovered a plaque with those words and how she bought it to constantly remind herself to implement that attitude into her daily life. The story also mentions how too often people put conditions on their own happiness. That's my problem. I tend to be a "glass is half empty" kind of person. Too often when things aren't going the way I plan, I basically take a back seat in my life and wait for everything to magically start getting better and work itself out on its own. Of course I am always disappointed when nothing happens or more often than not, things get worse.

I read the story a couple of weeks ago. It has stuck with me and I say the quote to myself several times throughout the day: "Life isn't about waiting for the storm to pass. It's about learning to dance in the rain." Just repeating that sentence over and over again makes me feel more positive and changes how I feel and react to situations that I am not normally happy with.

A couple of years ago my cousin Jenny and I had some sort of falling out. I am not even sure what it was about at this point. All I know was that Jenny had been my best friend, my maid of honor at my wedding and the godmother of my first-born child. I had thought of her every now and then. After our spat, I had been invited to her wedding but didn't go out of spite. I kept waiting for her to apologize or something. After reading the story I felt like a spoiled brat. How much time do we really have to cultivate relationships and do all the things we want to do? The fact is we really don't know.

I realized that I missed her friendship; this whole situation was completely silly. I was ashamed of myself for not going to her wedding. "Enough," I told myself. "This foolishness has to stop here and now. I am tired of missing out on my own life."

I sat down and wrote a note to Jenny. I told her that I wanted to start over, call a truce and I apologized for not being at her wedding. I mailed the letter and I waited. Would she return the letter unopened? Would she contact me? What if she didn't contact me?

A week later the phone rang. I asked my daughter to answer it because I was dealing with a flood in the basement. A sock had gotten stuck in the washing drain and I was busy reminding myself to dance in the rain! Jenny was calling to thank me for my letter. She was happy to hear from me and we talked on the phone for over an hour, until the battery died in my phone. She is planning on visiting us in the next couple of weeks. I will finally get the pleasure of meeting her husband, son and daughter for the very first time. I have learned to move forward now and to actively pursue my happiness. After all, "life isn't about waiting for the storm to pass. It is about learning how to dance in the rain."

— Catina Noble —

20

There for Each Other

There's no other love like the love for a brother.
There's no other love like the love from a brother.
~Astrid Alauda

My father is funny, smart, hardworking and loving. He taught me to drive, throw a baseball, and fish. One other thing my dad's good at is holding a bit of a grudge. For most of my teen years, he didn't speak to his younger brother, although they were at many family functions together.

I was never sure why my dad was so angry with my uncle in the first place. But they spent many Christmases, Thanksgivings and Easter Sundays seated at opposite ends of the table. It was simply something that we all accepted at the time.

When I was nineteen, I got a call in my college dorm that my dad was having serious medical problems. My mom and grandmother picked me up in the middle of the night so I could be there the next day when he was scheduled to transfer to a better hospital. I didn't sleep that night, not a wink. I tossed, turned and was almost delirious when we arrived at the hospital early the next morning before the transfer.

That morning, as my mom and I walked down the hallway of the hospital, we could see straight into my dad's room. A tall man wearing a stylish suit stood over my father's bed with his back to us. Casually, my mom remarked how nice it was for the doctor to come by to see my dad so early in the morning. But through my sleepless fog, something about the scene struck me as odd. The man with his back to us was standing very quietly and still, looking down, but he was holding both of my dad's hands in his own. Not typical doctor behavior.

I stopped cold in my tracks and whispered softly to my mom, "That's not a doctor." I knew right away it was my uncle. But, little did I know, I would continue to reflect on that quiet moment for decades. And it would be the beginning of something truly wonderful.

The hours and days that followed were some of the most trying of my young years. My dad had had a brain aneurysm and ended up in the hospital for quite a while. My uncle stayed with my mom and me the entire time. He forced me to eat, bringing me healthy snacks and making sure I actually ate them even though I had no appetite. He gave me his mobile phone, a novelty at the time, to check in with my best friend. He supported my mom as she tried to stay strong for me. Honestly, I don't recall him leaving our side once through the entire ordeal. When I think back on those uncertain days, I remember two things: being scared, and my uncle by our side.

Thankfully, my dad pulled through beautifully. He didn't even need surgery. Somehow, the brain aneurysm healed itself. I don't have much medical knowledge, but it always seemed like a miracle. The other miracle was my father's new relationship with his brother. He couldn't hold a grudge anymore. Not only had my uncle helped him but he had helped my mom and me get through the hardest days of our life. It was the true definition of a clean slate.

After that, my dad and his brother became as close as can be. It was incredible to watch them get to know each other again, and become the best of friends. We got to know him, his wife, and his three amazing sons. Eventually, my dad even went to work for my uncle.

Years later, when I was pregnant with my son, my uncle offered me a job where I could work from home so that I wouldn't have to leave my son in daycare. Being a stay-at-home mom was my dream come true, and he made it possible. It is still one of the greatest gifts anyone has ever given me.

Four years ago, my uncle died tragically at the age of fifty-eight. I can't even put into words the great loss our family has experienced through his passing. Though devastated at the loss of his brother, my dad was there for my uncle's wife and three grown sons, the same way my uncle had been there for me and my mom two decades earlier.

I miss my uncle every day, especially seeing him and my father together. They always reminded me of the importance of forgiveness, and that all things are possible with love. I'm thankful they had twenty good years together, and I'm so very grateful that I have this story to tell.

— Lauren Magliaro —

Chapter
3

Help Someone Else

What You'll Find in This Chapter

The best way to make yourself feel great? Do a random act of kindness for someone. Studies have shown that "doing good" is not only beneficial for the recipient of the good deed, but also for the person doing it, making that person happier and healthier. When you help someone else, you feel elevated yourself—more blessed and more empowered.

There's a story in the original 1993 *Chicken Soup for the Soul* that is one of my favorites. A tourist walking along a beach in Mexico sees a man bending down every so often to pick up a stranded starfish and throw it back into the sea. The tourist asks the man why he is bothering. He can't possibly save the thousands of starfish that have washed up on shore. How does he expect to make a difference given the immensity of the problem? The do-gooder bends down, picks up another starfish and tosses it into the water, saying, "Made a difference to that one."

That man undoubtedly felt terrific as he helped one stranded creature at a time. And that's a perfect way to start this chapter of stories about helping someone else, and how good that makes you feel. Everyone finds that the *donor or volunteer* ends up feeling even better than the *recipient* of the act of kindness.

Aimee Mae Wiley learned that on her fortieth birthday, as she describes in her story, "A Be-the-Gift Birthday." She celebrated her big day by giving small gifts to other people. She handed out flowers and cookies to friends, her favorite bank teller, the librarian, and the mail carrier, among others. In doing all this, Aimee says, "I discovered an unprecedented joy on what could have been a difficult birthday."

Filling a need can be as simple as weeding a cemetery plot on your daily walk, as Stuart Perkins describes in his story, "Weeding Baby Wendell." He doesn't think it's a big deal, but he does so much weeding in the cemetery that the family members who visit the graves always confuse him for staff. Stuart is just doing what his grandmother told him when she said, "If you see a need, fill it, and don't worry about who gets the credit."

At Chicken Soup for the Soul, we are big proponents of adopting dogs and cats from shelters, and we count numerous rescues among our own pets. So, I was pleased to include "Bed, Bath and Way Beyond," by Lisa Fowler, about how volunteering at her local Humane Society shelter changed her life... and that of an adorable puppy who found her forever home with Lisa.

I think these stories will make you feel good. These examples of kindness are particularly heartening now, what with the pandemic, divisiveness in our society, and conflicts around the world. A renewed focus on what is good about humanity is just what we need. That's what this chapter delivers — plenty of good news and good behavior, with stories about a wide variety of good deeds and how those acts of kindness made the people performing them so much happier!

Each story is unique, but we learn this universal lesson from all of them: We are all capable of providing help. And it is this ability that makes us part of a united community of people who really do care about one another. No matter what divides us, our basic humanity reunites us.

A Be-the-Gift Birthday

*Happiness is a perfume you cannot pour on others
without getting a few drops on yourself.*
~Ralph Waldo Emerson

On October 16, 2014, I turned forty years old. I wasn't entirely certain how to feel about this milestone — empowered or depressed, invigorated or old. But, after reading a blog post entitled "How to Have the Best Birthday, the Best Today, the Best Anyday…" several months earlier by Ann Voskamp, author of *One Thousand Gifts*, I was determined to celebrate my birthday differently. In preparation, I printed out her "Be the GIFT" tags which I would attach to the flowers I purchased and the cookies I planned to bake on my birthday morning.

I would make my birthday about blessing others instead of expecting something for myself. In doing so, I discovered an unprecedented joy on what could have been a difficult birthday.

The day began when I woke up for an early visit to the gym. In the 5:30 a.m. darkness, I approached my van, startled to see something large looming in the driver's seat. My heart skipped a beat as my eyes adjusted, and then I laughed with relief as I realized it was a gigantic birthday balloon. I climbed in with my oversized companion and drove to the gym, my first venue for the "Be the GIFT" experiment.

Along with my gym shoes, phone and ear buds, I also carried a little flower tube stuffed with vibrant pink, blue and yellow daisies with a "Be the GIFT" tag attached. I hung it on the personal trainers' door file holder and stepped onto the treadmill.

Scott, my personal trainer, arrived shortly thereafter. I watched him in the window's reflection as he headed to the door and stopped to examine the strange item before him. He looked at it, then opened the door, then came back to look at it again, removing it from the file holder. I later found that he had put the flowers on one of the meeting tables and taped the gift tag to his desk facing anyone who might come in for consultation, thereby sharing my joyful message with countless others.

After returning home and getting everyone fed and lunches made, I dropped off the boys and another flower bouquet for a surprised and smiling secretary at school. Then, I returned home to bake cookies and assemble more bunches of flowers. I finished baking just in time to place a package of cookies and flowers out for the mail carrier.

Shortly after, I began to notice that for every good deed I did, another came my way.

> *I began to notice that for every good deed I did, another came my way.*

My first visitor arrived as I was stepping out of the shower. My friend Sarah had shown up unexpectedly, gift in hand, and we sat and enjoyed a visit together while my children snuck away to the basement to play. I unwrapped the beautiful wrapping paper, which contained a lovely relaxation package of lavender-scented oil, Earl Grey chocolate, and a bag of herbal tea.

As Sarah rose to leave, my friend Kristina and her children arrived. We also had a pleasant visit, and she presented me with a peace lily plant to add to my budding indoor plant collection. It was planted in a hand-painted pot that says, "Your Friendship is a Blessing." I sent both friends home with flowers.

When the mail carrier had taken her gift and turned the corner, I retrieved the mail for the day. My mailbox was full of birthday cards, the most I'd ever received. I have a sneaking suspicion that a dear friend of mine recruited a bunch of sweet women from church to bless me with birthday cards, and they did. I was nearly in tears looking through the stack filled with such beautiful sentiments.

After lunch, the kids and I were on our way to deliver our surprise gifts for my birthday. We trooped into the small bank lobby, where we shared our birthday joy with our favorite bank teller, who always gives my five children the same flavor suckers so they don't fight over them. Next, we stopped with flowers and cookies to cheer up our unemployed neighbor. Then, we headed across the street to bless our pediatrician and his wonderful assistant with flowers, a plate of cookies, and a thank-you card.

Another special stop was our home away from home, the library, where our gifts were met with genuine gratitude. I think they even fast-tracked a book request I made; it arrived the next day. After school, I caught up with a few random parent friends and surprised them with flowers, too. One mom said that she was going to pass hers on to a friend who was having an especially difficult time. Another mom sent me a card a few weeks later to thank me for my little gift of encouragement on a stressful day.

From there, the kids got to be more directly involved. I took my five children to the park, where they sprinkled quarters on the playground equipment for unsuspecting children to find. Then, we headed to ShopKo, where they filled all of the 25-cent candy machines with quarters. Finally, we stopped at Goodwill, where I gave each of the children one dollar to hide in a piece of merchandise. We had attached our "Be the GIFT" tags to the dollar bills.

For the first time since I was a teenager, I bought my birthday cake instead of making it. When we returned home, another friend arrived unexpectedly, bringing me a personal birthday cupcake! Of course, I sent her off with a little bouquet of flowers.

Dear friends watched our children so that my husband and I could go out for dinner. When we returned, all of my children shared their sweet cards and gifts with me, and we sang and enjoyed the store-bought cake.

As the day came to a close, I reflected that, unlike so many birthday celebrations in my life, on this day, I made a point of being joyful and relaxed about the schedule. I chose not to live with expectation but to embrace with gratitude whatever came my way. In the process, I was able to do all of my favorite things: bless others and make them feel special, spend spontaneous time with friends, and celebrate with my family.

Giving to others and being the gift, especially on my fortieth birthday, helped me to avoid any tendency to focus on myself. Seeing the surprised and thankful looks on others' faces and sharing the fun of giving anonymously with my children made my day better than I could have hoped for.

—Aimee Mae Wiley—

22

Never Too Poor to Give

No one has ever become poor by giving.
~Anne Frank

"**D**on't you have any toys you want to share?" I asked my son during our church's Christmas toy drive. "What about all those things in your closet you haven't used in years?"

"I don't have anything," he said. "We're so poor."

We're only "poor" because we refuse to buy him the texting phone he wants for Christmas, which would also require a monthly texting charge.

"You're never so poor you have nothing to give," I found myself saying to him, a phrase my mother often used on me.

How could I help him understand, when I myself still whined about things I wanted, like the *Fowler's Modern English Usage* book that cost nearly $40? I knew Santa Hubby wasn't going to pony up for that one. What about that Vera Wang coat I wanted from Kohl's, the one with the $150 price tag? No, that wasn't happening, either.

> *"You're never so poor you have nothing to give."*

At work the next day, one of my students said, "I didn't spell your name right," as she handed me a Christmas gift — a beribboned box of chocolates. No wonder she hadn't spelled it right — I had only worked at the center for a couple of months, and my name is not easy to pronounce, even in English, which is this woman's second language.

The woman had been out of work for months!

"Thank you, Joanna," I said, trying to hold back the tears as I hugged her.

I hadn't expected a gift—I work at an adult education center, where we deal with people every day who struggle economically. The economic downturn is not new to those who come in our doors—those who are laid off, without work, and need an education to get ahead or for a sense of pride. When I was hired, my boss told me she tries to keep snacks around the center and cooks "stone soup" once a week, where whoever can bring something in does, because "You will hear growling bellies here. They give their food to the children before they themselves eat."

"Some of them get food stamps," my boss continued, "but by the end of the month, things are tight. We try not to plan field trips where they would have to pack a lunch because sometimes they just won't show up because they don't even have a sandwich to bring along."

And yet these people, so grateful for a second chance at getting an education, unable to sometimes even afford the gas money to come in, manage to do something for us nearly every week. Some bring in food; others do chores around the center. They help and encourage one another, and us. They give what they are able to give.

When I looked at my Christmas gift from my new friend, I wondered if it had been an offering out of a meager food budget, and I wanted to refuse it. Instead, I said "thank you."

When I brought the candies home to share with my family, I told them just how precious each chocolate was if you thought of how much the unemployed woman's family makes a year. Why, it was the equivalent of a *Fowler's Modern English Usage* book! I said it again, understanding so much better in my heart, "You're never so poor you have nothing to give."

Perhaps the way I could help my son understand best was for me to understand first.

Immediately, I went to my bookshelf and chose several of my favorite novels to share with the center. When I had them boxed, I turned to find my son nonchalantly lugging a white laundry basket of toys he had played with when younger. "I don't want these old things," he said.

I saw among them his beloved Buzz Lightyear and his favorite stuffed dog, Squishy. I set them aside for the toy drive and kissed him on his forehead. He had learned the way I had—by example. Now the students had not only impacted me, but my family as well. Here I had thought I was the teacher, but Joanna and the rest of the students at the center are the ones teaching me. Because you're never so poor you have nothing to give.

—Drema Sizemore Drudge—

23

Always Be a Friend

A good friend is a connection to life — a tie to the past,
a road to the future, the key to sanity
in a totally insane world.
~Lois Wyse

Sitting in church pews all my life, I've listened intently to dire warnings about the war between good and evil. How we as fallen humans are evil by nature, and good only by the grace of God. How we must fight daily against the evil we are inclined to do.

Frankly, it's a message that's hard to digest because, really, do any of us think of ourselves as evil? I have to admit, I don't. I've never stolen from anyone, picked up a knife or gun to harm anyone, or even reported anyone to the IRS. I pay my bills on time, volunteer at the library and recycle.

But some years ago, I stumbled across a brief essay that made clear to me what all those preachers were talking about.

One day on the NPR radio show, *This I Believe*, Deirdre Sullivan read her essay, "Always Go to the Funeral." In it, she relates how her father made her attend the funeral of her fifth-grade math teacher. Just sixteen years old and uneasy about death, Deirdre tried to get out of going to the service — the condolence line was just too uncomfortable to contemplate.

"Deirdre," her father said, "you're going. Always go to the funeral. Do it for the family."

Like Deirdre, I feared these encounters. I'm great on paper — I write a good and genuinely sincere sympathy note — but standing face-to-face with a grieving person and saying something meaningful? I stumble and stutter. I'd rather just sign the guest book and slip out the back door.

But then, four years ago, my best friend died. I had met Rebecca after she and her husband started attending our church. We became close rapidly — she had an only child, a son, and so did I. She was outgoing and loved a good laugh. Our friendship grew deep over coffee, movie nights and long phone conversations.

Rebecca suffered a massive heart attack one night and died instantly. She was only in her fifties, but her family genes had claimed her. Her husband called us that morning, choking on his tears, and asked my husband and me to come over. There, I perched awkwardly on the couch, trying to think of what to say and coming up with nothing. I felt so inadequate.

Rebecca and her husband lived hundreds of miles away from their families and had only been in the area for a few years, so when it came to the memorial service, I was worried that no one would have known her well enough to say anything. I realized that I needed to say something.

For days, I prepared what I was going to say. I memorized and rehearsed it. Still, I was afraid nerves would get the better of me, and my mind would go blank.

On the day of the service, I took my seat and waited for the invitation to share memories. My skin was ice cold, and my heart raced. My hands trembled, and the strength drained from my knees. I desperately wanted to back out. But I thought about the advice Deirdre Sullivan's father had given her — do it for the family — and found my courage.

I opened by recounting how Rebecca and I had been planning an outing to shop for swimsuits. To me, that was the best way to show how close we were — only a really good friend can be trusted to tell you the truth in that dressing room.

I went on to share how Rebecca lavished her time on others and bestowed her friendship generously. She encouraged others and lifted their spirits. In closing, I recited words about true friendship from the Scottish author George MacDonald: "If instead of a gem, or even a flower, we should cast the gift of a loving thought into the heart of a friend, that would be giving as the angels give."

As I spoke, I heard sobs from Rebecca's son in the front row. His pain made my heart ache. But I sat down certain I had done right by my friend.

In truth, Deirdre Sullivan's message isn't just that we ought to go to the funeral. Her message is a call to not give in to laziness and indifference. "In my humdrum life," she says, "the daily battle hasn't been good versus evil. It's hardly so epic. Most days, my real battle is doing good versus doing nothing."

That's it! I thought when I first heard those words. Evil suddenly made sense to me. Doing nothing — nothing to comfort the grieving, nothing to alleviate suffering, nothing to bring a smile to someone's face, nothing to make someone's life better — is a kind of evil. It's a selfishness that elevates our own desires above everything else. It's a miserliness of spirit that deprives others of the love and attention they crave from us.

To me, "always go to the funeral" means doing that thing you don't want to do when that inner voice nudges you to act. Do it when you'd rather queue up another show on Netflix. Do it when you'd rather scroll through your Facebook feed. Do it when you'd rather do nothing at all. Always write the note; always make the phone call; always extend a kind word; always offer up a listening ear. Always be a friend.

— Nancy B. Kennedy —

24

Bed, Bath and Way Beyond

It is a happy talent to know how to play.
~Ralph Waldo Emerson

olunteering wasn't my cup of tea. The thought of giving up my precious time in exchange for nothing didn't interest me. But then, at the ripe young age of fifty, I unexpectedly found myself unable to work as the result of a medical condition. Suddenly, I had way too much time on my hands.

The first year or so of my forced retirement was spent mostly sitting for hours alone feeling sorry for myself. The second year I spent my time cleaning out more closets, junk rooms and cubbyholes than I'd ever realized one home could have. There were times I was so bored with life that I actually contemplated knocking on my neighbors' doors to beg them to let me clean their forgotten spaces. The "postal lady" dreaded seeing me sitting on the porch when delivering the mail. I so longed for conversation I'd talk with her about anything that popped into my mind. The librarians at my local library called me by name because I'd spent so many hours bothering them.

By the time the third year rolled around I was still moping a bit, but with the tidiest garden on the street, the most organized pantry shelves, and the cleanest nooks and crannies on the block, I realized the thing I'd valued most in my life I'd been squandering.

One Sunday afternoon I saw an advertisement in the newspaper asking for community volunteers at the local Humane Society shelter. I'd always loved animals, and having lost my own best friend and beloved Pit Bull a few months prior to my sudden illness, the idea of working with dogs that needed homes seemed a perfect fit. There was no time to waste. After all, if I procrastinated they'd surely find someone else to fill the open slots. I dashed off an e-mail to the shelter letting them know of my interest and before the day was up had a return e-mail telling me where and when to "report for duty."

After sitting through a two-hour orientation, my reluctance to volunteer was back in full force. Each volunteer was asked to complete a three-hour stint in "Bed, Bath and Beyond," a fancy title for scrubbing food bowls and litter pans and washing trash bins stuffed with dirty, smelly laundry. Who knew animals could dirty so many blankets in one day? But with all the determination I could muster I told myself to relax and enjoy the task at hand. After all, this was only the beginning of a long list of volunteer opportunities available at the shelter, a way of weeding out those not truly interested in giving their time. Once this task was complete I'd be promoted to bigger and better things, right?

With all the diligence and enthusiasm I'd become famous for at the shelter, I went right to work. There was never a dull moment and always a new animal that needed love and the reassurance that it would soon find its new home. There was the occasional shy, grown cat that just needed company while it waited for its new owner to arrive. There were dogs of all sizes and breeds — some excited, some scared, some wanting to play, others simply needing a bit of space while they adjusted to the new surroundings.

One blustery January morning I pulled open the shelter doors, punched the volunteer time clock and went to work. As I'd come to learn, no day is considered normal at the Humane Society, and this one was no different. I began by washing dishes and shoving a load of laundry into the washer — a rather mindless task I'd actually come to enjoy, especially after seeing firsthand what a benefit it was to the paid staff for a volunteer to do the "grunt work" so they could spend more time teaching the animals basic commands in preparation for their new owners.

With the laundry packed away and the dishes drying, I made my way through the shelter in search of a "newbie," a dog or cat just introduced to the shelter that needed a bit of extra tender love and care. I found an unexpected surprise. With her lipstick mouth, spotted floppy ears, and paws that seemed perfect for a dog four times her size, she was packed in a twelve-week-old package of energy and excitement, with hazel eyes that screamed, "You need me, you just haven't realized it yet!"

Just looking at her brought a long-forgotten smile to my face. Around and around the pen she ran, chasing her tail until she fell over from dizziness. She would grab her tail between her teeth and growl at it like it was an enemy she'd finally conquered. I laughed, and the sound of my own laughter startled me. It had been years since I'd laughed out loud.

I stood watching the puppy for what seemed like hours before I finally reached in and pulled her to my chest. She sniffed, wiggled her way up my shoulders to my face, and began licking me with her warm, wet tongue. After a while she calmed, laid her head on my chest and stared into my eyes. Then she closed her eyes tight and sighed as if to say, "I'm at peace now, you're here." She knew it before I did. We needed each other.

A fresh zeal for a changed life can often be found in the strangest places. Mine was found in the eyes of a pup I named Hazel, and I would have missed the opportunity altogether had I not been willing to give of the most precious thing in life — my time.

— Lisa Fowler —

25

Weeding Baby Wendell

You can't live a perfect day without doing something
for someone who will never be able to repay you.
~John Wooden

I walk nearly every evening, rain or shine. Although the area where I live has sidewalks, ball fields and open spaces where most people do their walking, I prefer to walk in the cemetery across the street. It's nearly forty acres of rolling land full of mature trees and all manner of wildlife. It's filled too, with many graves. Toward a back corner, just a few feet from a rusted section of chain-link fence choked with honeysuckle, is Baby Wendell's grave.

On my daily walks I began to stop now and then to upright a vase, pull a weed or pick up trash. I don't always take the same route, so I never focused on any grave in particular. I just did what little thing needed to be done if I noticed, and kept walking. It was obvious when family or friends would tidy up around a grave, and it became clear that some graves never got attention other than the general maintenance by the cemetery staff. No one ever visited Baby Wendell. The little granite urn on his tombstone would fill with old leaves, grass clippings and spider webs. The day I noticed wiregrass smothering his tiny tombstone, I decided to make Wendell a routine stop.

My daily walks also meant that the many visitors who came regularly on Sunday afternoons or holidays would see me at one place or another on the grounds. I'd often be mistaken for an employee as they stopped to ask, for instance, where section L was, which gate exited where, or how to find the main office.

One Sunday evening, two elderly women who I later realized had seen me there many times, drove up as I was bent over picking a dead wasp out of Wendell's urn. Not wanting them to think I was up to no good, I stood and walked toward them to say hello. They were all smiles and I was surprised as they began to thank me.

"We see you out here real often. How long have you worked here?" the first woman asked as she adjusted the bouquet of artificial flowers she held in her hand.

The second woman added "Yes, and after that last storm you were the first one we saw out here picking up sticks. It's just so good that you work here."

I watched the first woman struggle with her bouquet and said, "Oh no, Ma'am. I don't work here. I just walk here."

As it turned out, they were sisters who had come to put flowers on their brother's grave. His is located just a few sites over from Baby Wendell, between a dogwood tree and a very old azalea.

"But you're here just about every time we come by," the first woman said, still fighting to get a grip on the bouquet in her hand, and looking puzzled that I didn't work there.

"And looks to me like every time we've seen you, you've been working," the sister added.

I explained to them how I might randomly pick up a stick now and then, or put some wind-blown trash back in the can, but that they only saw me so often because I had one day noticed the wiregrass that nearly covered the tiny tombstone near their brother's.

"I'm just weeding Baby Wendell," I said.

"Why? All that and you don't work here?" the first woman asked.

I'd never given it much thought. I walked there nearly every day and it was just part of my walk to upright a geranium now and then. I had occasionally remembered what Nannie, my grandmother, used to tell us kids: "If you see a need, fill it, and don't worry about who gets the credit."

"Well, we can't thank you enough for all we've seen you do," the first woman said, as a little piece of her bouquet of flowers broke off.

"Oh, it's just wonderful that you would help for no reason," her sister added.

They both seemed about to tear up as they walked away. I never thought about needing or getting credit for any of the random things I only sporadically did as I walked, but these two women had noticed and they had thanked me. Those tiny efforts took so little on my part, but to them they meant a lot. They noticed and they appreciated.

I suppose we all do random nice things because we know it's right and it's kind. Baby Wendell could never thank me, and none of us imagine we'll ever be thanked for the tiny things we do, and we may not believe anyone even notices. But out there for each of us is the equivalent of those two old ladies, noticing and appreciating.

I reached down and picked up the tiny piece of bouquet the woman had dropped as she thanked me. I finished weeding Baby Wendell and put those flowers in his little urn.

"No need to thank me, Wendell. You're welcome."

— Stuart M. Perkins —

Out of the Blue

Be happy when God answers your prayer but be
happier when you are an answer to others' prayers.
~Author Unknown

My friend Patty once shared the story of how she got over a bad case of "the blahs," and within her account was the best advice I have ever received. It was a simple bit of wisdom, casually conveyed, but has since become a precept I try to live by every day.

Her tale began on a gray afternoon in late February, when winter's drab skies, barren trees and numbing cold had left Patty feeling forlorn.

"I was down in the dumps and just couldn't perk up," she recalled. "I tried giving myself a manicure, watching a bunch of sappy rom-coms, making double-fudge brownies — nothing helped; I was stuck in the doldrums."

Desperate to overcome the gloom, Patty decided to try "retail therapy," but even an impromptu shopping trip left her hollow. Weary and defeated, she retreated into the comfort of her favorite coffee shop for a caffeine boost.

As Patty sat sipping a double cappuccino, she noticed an older woman walk into the café, struggling with a half-dozen overstuffed grocery bags. The lady looked to be about sixty, well dressed but slightly disheveled, and something about her was vaguely familiar. Patty kept glancing over, trying to place her, and it seemed the woman was doing likewise. After a few minutes, the stranger came up to Patty's table.

"Excuse me," she said timidly. "I hate to bother you, but I think I've seen you at church…"

Of course, that was it! Patty recognized her as one of the ladies who sang in the Sunday choir. The woman introduced herself and they chatted briefly before she asked for a favor.

"My car is in the shop, but I really needed to get to the store today so I walked," she explained, setting her bags down on the table. "Now it looks like it's going to rain any minute. If it isn't too much trouble, would you mind giving me a ride home? It's not too far from here."

Patty told her it wouldn't be a problem, and the two headed out to the van. Before they left the shopping center, Patty asked if there was anywhere else she needed to go, and the woman admitted she had hoped to get a few more errands done that afternoon. In the end, their trip included a visit to the pharmacy and a stop at the dry cleaner's to pick up her husband's shirts.

And sure enough, just as they pulled into the woman's driveway, an icy sleet began drizzling down. If the woman had walked home, she would have been caught in the storm long before reaching her house. The two joked about the timing of the wicked weather, and then Patty helped carry the thankful woman's parcels inside.

"I had so much to do today. I was praying God would help me make it through," she told Patty as the two were saying goodbye. "You were the answer to that prayer."

Patty smiled, hugged her and returned to the van, feeling better than she had in months. The blues were gone, replaced by a deep and dynamic jubilance. She turned on the radio and sang along with the music, her mood a complete contrast to the dismal day around her.

"I felt wonderful!" Patty exclaimed, relating the story to me. "All the while, I had been trying to cheer myself up and nothing worked because I was going about it all wrong. That day, I realized that the way to feel better is to be someone else's blessing."

Be someone else's blessing.

Over the years, that simple, straightforward concept has become a goal I try to meet every day. And whenever I've been fortunate enough to accomplish it, I find that helping others not only gives me a sense of purpose, but also reminds me of the many, many things I have to be thankful for in my life.

> *"I realized that the way to feel better is to be someone else's blessing."*

There are always plenty of ways to be someone else's blessing. Some are big opportunities like volunteering at the local soup kitchen or leaving a huge tip for the server who looks exhausted and overwhelmed. Others are small gestures that can have a big impact, such as letting the frustrated driver cut into the lane, or offering kind words to the mom whose toddler is having a meltdown. Oftentimes, these actions begin a ripple effect, with one good deed setting off a chain reaction of kindness, until it's hard to tell exactly where the blessings began and knowing they may never end.

— Miriam Van Scott —

27

Shelter in a Storm

My mother had a slender, small body, but a large
heart — a heart so large that everybody's joys found
welcome in it, and hospitable accommodation.
~Mark Twain

The rain started as I got into the car. The weather reflected the storm of emotions I felt. Three days earlier I had buried my mother. Now, as I prepared to go home, I knew I'd never return to this house again and find a parent waiting for me.

I saw the little family out of the corner of my eye through the haze of tears and a foggy window. The pungent aroma of funeral flowers was my only company, and they took up every seat. Steady traffic required that I wait, so I watched them make their way up the street in the pouring rain.

As they crossed the street, the tiny, young mother held one of the babies close to her, trying unsuccessfully to shield her from the rain. The father carried the other on his back. Rivulets of water running through his dreadlocks dripped into the face of the baby who held tightly to his neck.

I looked around the car as they passed in front of me. There was no room — flowers and knick-knacks from my mother's life filled every space in my car. Then I saw my mom's leopard print umbrella. I blew the horn, beckoning the father to come. His look of hope said he thought he had a ride.

A quick glance in the car revealed that my invitation was not to offer him a ride.

"Would you take this umbrella, please?" I asked.

"Oh, yes ma'am," he said softly. "Thank you." Then he hurried back to his waiting family.

The young mother quickly gathered her babies under the shelter of my mom's umbrella. For them the rain had stopped. They continued on their way with a souvenir of my mother's doing what it had always done for me, providing a cover of love.

— Trudie Nash —

28

Delivering Love, Receiving Hope

One of the great ironies of life is this:
He or she who serves almost always
benefits more than he or she who is served.
~Gordon B. Hinckley

After my partner passed away from AIDS, I was deeply depressed. I didn't know what to do. It seemed that I had lost my purpose in life, despite being a social worker in homeless shelters. At a staff meeting, one of my colleagues mentioned God's Love We Deliver, a group of volunteers who were delivering meals to people living with HIV/AIDS during the height of the epidemic. I saw this as an opportunity to honor my partner's memory by helping others who were struggling in much the same way that he had struggled.

Inspired by this idea, I made my way to the Upper West Side to meet the founders of God's Love We Deliver — Ganga Stone and Jane Best — and to learn how I could get involved. That was twenty-eight years ago, and I've been a God's Love volunteer ever since.

Those early years were critical — people living with HIV/AIDS were suffering and desperately needed help. As a volunteer for God's Love, I would pick up donated meals from restaurants and deliver them to our clients in time for dinner. Sometimes a client would invite me in to sit and talk. I was always glad to spend time with them, knowing they were not only hungry, but lonely, too. In those moments, I'd be reminded of my partner, and I'd feel as if by helping others I was also helping him. So many family members, friends and strangers had been there for us when we were going through difficult times, and now I, too, was making a difference. Giving back was giving purpose to my life.

Ever since that day in 1987 when I began volunteering with God's Love, I have been blessed with the opportunity to help those in need. So many of their faces are imprinted on my memory — a young mother, nearly blind from AIDS, and her son standing in their small, meagerly furnished room as I delivered their meals. Christmas was approaching, and my heart broke as I listened to the little boy recite the list of toys he hoped to get from Santa. I suspected the toys would never materialize. Again, I was inspired by the chance to be there for this family. I submitted their letter to "Santa Claus," otherwise known as the generous New Yorkers of the Operation Santa Claus Project. A few weeks later the young mother and son received three shopping bags filled with toys. I was thrilled to help make their Christmas a little brighter.

I'll always remember the client in Staten Island who had no food or money. When I arrived at his home with a weekend's worth of food, I saw that he was severely ill. He asked me to stay, so I did, for four days. As I watched his health decline, I urged him to go to the hospital, but he refused out of fear. Finally, after I told him it was time for me to go home, he changed his mind and we rode together in an ambulance to the emergency room. At the hospital he learned that he had a blockage in his kidney, which was, thankfully, treatable. It has been an honor to be a point of contact through God's Love for so many people who are sick and don't have anyone else to assist them in getting the help they need.

Now, I am one of over 8,000 volunteers a year who support God's Love We Deliver and the clients they serve. The chefs and kitchen volunteers cook nutritious meals for people affected not only by HIV/AIDS, but by a variety of life-altering illnesses, who can't shop or cook for themselves. I have seen many changes at God's Love and in New York City over the past twenty-eight years, but one thing remains constant: the God's Love community has so much heart. The love we put into our work, and the love we put into the meals we deliver, always reaches the clients. It is an honor and a privilege to be a part of it, and I know I gain more from volunteering than I will ever be able to give.

—James Strickland—

The Strength of Vulnerability

Nothing is so strong as gentleness,
nothing so gentle as real strength.
~St. Francis de Sales

I have never used the words strength and vulnerability together before. Strength essentially means great power, and vulnerability is about being open or exposed. Somehow I had not thought the two words could go together, but recently I felt the strength of vulnerability through one simple act of kindness.

It was Thanksgiving weekend and my family had decided to have our turkey dinner on the Saturday night. I had to work until 7:00 p.m. so the plan was that my mother and husband would have the dinner timed for around 7:30 p.m. The mall was quiet that evening and I was able to lock the store right at 7:00 p.m. I gathered the garbage and as I looked forward to our family gathering, I did not even notice I had not taken my usual route to the garbage bins.

An agitated young man who had missed his bus stopped me. He needed a ride and if he waited for the next bus, he'd miss his curfew and his bed at the Salvation Army. He'd be forced to sleep outside and he didn't have a sleeping bag. He needed to get there before they locked the door.

The voice inside my head got very loud as the survival instinct kicked in and quickly reminded me of all the reasons why giving this man a ride was a very bad idea. My family was waiting, my cell phone had a 2 percent charge left on it, I might get mugged or raped and on and on. I asked him a few questions and even wished I had some cash on me, to send him off in a cab so that this problem would go away.

As these thoughts whirled through my mind, I looked into his eyes. I saw desperation, but more importantly, I saw a person. I saw him. I heard a small voice that quietly said, "He's someone's son." In that moment, I just knew I had to give him a ride. The embarrassing thing was that I couldn't even remember where the Salvation Army was.

He promised directions and offered to take the garbage bag I still held, while I called home to say I'd be another hour. As we drove downtown we chatted. He was trying to get clean and turn his life around. He got kicked out of the house he was living in. I told him to look into going back to school, unsure of what other motherly advice I could give him.

Eventually, he asked about me and found out that I was missing my Thanksgiving dinner in order to drive him. He began to cry. Perhaps his faith in humanity was restored in that moment; I don't know. All I could think of to say was "Don't cry for me, my dinner will be there when I get home and it's more important that you get your bed. If I was in your position, I'd want someone to help me."

Somehow I knew our roles could easily be reversed. His name was James. We made it to the Salvation Army on time and he had a place to sleep that night. I felt alive and our dinner was made more beautiful by sharing this story. Interestingly enough, if I had taken my usual route to the garbage, I wouldn't have this story to share.

I am not saying we should all run out and give strangers a ride. In this case, however, in finding the strength to allow myself to be a little vulnerable, I opened myself up to a life-changing experience. I made an important human connection that I wouldn't have made if I had taken the safe and fearful route.

—Mary Anne Molcan—

It Was Nothing

*To give and then not feel that one has given
is the very best of all ways of giving.*
~Max Beerbohm

My first lesson is at a meeting. As we settle around the table, I hear Meg, who is recovering from surgery, talking to Judith, the manager of our project. "Thank you so much for driving my daughters to all their dance and music lessons last week. I can't tell you how much that meant to me."

Judith checks her planner for the time of her next meeting. "Don't mention it," she says. "It was nothing."

I listen with awe, knowing how crammed Judith's schedule is, with her work, meetings, kids, and aging parents. Driving someone's children to lessons seems incredibly generous to me, bordering on the angelic.

The meeting is just beginning when Donna hurries into the room. "Sorry I'm late," Donna says, pulling out a chair. "I was hosting my semi-annual lunch for my friends who are over seventy. A few of the ladies lingered a long time."

I envision Donna, surrounded by white-haired ladies, each beautifully coifed and bejeweled.

"How many people came?" I ask.

"Eight. We have a lot of older people in our apartment building and they don't get out much, so I fix a fancy luncheon for them. The stories they have to tell are truly fascinating."

I think of my own neighborhood and realize that several of my neighbors don't get out much anymore. I never thought of inviting them over for a meal.

"That is so nice of you," I say, knowing how busy Donna is, how she doesn't really like to cook and clean.

"Oh," she says, waving her hand, "it was nothing."

Meanwhile, I am moving into a new house. Between unpacking and working, I feel fried and frazzled. That feeling lifts instantly when I come home from work and find two fledgling rosebushes on the front stoop. The note from Nick reads, "I know you like roses. Don't worry if you kill these. I have more." I pick up each plant and smile at the world. Roses are my favorite flowers and it is quite possible these magnificent plants will not survive under my care. Nick's note assuages my guilt. Despite the gathering dark, I plant the bushes and call Nick, spilling over with gratitude.

"Hey, it was nothing," Nick says. I hear the pleasure in his voice. He loved bringing me those plants. As a master gardener, he was sharing one of his great gifts.

I start thinking about this concept of "nothing," this serene and generous way of living. While I am in the middle of this pondering, Terri calls. She is giving an important speech and is very nervous.

"Can I practice in front of you?" she asks.

"Sure," I say. I know how terrifying public speaking can be.

Sunday afternoon, Terri stands in my living room and gives her speech. She sounds shy and uncertain. Her beginning is long and stumbling; her ending is abrupt. I have a few ideas.

"I think you could start with that great story you told in the middle," I tell her. "And you could look at me more often."

She tries the speech again, her voice stronger, her eye contact good. We discuss the opening story and she tries again. After the fifth try, I give her a rousing round of applause. "It's great," I tell her.

"I can't thank you enough," she says.

I smile and shake my head. "It was nothing," I say.

Then I stop — had it really been nothing or am I just saying that? I think about the afternoon. I was tired when we started, still worn down from working all day Saturday. Now, I feel alive and energetic. I feel confident, smart and talented! And looking at Terri, I can see she feels pretty good too.

"I was wrong," I tell Terri. "Helping you was really something to me."

And so, I learned that giving from the heart doesn't have to mean sacrifice and hard work. The trick is finding something we love to do and finding someone who needs that something. We can be generous to others and to ourselves at the same time! Once you get the hang of it, it's nothing. And it's really something.

— Deborah Shouse —

Have Less Stuff

What You'll Find in This Chapter

We all have too much stuff. We know it, we feel the weight of it, but we don't always do something about it. However, when we do clean something out, even if it's just one drawer in one chest in one room, we notice we feel better. So how do we motivate ourselves to do what we know would make us happier?

Start by donating some of that extra stuff. The fact that you might be holding onto something in your closet or basement or garage that you will never use, and that could be of benefit to someone else, is probably the best reason of all to de-clutter your home. And the longer you hold onto them, the less valuable those items will be to the next person. If you're never going to wear that clothing again, why not give it away while it's still at least somewhat in style?

What I do is create a mental image of the person who will pick up my excess stuff from the church thrift shop. And when I'm organizing my donations for my imaginary friend, I'm excited that these items that once were special for me will now be special for her.

We all know the drill. Make a pile to donate, a pile to throw away, and a pile to offer to friends and family. After they say no, you can add those items to the "donate" pile. You'll feel freer with less stuff, and you'll derive more joy from what you've kept because it's the stuff you'll really use.

You'll meet some good role models in this chapter, people who either voluntarily got rid of their stuff, or people who lost their possessions through fire, or financial ruin, and realized they were absolutely fine, and even happier, without all those things. In Pam Phree's story, "The Right Dream," she tells us that she and her husband had been living the good life, pursuing the American Dream. They were forced to dramatically downsize after their business failed, giving up their fancy home, cars, and expensive possessions. She says, "Now, our home is modest but fully paid for. We don't have a lot of things that need dusting and maintenance—only the necessities… Now I can honestly say my husband and I are truly living—and enjoying—the American Dream."

If you're holding onto too much stuff for sentimental reasons, you'll want to read Amelia Hollingsworth's story, "The One Thing We Didn't Have to Unpack." She tells us that as she was packing up her young family's home for a cross-country move, she had a hard time letting go. So much of their furniture held special memories for her, but not everything would fit in their new, smaller home. She couldn't decide what to take and what to leave until her mother put it all in perspective. "The stuff isn't the memories," Amelia's mother told her. "And you don't have to worry about losing the memories when you leave your stuff behind. Those you take with you." And she was right. Even though Amelia had to leave a lot of items with sentimental value behind, she doesn't miss them. "We have not lost the happy memories of our old home," she shares. "Those came with us, and they were the only things we never had to box up or unpack."

31

The Right Dream

The clearer you are when visualizing your dreams,
the brighter the spotlight will be to lead
you on the right path.
~Gail Lynne Goodwin

After working for nearly a decade at the same dead-end job with no advancement and no pay increases, I was contemplating leaving the profession for good when I got a job offer I couldn't pass up. I was offered the position of Office Manager for a struggling company that had been operating at a loss for over a year. My job would be to organize the office, hire and fire as needed, and help turn a losing operation into a profitable one. The owner knew that would be no easy task and because of same, he offered me a salary I had only dreamed of, paid vacation, sick leave and a 401K. Since my current job offered zero benefits, it took me only two seconds to accept.

I had colleagues in the business who were willing to come aboard for the benefits alone, and with the owner's permission, I hired friends and family (including my husband) who shared the same vision I did: to make the firm the biggest and best in the business.

When we became profitable, I was promoted to State Manager with a substantial salary increase. I managed two offices with forty-four employees working in five separate departments, with plans to open a third office on the drawing board.

As sometimes happens when one goes from rags to riches, as our income increased, so did our spending. My husband and I moved from our small apartment to a large, beautiful home near my office. Since the job entailed a considerable amount of entertaining, our house was filled to overflowing with high-end quality furniture which I had purchased on the installment plan to improve my credit rating. We had two beautiful cars in the driveway.

By all appearances, we were living the American Dream.

I'll never forget the Friday that I was walking around the office, looking forward to the weekend, and encountered our company attorney. He wordlessly handed me a sealed envelope.

The letter inside was brief. It stated that due to the recent downturn in the economy, the company had reorganized and my position had been eliminated. Effective immediately, I was to leave the premises.

When I looked up after reading it, I noticed that seven other employees had been given the same envelope — including my husband.

The aftermath was devastating. We got new jobs, but in a different profession and only making minimum wage. We were forced to move out of our house into a tiny apartment. The furniture and one of our cars were repossessed.

Even worse than the loss of our possessions was the loss of self-esteem. Somewhere along the way, I had equated my identity with my job; i.e. since I had such an important job, then that made me important. And somewhere along the way, I measured personal success by how many big and expensive things I owned; the more possessions, the more successful I was. Without that important job and without all those possessions, I thought of myself as unimportant and unsuccessful.

> *I measured personal success by how many big and expensive things I owned.*

The sudden loss of our jobs was heartbreaking but as with most misfortunes, it turned out to be a blessing in disguise. It forced us to come to a complete stop and analyze what we really wanted out of life and what we needed to do to get there.

We realized we had worked 24/7, 365 days a year to keep that company afloat and profitable. We had sacrificed time with our friends, families and even each other to advance in a corporate world that in the end, didn't appreciate, deserve or value our efforts. We had missed important births, funerals, graduations and weddings.

It's been years now since we both lost our jobs. And our lives did change — for the better.

Now, our home is modest but fully paid for. We don't have a lot of things that need dusting and maintenance — only the necessities. We don't finance or use credit cards anymore. If we don't have the cash, we don't buy it.

Now I can honestly say my husband and I are truly living — and enjoying — the American Dream.

— Pam Phree —

32

The One Thing We Didn't Have to Unpack

A memory is what is left when something happens
and does not completely unhappen.
~Edward de Bono

I

t was two days before we had to leave our large four-bedroom house and move out of state. I loved this house and all the memories we had made in it. I thought back to raising our son and daughter there. We had brought them home from the hospital to this house. This was where they learned to walk and to talk. This was where we watched them play on the lawn as we rocked on the welcoming porch on beautiful spring and autumn days. I had picked apples from the trees in the back yard and learned to make apple pie from scratch in this house.

And now we were saying goodbye.

My husband announced that our things would not all fit in our POD. I stood in our driveway while the cicadas screeched like a car alarm. "What's not going to fit?" I asked.

"The sage couches, the kitchen table, the coffee tables, the treadmill, the rocking chairs…"

"We have to take the porch rockers!" Thunder was starting to rumble in the distance, and the wind was picking up, only adding to my sense of urgency. "I nursed our babies in those! We sat in those and counted the fireflies every summer."

"Honey," my husband continued patiently, "they're not going to fit. And even if they did, we're not going to have a porch in California."

We lived east of the Mississippi and all our family was out West, so we were moving out there to be with the people we so desperately missed. We needed our children to be surrounded by people who loved them unconditionally the way only grandparents can. We needed to know that someone had our back and would move heaven and earth to be there if we called. We had flown solo for five years, and although we had made dear friends, there was just no substitute for our parents, Grandma and Grandpa for our kids.

When an opportunity came for my husband to transfer west (to a town that was just a few hours from my parents and a day's drive from his), we knew it was time. We were excited. We would be living in a house half the size of this one, but we didn't care. We would never have to spend Thanksgiving or Christmas alone again. Our children would be able to grow up with grandparents, aunts, uncles, and cousins in the picture.

"Could we get a bigger POD?" I asked, still trying to bring everything along with us.

Jason sighed. "Amy, this is as big as they come."

"But I love the kitchen table," I said.

"Do you want to bring that one instead of the dining room table?"

I thought a moment. "No."

"Honey, we can't take both!" My husband took off his work gloves. He wiped the sweat from his forehead and locked the doors to the POD. The wind was blowing the branches of our pear trees sideways. The thunder boomed. "We have to wait until the storm passes before we can load anything else in the POD. Okay? You think about what you want to take with us." He slipped quietly back into the house.

I stood in the garage and watched the rain run off our driveway. I felt like the sand was running out of our hourglass. We had to say goodbye to the home I loved and the furniture I loved, too.

I sat down on the bumper of my car and called my mom.

"Hello?"

"Hi, Mom. It's Amy."

"Hi, honey. What's new? How's the packing going?"

"It's not all going to fit," I said, trying to keep my voice steady and not burst into tears.

"What's not going to fit?"

"The treadmill, the kitchen table, the couches, the porch rocking chairs." I felt hot tears spill down my cheeks. "And I know it's just stuff, and I know stuff doesn't matter, but it's hard! I sat in that rocking chair and read stories to Azure when I was pregnant with Seamus. And I lost the last thirty pounds of my baby weight walking on that treadmill at night after the kids went to bed. And I've sat at that kitchen table every night with my family since we moved into this house…"

"Amy, honey. The stuff isn't the memories. You don't need the rocking chairs to remember reading books to Azure on the front porch when she was small. You don't need your kitchen table to remember family dinners. You will always have those memories, whether the stuff comes with you to your new house or not. And you don't have to worry about losing the memories when you leave your stuff behind. Those you take with you, and you don't even have to worry about boxing them up. Okay?"

"Okay," I said.

"How's your weather?" my mom asked.

"We're having an afternoon thunderstorm." I looked up at the skies. The clouds had thinned and bright blue sky bent around them. "But it looks like the rain has stopped."

"Yeah. You are going to be just fine. Moving is tough, but we are so excited that you are going to be closer."

"We're excited too."

My mom was right.

We've been very happy in our new home, half the size of our old one. We have half as much stuff as we did before. We don't miss it, and we have not lost the happy memories of our old home. Those came with us, and they were the only things we never had to box up or unpack.

— Amelia Hollingsworth —

33

The Liberation of Liquidation

Reduce the complexity of life by eliminating
the needless wants of life, and the
labors of life reduce themselves.
~Edwin Way Teale

Annie and I had been living in a sprawling, three-bedroom, two living area house for over ten years. The house was a rental, but we had been in the place so long it felt like home. We'd originally intended to buy the place from the owner, who had passed away from old age. Now her relatives were ready to sell but we weren't ready to buy. It was time to move.

"You know," my sweet wife told me one morning after we'd gotten the news that it was time to move on. "We've spent over a decade mowing the lawn, trimming the hedges, pruning the trees, and all the other yard work that comes with living in a house. Don't you think that's enough?"

I nodded, standing next to her and pondering about paying rent on yet another house. All our children had grown up and gotten married, and my mom, who had come to live with us, had passed on two years before. I supposed we could rent a smaller house, but they seemed a bit hard to come by, and we weren't yet ready to buy our own house.

"Why don't we rent an apartment?" my wife said softly at my shoulder. "There would be no mowing, no trimming, and no pruning to do."

I don't know," I argued, immediately thinking of living next to people who would be to the left of us, to the right, down below, and up above. "An apartment is not a house."

"A cozy, little apartment," my wife continued, "for just the two of us, a sweet little nest where we could be together."

"A small apartment would mean less cost," I conceded. Then I did a reality check and looked around. "But what would we do with all our stuff?"

And did we have a lot of stuff! We had rooms stuffed with stuff. The garage was stacked with boxes. There was so much stuff we didn't even know what we had.

"What are we going to do with all of our things if we move into a little apartment?" Annie asked. Then her eyes brightened. "Why don't we put what we don't need in storage and save it for when we buy our own house?"

So that was the plan. We found a wonderful apartment that was exactly the cozy, beautiful little nest my wife and I were looking for. It was only one bedroom, and so most of our things would have to be packed up and put into storage. That's when I got the bright idea to just let everything extra go. Everything we had slated to go into storage would be sold or given away instead.

"So you're serious," Annie said after I told her my idea. "You want to get rid of everything we can't take with us?"

"Why not?" I replied. I looked at all the furniture and boxes that wouldn't see the light of day for a few years. "What happens if we get to like apartment life, or it takes somewhat longer before we can afford to buy a house? Or what if we decide to wait until I retire? That stuff might be in storage forever."

"True," Annie replied. "We might not get around to it for a long time."

"Then again," I pointed out, "Let's say we stay in the apartment. We'll get used to having less very quickly, and all that extra stuff will just be like an anchor around our necks. Why not keep the most important things, things that we treasure, and let someone else have the rest?"

Annie smiled at me. "I think I know who might be able to help."

So we hired a person who liquidated estates, let her take care of selling or donating three-fourths of everything we'd once thought we couldn't live without, and moved forward. Walking away from all the stuff we had acquired during our life together was hard, but it was also liberating.

Now, here in our tiny little nest, where it's just the two of us and those things that are dearest to our hearts, life is a different kind of adventure. In finally getting down to the basics, letting go of the need to have "stuff," Annie and I are better able to concentrate on our family and each other, and on living a life where what we have isn't as important to us as who we have in our lives.

—John P. Buentello—

34

From Tragedy to Triumph

When I chased after money, I never had enough.
When I got my life on purpose and focused on giving
of myself and everything that arrived into my life,
then I was prosperous.
~Wayne Dyer

etal crushing, glass shattering and the acrid gun-shot smell of airbags deploying are all I remember of the single minute that took me from an upper middle–class life to poverty-level, surviving on less than fifteen percent of what I previously made. For the first six months after the accident, I spent every day curled up on my bed, unable to move, and shocked at how much of my identity had been tied to how much I made and how much I spent.

I finally faced the fact that although I had worked hard my entire life, everything I had was gone. I now had to learn how to live on almost nothing. Even if I did receive permanent disability, it would still be less than twenty percent of what my six-figure income had provided.

At first I was angry, resentful and fed-up. I no longer had the option to make any decisions about discretionary spending. There simply WAS no extra money available. Everything had to be prioritized so that only the necessary bills were paid. The rent was first, utilities second. After that it became a game of spreading the money between groceries, caring for the animals I had adopted, and medicine for me. It was a miserable existence, and then two things happened in the same week and broke me out of this rut.

The first was receiving a series of pictures showing how much people in various cultures got to spend on food in a week. When I saw a family in Africa making do with their single bag of rice and a few wilted vegetables I gained a new perspective on my own situation.

Then I had a conversation with a neighbor who was going through essentially the same process as me and I realized that I had already survived the worst of my debacle. I hadn't lost my home; my utilities hadn't been shut off, and although I hadn't eaten the sumptuous restaurant meals I was used to consuming while working two jobs, I also hadn't starved. I had, by sheer stubbornness, found ways to make the reduced income do double duty and survived.

The accident had taken away my purpose in life. But as often happens, what doesn't destroy us makes us stronger and wiser. I knew that finding a new purpose was mandatory, and that instead of feeling angry and resentful, I could begin to look at the need to live successfully on significantly less as a challenge. If I could win this game, I could help others do so too. That gave me a new focus.

I cut up all my credit cards and sent them back to the credit card companies. I paid them only what I could, when I could. I sold all the high-priced examples of over-spending I had accumulated over the years: fancy collectibles; expensive jewelry, too-expensive automobiles and anything else that had a value. By doing so, I was able to keep going and pay off much of the debt I had. A second benefit was that I began to have a lot less to clean, and began to truly find a lightness in my spirit that the weight of "stuff" had held down all those years.

> *I began to truly find a lightness in my spirit that the weight of "stuff" had held down all those years.*

Being freed from caring what anyone else had or did allowed me to become my own person. Instead of trying to keep up with anyone else, I got to concentrate on what really mattered to me. Amazingly, over a five-year period, I learned that living in the finest home, driving the newest car and/or having the latest gadgets were simply no longer important to me. Even when I got an increase in my disability check, I no longer desired to run out and replace any of the "things" I previously had found so important.

Little by little I cleaned out and downsized to the point where I now have a minimalist home that I can take care of pretty much by myself. Interestingly, if the dogs do something that creates a mess, it no longer stresses me out. There's nothing so important that it's worth having a meltdown about anymore. I also have so much more of that illusive item that most people running on the hamster wheel of ambition have almost none of — time.

I now focus on spending time with family and friends. We talk about the olden days, the days of lavish Christmas presents, of eating out every night, and of buying new clothes, toys and décor almost monthly. Amazingly, my kids don't remember most of what I gave them or they played with. Instead, their memories are of the days I couldn't attend their ceremonies or my coming home from work after they were already in bed asleep. Time with people can never be replaced by stuff.

Granted, there are still days I wish I had more income to accomplish a cherished goal or make a repair to my home. But I've found that if the goal is meant to be, eventually it will happen. God provides in interesting and unique ways, and helping neighbors with their problems has opened avenues for them to help me with mine. By not being able to buy myself whatever I want, I've learned how to develop deeper and richer relationships, networks and friendships.

And a lot of the resentment my children once felt at my quest for the best and brightest has gone by the wayside. We were recently all just talking over a simple salad and tea — realizing that we were closer now than many families who have much more materially, but spend no time connecting emotionally.

Would I have voluntarily gone through what happened? Possibly not, but since I was allowed to experience it, I have been able to help many others make wiser financial decisions and survive in the face of traumatic events. I am now at a place in life where I can truly say that I wouldn't exchange the life I have for my old one. Living on less allows you to truly live — a rare gift that many miss out on.

— Kamia Taylor —

35

Mountain Dreams

Get excited and enthusiastic about your own dream.
This excitement is like a forest fire — you can smell it,
taste it, and see it from a mile away.
~Denis Waitley

O ur family had enjoyed a happy home in the small community where we lived. Yet, as life often does, our situation changed. The town had grown, but we had not. We decided to move and start fresh.

That night, unable to sleep, my husband and I discussed our plans, or lack of them. We had no idea where we were headed or what we should do with our lives. The more we talked, the more I thought about one of our family's favorite Disney movies: *So Dear to My Heart.* This wonderful movie portrayed the lifestyle my husband and I longed for. We had always dreamed of owning a tiny chinked-log cabin like the one in the movie, but we'd live in the mountains. I'd spin wool by the wood stove, milk goats, make cheese, can food and work a garden. My husband would harvest wood, hike, fish, snowshoe and make maple syrup. We imagined our children thriving and pursuing their interests in the great outdoors. The longer we chatted, the more I felt our answer had been in front of us all along.

"Do you still want to live in the mountains someday?" I asked.

"Of course," he answered, "but we can't do it now."

When I asked him why not, he presented me with our usual collection of problems: east versus west, how we would finance our land,

and how we would make a living once we were there. "The bottom line is that we can't afford it right now," he said.

"That's how you felt when we wanted a baby," I reminded him. "If we'd waited until we could afford one, we'd still be childless today." He nodded. "Why not live our dream?" I continued. That did it.

We were excited and terrified at the same time. Naturally there were obstacles, but fighting for our dream made it worthwhile. The eastern mountains won. We financed and found land. We put our home up for sale while we built our cabin from thousands of miles away. Questions and concerns from well-meaning friends and family were addressed.

"Why such a hard, meager life?" my in-laws asked. "Why not move closer to a city? Why not move closer to us?"

"Because we've always dreamed of living in the mountains away from it all," we answered.

Eventually we packed up our three kids, six cats, seven parakeets, and one dog and we made the cross-country trip eastward. Living in the mountains had been our big dream, but there were plenty of mini dreams that we fulfilled along the way. Each dream required a separate leap. We homeschooled our children. I milked goats, made cheese, spun wool, grew my garden, ground wheat, and baked bread. We heated with wood stoves. We made maple syrup, picked berries, and canned our food. We hiked and enjoyed nature and our peaceful surroundings. But most of all our children thrived and so did we.

This year we celebrated the twenty-year anniversary of living our dream. I can't believe how quickly the years flew by or how many changes have taken place. We're older now. Our children are grown. We've got grandkids. Time moved on and now there are new dreams on the horizon. We are grateful that we took this risk. Not only did we survive — we thrived!

— Jill Burns —

36

My Kitchen in a Trunk

If you look at your entire house as one unit of junk,
you'll never do anything because the job is too
overwhelming. Take it one drawer at a time.
~Janet Luhrs

Kitchen remodels are not easy or fun, but sometimes they yield the most surprising benefits. Besides putting in a new countertop and sink, we were having our cabinets refaced, so I emptied all the drawers and cabinets.

By the time I was done, I was surrounded by boxes filled with dishes, glassware, gadgets and utensils. I had no idea where many of the things even came from, or what they were supposed to be used for. My kitchen had become quite the storage space.

I did what most sane people do at that point. I took a break and watched some television — not just any television, but one of the channels that dealt with home and garden issues. Episode after episode was filled with ideas for meals to prepare, renovations to complete and gardens to transform. When you are in the middle of renovations, I don't recommend watching others handling it better than yourself!

In the midst of these shows was nestled a little gem of an idea. The host talked about our obsession with utensils. Her advice was to eliminate all but the seven basic utensils that really are needed for cooking the majority of our meals: a slotted spoon, regular stirring spoon, spatula, tongs, measuring spoons, measuring cups, and peeler. The idea made me sit up straight and bring out the boxes of assorted utensils I owned. I dug out the seven items and set them aside. I was overwhelmed by what was still in the box. Each item had a specific purpose, but how often did I really use them, and could I accomplish the task with one of the seven instead?

I closed up the boxes of utensils and put them in the trunk of my car. I was about to conduct an experiment — one that would keep these utensils and kitchen tools close enough to retrieve, but also far enough away to make me think twice about reaching for them.

As I fit my seven surviving "essential" utensils into just one of my beautiful new kitchen drawers, I instantly felt lighter and freer. With that big step under my belt, I took the opportunity to lighten a lot of my other cabinets and drawers. Using the same thought process, I simply "put back" what I used on a regular basis, and left the rest in the boxes. Then I added the boxes to my trunk, which was now very full.

Over the next month my experiment yielded some very surprising and interesting results. First, I rarely faced a cooking project that couldn't be accomplished with what I had saved. Next, having my trunk handy allowed me to retrieve the few things that I needed to add to my streamlined kitchen drawers to keep me sane. Best of all, it was much more fun to cook without foraging in drawers and moving things on shelves to get to what I needed! And because it was more fun to cook, I was cooking more!

Having survived my kitchen experiment, I needed to decide what to do with the boxes in my trunk. Surprisingly, I kept coming upon people that were either in the process of starting out on their own, or in need of some odd kitchen item for a project. So, I would lead them to my car and watch them excitedly dig through the boxes like they were on a treasure hunt, holding up the items they found to take to their home. Little by little, news got out, and the boxes shrunk to nothing. What a fun time that was!

But it didn't stop there. At one point I decided to expand this newfound concept to my clothes closet and surveyed the crammed quarters. I took every piece of clothing out of the closet and piled it on the bed. Next I put back into the closet the clothes that I truly wore — yes the ones that fit and I enjoyed being seen in. The rest I placed in bags and took to the local thrift store. What an easy process that was, versus the normal mental anguish I went through as I evaluated and scrutinized each item in my closet!

Looking back over the whole episode, there is not much I would do differently. Occasionally I stand at the stove and miss a specific tool, but I only have to look at my orderly drawers and do some creative thinking to put the smile back on my face. It was a kitchen remodel that yielded the most amazing results ever!

—Joan Wasson—

Half Is More

Women usually love what they buy,
yet hate two-thirds of what is in their closets.
~Mignon McLaughlin

Being the mother of three active children, I enjoyed volunteering at their school and attending their music concerts and athletic games. That is why I was taken aback one morning at breakfast when my youngest son asked, "Mom, are you coming to my doo-wop concert tonight?"

"You know I am, so why are you asking?"

"Well, umm, please don't wear your clown blouse," he said.

"So what blouse are you talking about?"

Looking at the floor, he softly replied, "The bright blue one with the yellow confetti specks and it ties in a big bow at the neck."

He had just described my favorite blouse. Suddenly I started laughing and couldn't stop because I had to admit it did look a bit clownish. With tears running down my face and a big smile I promised him: "I will never wear that blouse again."

The look of relief on his face was unforgettable as he grabbed his books and ran out the front door to school. Reluctantly I went upstairs to get dressed for work. Since my favorite blouse was now definitely out, I had to choose another top to go with my navy blue skirt and heels. Stressed, I pulled on a red short-sleeve sweater that was too hot for the sunny September day, but there was nothing else that looked appropriate.

Off and on that day I couldn't stop thinking about all the clothes in my packed closet. After the birth of my first child I had started purchasing my clothes exclusively from clearance racks to save money. This plan had worked when I was a stay-at-home mother and for the past five years working part-time in the trade school's construction office. Jeans, T-shirts, and hoodies were my main wardrobe.

However, things had changed this school year. I had a new job working full-time in the school district's Public Information Office. This first week had been really stressful, between trying to get dressed each morning and learning my new responsibilities.

Knowing I had to make some major changes, I got up early on Saturday to take everything out of my closet, which I hadn't done in years. Methodically I tossed all the worn clothing and shoes, stretched out belts, and dusty purses into large trash bags. The items that were still in good condition, but didn't fit or I hadn't worn in a year, I put in boxes to donate to charity. I kept only the clothes and shoes that fit perfectly and were a solid color. Looking at the few remaining dresses, skirts, slacks, and blouses I could see there wasn't much left to wear to work.

As I carried the trash bags out to the garage and loaded the boxes into my car, I decided to buy at least two new tops. That afternoon, I went to the shopping center and carefully selected a long-sleeved white blouse and a structured beige tee that would go with everything. Unsure of what to buy next, the following week I signed up for an adult education class that was offered in October. It was for women like me who wanted to learn how to dress professionally for the office. When the big day arrived, there were thirty women in attendance. The instructor welcomed everyone and promised, "In the next two hours, you are going to learn how to put together a simple and basic working wardrobe for the business world."

She started off by instructing us to purchase a skirt, slacks, jacket, cardigan sweater, shoes, and a purse all in the same color like black, gray, dark blue, brown, or beige. "Whatever your budget, try to buy these basic items from the same manufacturer so the dyes and styles match."

I had never thought about details like this before, but this was definitely the information I was looking for. Her assistant wore a matching black skirt and jacket to show us the many different looks you can achieve by adding a scarf, belt, or jewelry. At the end of the class, the instructor summarized, "Remember to limit the color in your outfits to your tops and jewelry; and keep an up-to-date wish list of clothing you need or want. By following this easy plan, you will always have something to wear that fits every occasion."

This simple wardrobe strategy changed my life completely. Over time I bought the basics in black, dark blue, and beige. Of course I still shop the clearance racks, but I only buy an item if it is on my list and in the right color. With half the clothes, I am always amazed and relieved that I have so many outfits to wear.

—Brenda Cathcart-Kloke—

Life Reignited

When we lose one blessing, another is often most
unexpectedly given in its place.
~C.S. Lewis

October 19 started out like any other morning. A single mom, I rushed about the house getting my son and myself ready for work and daycare. I remember putting on my favorite pair of jeans even though I should have worn something a bit dressier for work. As we headed out the door that morning I tripped over some dinosaur toys strewn across the entryway. I told my son that when we got home that night we were going to have to really clean up the house so we didn't break a leg on all those toys. I dropped him off at daycare and headed to work.

I hadn't been at work ten minutes when the call came. My house was on fire. My boss rushed me to my home. As we turned onto my street, all I could see were fire trucks and police cars. We parked half a block away and I ran up the street. I reached my driveway to see the thick black smoke rolling out of my house. A fireman was chopping holes in my roof with an axe.

I remember officers talking with me, neighbors offering hugs, friends arriving, the fire chief explaining to me what would happen next, and the smell of the smoke.

Hours passed as I stood in the driveway and watched the firefighters work. They chopped holes in my home and threw burnt items out the windows.

As I watched I started to laugh. I didn't laugh because house fires are particularly funny. I laughed because I had told my son we had to clean the house tonight and now that seemed like an impossible task. I laughed because I was wearing my favorite jeans and we all know how hard it is to find a great pair of jeans. But most of all I laughed because I had two options in that moment.

I could give in to the pain and cry, or I could choose to find the joy and laughter in the darkest of situations. I made the choice in that moment, in my driveway, surrounded by smoke, to laugh. I made the decision to find the positive and focus on that.

The fire allowed my son and me to rebuild our lives. Our lives were spared that day. We had the chance to start over fresh, to create the best life possible for us. The possessions that I thought meant so much were gone. But the things that really mattered in our lives stayed intact. Joy, gratitude, laughter — those things can't be burnt!

In the weeks after the fire, we were blessed by the generosity of friends and strangers alike. Our new apartment was bare, but our hearts were full and we were happy.

I learned that you really need very little to survive. Instead of eating at a kitchen table, we had lots of picnics on the living room floor. All the toys my son had before were barely missed.

> *Our new apartment was bare, but our hearts were full and we were happy.*

Instead, we spent more time playing outside together, reading, and listening to music. All those knickknacks that I thought I had to have were replaced, but only with things I truly loved or that my son and I created together.

In our new life, we banned excess. When you each have only a few outfits, it makes laundry day much easier. Since I didn't have to spend so much time picking up the house, I actually had time to do some of the things I loved again. I sat and read a great book. I created art pieces to hang in our new place. I started getting a full night's sleep every night.

The fire simplified my life. The power that "stuff" had over me before was gone. My heart was more open and my mind was calmer.

Instead of just creating a new home I was able to create a new life. A life that I designed from scratch. This new life was filled with laughter, creativity, fun, gratitude, and very little stuff.

The fire lit a spark in me that had been out for a very long time. My passion for life was reignited and I was ready to live again. With my son beside me, and wearing my favorite jeans, I was able to laugh in the face of tragedy.

—Jessie Wagoner—

39

Take Two

For it is in giving that we receive.
~St. Francis of Assisi

When you're my age, you don't get many bridal shower or wedding invitations from your peers. Nieces and nephews, yes. Children of your friends, yes. But not too many wedding bells chime in my age category, especially among those who have already tied the knot once or twice before.

Therefore, when my friend Diane and her beloved, Jack, who are even older than I am, decided to combine their love, lives, children, grandchildren and the paraphernalia of three households (hers, her recently departed mother's and his), the joy among friends and relatives resounded from state to state and across oceans.

In one fleeting, dreamy-eyed moment during the planning of the wedding, Diane said wistfully, "Oh, I hope people don't bring presents. We do not need any more things. Our entire basement is filled, wall-to-wall, ceiling-to-floor, with things we don't need and can't possibly use in this lifetime. Nice things. Well, some of them are nice. Others are, well, too nice to throw away but too sentimental to give to strangers. And I can't bear to have another rummage sale."

Diane kept talking and planning and then she had a great idea: "Wouldn't it be nice to give each guest who comes to our wedding a gift to take home, instead of the other way around?"

I piped up, "Well, I'd be happy to give you a shower, and instead of playing those mindless games, we could wrap all your treasures for you to give away."

Diane practically shouted, "Yes! We'll number each present, and I'll put corresponding numbers on each place card at the dinner tables at the reception." Diane figured she could at least match up some of the more special heirlooms to the people she wanted to receive them.

And so, the bridal-shower invitations went out, requesting that the women bring gift wrap, tape and scissors instead of a gift for the happy couple. We gathered in the basement family room of the house that Diane and Jack had recently purchased.

The first thing the shower attendees got to do was choose three or four gifts from the hundreds in the basement that we, personally, would like to own. We were commanded to take, take, take! It was more fun than 70-percent-off day at the nearest department store. As we chose things we wanted for ourselves, Diane insisted that we take them to our cars immediately so they wouldn't get wrapped for the other wedding guests.

I chose a nice wooden tray that just needed a little lemon oil to remove the water stains, a small lead-crystal candy dish, and a china-faced floppy clown for my granddaughter.

Back downstairs after removing our own treasures, we giggling middle-aged women began to wrap the rest. There were candleholders wrapped in teddy-bear paper. Picture frames and egg cups decorated in purple foil. Decanters in festive holiday paper. Jewelry and mugs in birthday florals. Housewares, glassware, trays, books, linens, silver, and bric-a-brac wrapped to the hilt. One hundred presents in all. "Enough," Diane said, "to give a gift to everyone at the reception with enough left over to share with the wait staff."

While we wrapped, ate, laughed and talked about how we met Diane and what a joyous occasion this marriage would be, Jack sat upstairs with eyes as big as saucers wondering how his friends would perceive this crazy idea of handing out secondhand gifts at his wedding.

As I passed through the TV room where Jack was trying to ignore the cackling downstairs, I bubbled, "Jack, you're not going to believe how much stuff we're getting rid of! We're wrapping one hundred presents!"

"All I'm hoping for is an empty shelf downstairs where I can put a few of my own treasures," he mumbled.

"Jack, when we're finished, the entire basement will be cleaned out! You'll have tons of empty space!"

Diane wrote a poem that was printed and placed on every table at the wedding reception. Two of the five stanzas declared:

We love family and friends without measure.
There are even some things that we treasure.
But as three households merge, there are things we must purge.
So we gift them to you for your pleasure.

You may keep them and use them — or not.
You may love them or trash them or plot
Ways to recycle them, give your own requiem.
Love is wrapped in each piece in the lot!

And so it was that everyone who witnessed the joining of two hearts left with a gift, and a newly married couple went home to a nice empty basement.

— Patricia Lorenz —

40

Döstädning

Outer order contributes to inner calm.
~Gretchen Rubin

"Hey, Mom, the house looks great." My grown son nodded approvingly. "Seems like there's a lot less stuff around."

There was.

Two years before, my daughter had introduced me to the concept of döstädning. A recent convert to minimalism — perhaps out of necessity since she lived in a Washington, D.C. apartment — Abigail extolled the benefits of owning less. "Mom, you should try it," she said. "Not having so much stuff to take care of frees up time for better things."

Döstädning.

I might not have remembered it at all if I hadn't bothered to Google the term. Döstädning: Swedish for "death cleaning."

Now that was perplexing, and maybe a tad insulting. I wasn't exactly knocking at death's door.

It turns out that döstädning also means "decluttering." Maybe my daughter had a point. I mean, after three-plus decades of marriage, stuff piles up. Or, in my case, stuff comes in and goes out and comes in and goes out and...

Over the years, my husband and I had endured a half-dozen significant moves. Before any of the moving trucks pulled into the driveway, I divided our worldly possessions into three categories: pack away, throw away, give away. We parceled out van loads. Out went the furniture the children had outgrown. Decor that wouldn't fit well in another home. Coats, hats and boots that would never see another frigid winter. Books, CDs and DVDs, even the potted plants. But the way I found to make the new house a home always pivoted on accessorizing all over again. New pillows and throws. New scented candles. New seasonal decor. You get the idea.

Declutter? I hesitated. I clung to the view Myquillyn Smith teaches the reader to abandon in her book *Cozy Minimalist Home: More Style, Less Stuff*. I worried removing all this would make my home scream cold and cheerless. After all, didn't all my layers of stuff whisper warm and welcoming?

Maybe. Maybe not.

Perhaps, on occasion, I missed the mark trying to achieve that warm and cozy feeling. The time I decided the perfect holiday season included seven Christmas trees, grouped by theme, comes to mind. Or what about those emotion-driven shopping sprees, like when I ended up the proud owner of a porcelain vase collection large enough to fill two curio cabinets?

The same daughter who recommended döstädning had once suggested I add velvet ropes to cordon off rooms in that seven-Christmas-tree home. Maybe all my warm and welcoming accumulations hindered the very environment I strove to create. Maybe there was something to this döstädning.

Maybe.

But I like things. I like admiring them and touching them and, well, just having them. And I was going to need time to adjust to not having them. I made it easy on myself. I headed out to the garden shed and lugged things to the curb for the neighbors to pick up, which they did — with shocking speed. Next (only because most homes in the Deep South don't have basements, so that wasn't an option for me), I headed to the attic and my stash of holiday decor. Who has time for seven trees anyway? After that, I inventoried and culled the closets. Eager young crafters gobbled up supplies requiring nimbler hands and keener eyesight. Clothing refusing to measure well against my more mature self was shown the door (of a local charity).

Like Smith, I now ask myself a few questions about my possessions: Am I using this? Is the care it requires the best use of my time? If I move again, is it worth the cost and effort of packing, transporting and unpacking? Is there someone I know who would appreciate this object?

"No one wants our stuff," my college roommate said recently. Well, no one wants all our stuff all at once, but new homes can be found, piece by piece. Like the Aesop fable teaches, "Slow and steady wins the race." Opportunities presented themselves: a donation call for a church festival, a charity-run used bookstore, a school fundraiser, families in challenging circumstances, "adulting" millennials setting up new households.

And so it occurred to me that while I might not be at death's door, there was no denying that my allotted time on the planet was waning. Suddenly, it seemed selfish to wait for death to pass on heirlooms. Why not gift them now and add another layer to their meaning and history? Why not create new memories with new celebrations?

My goal is one laundry basket a month out the door. Döstädning. Basket by basket. If it's not worth giving away, there is always the recycling bin or, as a last resort, the trash bin.

My daughter hadn't been unkind when she suggested döstädning. For a couple of years, she vehemently denied ever recommending anything related to maternal mortality. She honestly thought döstädning was just Swedish for minimalism.

The process and the journey have been liberating. Even now, my home has more open places, more breathing space. There is less "stuff" clamoring for my attention, more time for living. Cleaning for life, not death!

— M. Elizabeth Gage —

Think Positive

What You'll Find in This Chapter

How do we choose the 101 stories that ultimately grace the pages of each of our books? There *is* an overarching imperative, and that is to introduce you to people whose stories illustrate the power of positive thinking. Positive people give us stories that are empowering and uplifting, encouraging our readers to look within themselves for the keys to being happy, productive, and purposeful. I love stories from people who have been through enormous challenges and yet have maintained a constructive attitude, filled with gratitude for the good things they still have.

You won't find any narcissists among our writers. They're not big complainers either. I think that my attitude toward people in general has changed after working on these books. I am still blown away after all these years by how positive, resourceful, and resilient our writers are. They are wonderful role models for all of us at Chicken Soup for the Soul. They make a conscious effort to find the positives in their lives, to find the silver linings even in the everyday hassles. But they weren't always that way, and many of them relate in their stories how they came to be positive thinkers.

Scott Martin had to learn how to think positively in a major way after he lost his hands and feet to "flesh-eating disease." This athlete had to give up playing soccer but realized he could remain part of the game — as a coach. In his story, "Moving Forward in Reverse," he explains how he redeveloped his confidence and his sense of purpose, saying, "As long as the players needed me — and hopefully wanted me — I would give them everything I had. Their canvas would become mine and I would teach them to paint."

Sometimes, a tiny, easy tweak is enough to set us on a different, more positive path. In her story, "Try a Smile," Ferida Wolff passes on a lesson that she learned as she was stomping through a parking lot after a frustrating visit to a crowded post office. When she saw another woman stomping toward her, scowling and looking grumpy, Ferida realized that's how she must have looked, too. That shocked her into smiling at the woman, whose body language changed immediately.

The encounter showed Ferida the power of a simple smile: "I became aware of people's expressions and my own, of the way we show our emotions so plainly. Now I use that awareness on an everyday basis, letting it remind me that when I am fighting the world, or see someone else in that position, I can try a smile. More often than not, the energy of the moment shifts with that one little gesture."

I could have called this chapter "Think Confident" instead of "Think Positive" because so much of positive thinking is about feeling confident. I think you'll love Laurie Davies' story, "All the World Is a Playground," in which she relates how a teacher helped her develop the confidence to go outside for recess. Her wise words? "Walk out onto that playground like it's yours." Laurie's been telling herself that ever since, approaching every challenge and scary situation as if it were a playground that she owns. That's the kind of positive thinking we can all implement in just one moment, and it's life changing.

Bank Owned

Where thou art — that is home.
~Emily Dickinson

I've lost my home. The home I bought, cherished, loved.

It now stands vacant. The bare picture windows stare out like hollow eyes. A bank owned sign sticks crudely in the overgrown, yellow lawn. The flowers I planted and watered religiously wilt, hanging low as if weeping.

Indentations in the carpet reveal the outline of furniture, of a life, of a family. Putty and paint cover the holes in the walls where pictures once hung.

Even though the house is empty, images flood my mind of a time when it was filled with life.

On the driveway, we showed our son how to ride a bike. In this house, both kids started school, learned to read and write. We taught our son to tie his shoes, and for several horrific months went through potty-training our daughter.

Since it was our first home, we set right out to decorate, make it our own. My arm still aches from painting my son's bedroom walls a bright blue that needed three coats before it stopped appearing streaky. I remember the plans to paint my daughter's room pastel pink that never came to fruition.

Many injuries and bruises accumulated over the years. There's the time my daughter tried to climb on top of her dresser and it fell over on her. Luckily, she wasn't badly hurt. Or the time my son fell off his bike and scraped his knee.

I remember the excitement about having a master bedroom with our own bathroom and walk-in closet. Many fond memories are associated with the room I shared with my husband. The room we talked in, embraced in, laughed in, loved in.

I'll never forget the time we found a lizard slithering through our hallway. I screamed and jumped up on a chair. My husband caught it and it became the family pet. I wonder now where Ben Casey went after we let him loose in the backyard. I'm sure he misses the excitement and noise back there since now there is only silence.

My heart hurts as we drive away from the house, leaving it in the dust like nothing more than a distant memory.

Behind me my kids' chatter fills the back seat. My husband at my side threads his fingers through mine. It's then that I realize I haven't truly lost my home. My home is not a structure with four walls and a roof. It's not something that can be bought or sold. My home is not the place I live. It's the people I live with. The people right here in this car.

My family is my home.

— Amber Garza —

A Positive Message from a Time Traveler

*It is often hard to distinguish between the hard knocks
in life and those of opportunity.*
~Frederick Phillips

Recently, I was cleaning out a closet and came upon several curious letters. They were all written on letterhead from various television stations around the country, all dated in late 1979. It took me a minute to recognize what they were, but as I read through them, I realized they were all rejection letters to me from various television news executives.

I wondered why I kept them. I vaguely remembered applying for the jobs. It was during a time in my television career when I was looking to make that next step toward more responsibility, a bigger city and a bigger salary.

I tried to get inside the brain of that 1979 version of myself to understand what I was feeling at the time. Why did I save these rejection letters? Was I trying to keep myself humble? Was there some hidden streak of masochism causing me to flog myself for my inadequacies?

Finally, I decided that I must have kept the letters specifically for this particular moment forty years later. I concluded that it might very well have been my version of time traveling, a way of sending a message to my "future self." Yet, at the time, I could not have been sure of what that exact message might be.

Strange as it sounded, that rang true. After all, there were many times in my life when I felt that a particular event held some sort of special meaning, but I wasn't sure of the full meaning at the time. The loss of a loved one, a failure in romance, a layoff, a poor invest-ment — they all were life events whose significance only my future self could fully appreciate. My younger self must have sensed significance in those letters, but also suspected that it would require a future self to totally understand what that significance was.

And my present-day self did understand. Each of those letters represented a path not taken — not because I didn't want to take it, or didn't try to take it, but because someone else decided that for me. It was a reminder that my future is not totally in my control; I am not the master of my own fate.

And there was a second part to the message: The fact that I am not in complete control of my life is not necessarily a bad thing. Closed doors guided me as much as open ones had. That's the message the present-day version of me now understands, but the 1979 version of me could only take on faith.

That 1979 version of me who was rejected for TV jobs in Green Bay, Wisconsin, Greenville, South Carolina, and Jacksonville, Florida, didn't

> *Closed doors guided me as much as open ones had.*

know that his 1981 version would get a job in a much bigger TV market in the Pacific Northwest. He didn't know that his 1985 version would marry a woman there who was to be his lifelong companion, and that his 1991 version would be given a new opportunity for advancement. That early version of me didn't know that my 1999 self would eventu-ally be laid off from that job and then move his family cross-country to take a job at a national network. But the present-day version of me can look back on all those events and see that, although none of them was completely under my control, each had positive results.

So I'm thankful that my 1979 self sent me that message, even if he didn't fully understand it at the time. I can't travel back in time to thank him, but what I can do is send a message ahead to my 2029 and 2039 selves. That message is this: Life is most productive when you make the most of the path you're on, not when you fret about what the other paths might have held.

So, to my future self: Stop trying to be in control. Don't dwell on what might be on the other side of that closed door. Continue to make the most of every open door. And, one more thing, future self... you're welcome.

— Nick Walker —

43

Maintenance Required

Good for the body is the work of the body,
good for the soul the work of the soul,
and good for either the work of the other.
~Henry David Thoreau

The yellow light flashed on my dashboard, illuminating the words: Maintenance Required. "I don't have time for this," I stewed. "I've got two jobs, a family to take care of, dogs to feed, exercise to get in, I don't have time for this. When can I squeeze in a four-hour window without the use of my car?" I crumpled the foil from the sandwich I'd eaten as I sped along the freeway.

For days I drove with the light illuminated and flashing. Normally after a couple of minutes it would relent and turn off, as if to say, "Okay you might not want to listen, but I'm warning you…" But the next morning when I headed for my hour-long freeway drive, the light came on and stayed on. It stared me in the face day after day gloating, glaring, and never going away.

I felt frazzled, juggling a new job that had me driving all over the city, eating in my car, and toting heaps of files with me. I was never good with paper organization and now piles mounted and papers slipped out of folders. Other piles accumulated and not just the literal ones, like bills and clothing, but the metaphoric ones as well. I was drowning in my "to-do's" and this "Maintenance Required" was putting me over the top.

I remember the last time I let the "Maintenance Required" light flash a little too long and ended up stranded on the roadside, only to be towed to the dealer and charged a whopping bill for repairs on an engine that could've been serviced by an oil change.

The light now had my full attention. It was obvious I was going to have to change my entire day. As a contract therapist, I am only paid for the clients I see, so canceling my appointments was going to cost me, but so would ignoring the light. As I searched for my cell phone to call the office, it rang from the depths of my purse. My client had called to cancel his appointment.

I made it to the dealer in time to drop off my car. I had at least four hours to "kill." And then it struck me, why would I ever want to kill this time? It was a gift I could never recover. I thought about waiting at the dealer, but that seemed like punishment. My car needed maintenance and so did my soul. I found out the dealer offered a shuttle ride that could drop me at a mall. Although I had no interest in shopping, I knew that the beach was about a mile from the mall. I had my sneakers, my iPod, and my phone so I set off on my adventure.

I discovered that everything, including waiting and distance, seems shorter and closer when I mentally use the word "only." It would only be four hours and I would have my car again. The beach was only a mile away.

I plugged in my iPod and grounded myself with the meditative chants from my yoga class. Then I listened to the self-help and motivational tapes that I'd heard before, but suddenly heard in a new way. As I walked, I dug my toes into the soft wet sand. I breathed in the salty fresh ocean spray. I felt the warmth of the sun and the gentle caress of the breeze. I was feeling so renewed and peaceful I almost felt guilty.

What a brilliant idea those carmakers have, I thought. "Maintenance Required." If only we came with such a light.

My phone rang. It was the dealer letting me know my car was ready an hour early.

"So soon?" I inquired. "Will it be okay if I come in a couple of hours? I'm still working on a little maintenance of my own."

— Tsgoyna Tanzman —

44

Try a Smile

The world always looks brighter from behind a smile.
~Author Unknown

I was at the post office early that morning, hoping to be in and out and on my way at the start of a busy day. Instead, I found myself standing on a line that zigzagged through rope-defined lanes and oozed out into the hallway. I had never seen so many people there and it wasn't even a holiday. Someone must have made an announcement that I obviously missed, welcoming patrons with as many packages as they could possibly carry to bring them in at the exact time I needed to have my own parcel weighed. The line moved excruciatingly slowly. My mood turned edgy, then annoyed. The longer it took, the angrier I became. When I got to the counter — finally! — I concluded my business quickly and curtly and strode past the line that was now extending past the front door.

"Excuse me," I said, trying not to be too pushy. Several people had to shift to make room for me to get to the exit.

I strode out grumbling under my breath about inefficiency and how I was going to be late getting to my dentist appointment. I was scowling as I headed into the parking lot.

A woman was coming across the lot in my direction. She was walking with determination, each step pounding the ground like a mini-jackhammer. I noticed that her brow was tightly furrowed and she looked as if she could breathe fire. It stopped me in my tracks. I recognized myself and it wasn't pretty. Had I looked like that? Her body

> *I smiled.*
> *In the space*
> *of a second*
> *everything*
> *changed.*

language said that she was having a really rough day. My anger melted away. I wished I could wrap her in a hug but I was a stranger. So I did what I could in the brief minute before she barreled past me — I smiled. In the space of a second everything changed. I could tell that she was startled, then somewhat confused. Then her face softened and her shoulders relaxed. I saw her take a deep breath. Her pace slowed and she smiled back at me as we passed each other.

I continued to smile all the way to my car. Wow, I thought. Look what a simple smile can do.

The rest of the day felt like a meditation on smiling. I became aware of people's expressions and my own, of the way we show our emotions so plainly. Now I use that awareness on an everyday basis, letting it remind me that when I am fighting the world, or see someone else in that position, I can try a smile. More often than not, the energy of the moment shifts with that one little gesture. The smile on the outside turns inward and the day becomes new again, turning a bright face toward the activities that are yet to come.

— Ferida Wolff —

45

Moving Forward in Reverse

The excursion is the same when you go looking for
your sorrow as when you go looking for your joy.
~Eudora Welty

I was full of joy and caught up in my thoughts, so I didn't have time to react to the two girls who came sauntering around the corner, engrossed in conversation. I stumbled to my right, trying to avoid a collision. But I wasn't fast enough: our shoulders jostled and I staggered sideways.

"Excuse me," I called as I righted myself.

The girl I had bumped gasped and lifted one pink-manicured hand towards her friend for balance. "Ew!" I heard a voice cry behind me. I started to turn, curious what had caused her disgust.

"That man with no hands touched me!"

I froze. Her words seemed to reverberate towards me and through me. I was the thing causing her disgust, despite the appearance of the girls, with their bleached blond hair and overdone make-up.

Shrinking in on myself, I put my head down and subconsciously pulled my myoelectric hands towards my stomach. My emotions shut down. Sweat began to break out across my forehead. Fight or flight? Fight or flight?

I felt my heart race and dove for the sanctity of my office. The door was locked. I fumbled with the keys in my robotic hands. It took too many tries and too much concentration to single out the correct one. A screech like the yowling of a cat emanated from my hands with every motion of my fingers. I shied away from the sound, recoiling at the way it seemed to echo down the hallway. Once I had the key pinched between two fingers, I fought to navigate it into the keyhole and turn the lock. Without the use of a wrist, it was a trying feat on the best of days. And today was not the best of days.

Where had my confidence gone? I felt deflated and traumatized by what had just happened. I could feel the eyes of the other students on me, staring at my mannequin-like hands, judging me for my incompetence and handicap. I felt utterly inept and completely isolated.

When the key finally slid home and I managed to turn the latch, I rammed my shoulder into the door with unnecessary force. I stumbled across the threshold and quickly shut the door behind me, locking everyone else out.

My hands were shaking as I set the key on the edge of my L-shaped desk; my legs wobbled as I lowered myself into my chair. The only sounds were my panting and the creak of the hands as I laid them flat across my legs. I looked down at my lap, staring at the off-colored rubber that hid the metal fingers beneath. My handicap. Just when I thought I had made real progress in overcoming the hardships and self-consciousness having no hands or feet caused, something happened to knock me back down again. Hearing her words forced me to glimpse into the mirror reflecting my shattered self-image, and the broken figure I saw revolted me.

Maybe this is the new normal, I thought as I stared at the white, concrete wall before me. *The rest of your life is going to be spent as the object of other people's ridicule. Might as well get used to it, buddy. No one likes a handicapped person. Children gawk at you; adults avoid you; teens scorn you.*

I lowered my chin to my chest and closed my eyes against my unfair reality. From a successful collegiate soccer coach and player to this: Could life take any larger a turn for the worse? Six months ago I would have gone out to the soccer field to kick the ball around after something like this. But six months ago I had hands and feet and "the flesh-eating disease" was a term reserved for medical dramas. Now it was the illness that threatened to deprive me of the thing I loved most: soccer.

Playing soccer had been my greatest form of expression — my art form. A soccer field was like a blank canvas and the ball my brush. With them both I could create any masterpiece I dreamt of; I could funnel my emotions into the creation of my design and leave them on the field when I was done.

Now I couldn't even take the ball for a walk like I taught kids to do.

At least you still have a coaching career. This was true. I was still coaching and I still had my team. It seemed that was the only positive thing left in my life. But one positive is still better than none. As long as the players needed me — and hopefully wanted me — I would give them everything I had. Their canvas would become mine and I would teach them to paint like Jackson Pollock. If the rest of the university campus wanted to fear or ridicule me, so be it. I was a thirty-five-year-old man. I could handle a little bullying.

That was the last time I let myself think about the torments that threatened to pull me under. I put everything I had into developing the soccer program. I was able to recruit a few more strong players and implemented a new playing style to make up for our lack of a pure scorer. Long hours in the Soccer Office and as an Assistant Hall Director left me mercifully little time for self-pity and reminiscing.

It may have been avoiding a problem rather than confronting it, but I found that focusing on the good things I had going for me was better than worrying about the countless things stacked against me. Coaching was something I could excel at with or without hands and feet. As long as I was on the field or thinking about being on the field, I forgot that I had lost so much: I wasn't The Man with No Hands or severely handicapped; I was just Scott Martin, coach and mentor. The longer the hours I worked, the more time I was able to live as only Scott, and the less apparent my poor self-confidence became.

My dedication paid off when we cracked the Top 10 ranking nationally that season and I was nominated for National Coach of the Year. I reveled in my team's success and realized it didn't matter if I wasn't the man I used to be on the outside, because I still had it on the inside. Life wasn't perfect: I still missed playing terribly and regularly dreamt I was running — more than once I woke after kicking the wall because I was playing soccer in my dream. In some ways, losing soccer was more devastating than the loss of my hands and feet. I could forget that I was handicapped at times, but I could never forget my longing to run the ball down field or the devastation at never being able to play as a part of a team again. But loss is a part of life and those who choose to focus on what is lost lose sight of what they have. And I still had a wonderful thing — myself.

— Scott Martin —

Rewriting My Story

*The world is round and the place which may seem like
the end may also be only the beginning.*
~Ivy Baker Priest

had heard the old adage that insanity is doing the same thing
over and over but expecting different results. In fact, I was getting tired of my own "insanity." I knew I needed to do something
different in order to achieve a different outcome.

The solution came to me while driving to a conference in
Philadelphia during Friday afternoon rush hour. I had been reciting a litany of frustrations — the traffic, the other drivers, the road
repairs — when a light came on in my heart and soul.

"Okay," I said to myself. "It is a lovely day. I am headed to a
conference I want to attend. I have an entire weekend to learn new
things and enjoy myself. I am safe. All is well here. I choose to see this
situation differently, right NOW!"

I relaxed, and traffic inched ahead. At that moment, my life began
to change for the better.

I'd had inklings in my long years of marriage that my husband
was not as committed to our relationship or to me as I was to him.
After the children were born, late in our life together, this became
more apparent. But still it shocked and wounded me deeply when he
announced he was leaving me for a new life with someone else.

I tried to pick up the pieces of my life, parent my two young
children, grieve for my marriage. I also mourned the loss of my father,

who died right around the same time. My children and I moved to a new town. After several years at home, I went back to work. With depressing regularity, I ran through all these emotions and more: hurt, betrayal, fear, anger, sadness, loneliness, despair.

Friends who had known us as a couple said the usual supportive things to me, things like they had never liked or trusted him anyway. These comments were intended to help me, but they only made me feel more like a victim. I was able to tell the story of his shortcomings, although this never made me feel any better. Most of me blamed him. Part of me blamed me. Either way left me feeling hurt and angry, and did nothing to enhance my life in any way.

Suddenly, I realized that sitting in Friday rush hour traffic was a metaphor for my life. I couldn't change my circumstances, but if I could tell myself a different story, I could have a different outcome. And if I could rewrite the story of urban traffic, why couldn't I rewrite the story of the end of a marriage, and tell a story instead that ended with my own rebirth?

The traffic was simply an obstacle I needed to overcome to get to a wonderful weekend of learning. The end of my marriage was, in truth, a huge gift to me. When I stopped blaming, I could see the possibilities ahead of me for my life.

> *The end of my marriage was, in truth, a huge gift to me.*

Instead of focusing on my former husband being the villain and me being the victim, I could rewrite my story to make myself, or even BOTH of us, into people simply trying to travel the road of life as well as we could. It was as if I had found the key that unlocked my heart, and just like the Grinch's once did, my heart grew three sizes that day. I felt compassion for myself as well as for the man I had been married to for so long. We had never been well matched, and so eventually the marriage ended. It no longer mattered who left whom.

As I told a different story, in which I chose to be uncoupled from someone who made me feel small and unloved, I grew larger and more empowered in my own story. My marriage ended because we were headed in different directions, with differing values and goals. I could let this be okay. In fact, it could be fine. *I* could be fine.

Now that I have let go of my old ending and focused on my new beginning, I feel hopeful and I've become happier. In my new story, I am not carrying around with me the slings and arrows of old wounds. In this story, life is rich with possibilities. I have discovered I am capable, strong, adventurous, smart, and I have a quirky sense of humor. I have made new social connections, found new interests and hobbies.

Since that day when I was stuck in traffic (in more ways than one), I've turned my life around. I feel empowered and optimistic. And life reflects this back to me at every turn.

— Deborah K. Wood —

Bloom Where You Are Planted

Things turn out best for the people who make the
best out of the way things turn out.
~Art Linkletter

I was smitten from the moment I laid eyes on that adorable condo, with its sunken living room and the gorgeous French doors that opened onto the flagstone patio. I convinced my husband Joe that "happily ever after" awaited us on the other side of that threshold. The threshold with the elegant front door flanked by full-length beveled glass windows. The one located at 6823 Crooked Lane.

Right away we put our house up for sale and in less than a week someone made us an offer. I took it as a sign from Heaven and mentally started feathering our Crooked Lane nest. The same day we accepted the buyer's offer we put a deposit down on our dream house. Let the packing begin!

As I filled each box I pictured myself cooking sumptuous suppers in that beautiful wide-open kitchen, or soaking in the luxury of the Jacuzzi after a long day at work. Yep, living was going to start just as soon as we were settled into our new home, and I could hardly wait. Joe, on the other hand, had his own fantasy list of activities (or lack of them) that he mused over. The thought of being relieved of his responsibility to mow the grass and shovel snow made him practically giddy.

As we packed, the usual paperwork and appointments ran their course. We were approved for our new mortgage without a hitch and our house on Spring Mill Avenue passed all routine inspections. Not a snag in sight. Settlement day approached and with it our excitement about moving to Utopia grew steadily. We counted down the days and never counted on trouble, but trouble was waiting right around the corner.

I stared across the table at the empty chair just as the grandfather clock in the corner of the real estate office struck three o'clock. The buyer of our home was now officially thirty minutes late. This seemed unusual since he was a real estate agent himself.

Our own real estate agent frantically called the buyer's office and cell phone. When we had waited a full hour my husband stood up and said, "We've had enough. We're leaving, and unless you can prove that the buyer has come to some physical harm that prevented him from contacting this office, the sale is off." Then we walked out.

We drove home in shock. Well, I was in shock. Joe barreled past shock and didn't put the brakes on until he got to rage. The whole time we ate dinner I'm certain there was smoke coming out of his ears. Neither of us could accept that the sale of our house progressed to the point of settlement without our own real estate office following up on the legitimacy of the buyer. We never asked questions because, well, because we had no experience selling a home and when our agent said everything was fine, we believed that everything was, in fact, fine. Silly us.

At about seven o'clock in the evening our real estate agent called to say that he finally spoke with the buyer, who confessed he had too many irons in the fire at the moment and was having a little difficulty securing a mortgage. Of course our agent George assured us that if we would just grant the buyer an extension of a few weeks all would work out.

Joe put the phone on mute and said, "What do you think, Annie?"

There I stood among stacks of packed boxes, having hitched my wagon to the house on Crooked Lane with "Let's give him another chance" right on the tip of my tongue. The look on my financially prudent husband's face spoke volumes. I drew in a deep breath, and

Think Positive | 153

then said, "No way, Joe. He had his chance and I don't think we should bank any longer on his empty promises. There's something crooked going on here and I don't trust this guy."

Joe gave a sigh of relief, delivered the news to George, and then hung up the phone.

"It's official, Annie. The sale of this house is off."

"What do we do now?" I asked, hoping Joe had an ace up his sleeve, but in my heart I knew better.

"This," he said, as he dialed the number for the real estate agent of our condo on Crooked Lane.

I had to leave the room. Just thinking about having to swing two mortgage payments until our house sold was making me sweat in places where I didn't even know I had glands. I knew for sure Joe would never agree to a swing loan or any other high interest quick fix, and I shared the same mindset. At this point the odds were no longer in our favor. Even without being in the room, I knew Joe was going to explain our situation and ask if we could be released from the agreement to purchase the condo on Crooked Lane.

When Joe hung up the phone he came into the living room and flopped down on the couch next to me.

"What a mess, Annie. What a big, fat, exhausting mess."

The owner of Crooked Lane agreed to let us out of the contract as long as our real estate agent's office sent a letter explaining what had happened. They were disgruntled but cooperative. Though our agent would much rather have talked us into giving the buyer another chance, he agreed to send the letter all the same.

When the dust settled, Joe and I decided to pretend that our little house on Spring Mill Avenue was Crooked Lane. And that's just what we did—mortgage-wise, that is. The mortgage payment on the new house figured to be almost twice what we were paying on Spring Mill Avenue. So every month we wrote a check that was almost twice the amount of our scheduled payment.

We've made some cosmetic changes over the years, like tearing down the old wood paneling and installing hardwood floors, but we certainly have no Jacuzzi. And all these years later my husband still grumbles when the grass needs cutting. The amazing news is that last December we made our final mortgage payment on this little house of ours, fifteen years ahead of schedule. That's quite a positive outcome in a world where top-heavy mortgages abound. We don't have a mortgage. We have a deed and equity. We have pride and peace of mind, in a cozy and comfortable home that we have grown to love. But mostly we have firsthand knowledge that sometimes you just have to look on the bright side and bloom where you are planted.

— Annmarie B. Tait —

All the World Is a Playground

Each time we face our fear, we gain strength,
courage, and confidence in the doing.
~Theodore Roosevelt

Growing up, I hated every girl who could skip. I sat inside at recess, watching all the skippers. No matter how hard I tried or cried, I just couldn't get the steps and rhythm right.

I felt so uncoordinated. So clumsy. My older sister tried to teach me, to no avail. And when I asked one of the girls at school to show me? Let's just say the snickering stopped me from asking again. Childhood can be brutal.

So can adulthood. I miss steps. I misstep. I watch others breeze by with more talent, connections, looks, and likes. I watch all the skippers skip by. Skipping.

Now in midlife, I am still tempted sometimes to stay inside at recess. I'm inclined to draw smaller, safer circles where I won't get hurt. It's tempting to believe I'm better off there.

But the fears never last long, thanks to the no-nonsense, no-frills fifth grade teacher named Miss Lyon who stopped all that in its tracks for me when I was just a kid. Miss Lyon was actually my older sister's teacher, but she was having none of my recess rejection. She sat down in the hallway during recess with me one day and said, "It can be rough out there, can't it?"

I nodded, holding back my tears.

She took the cue. We sat silently.

The sounds of bouncing balls, whistles and squeaking swing sets from outside punctuated the quiet. It sounded so far away. I had to admit, it also sounded like so much fun.

After a few minutes, she looked at me and promised I would find my people. Then she gave me some advice that I have never forgotten: "Walk out onto that playground like it's yours." And she opened the door to the outside and beckoned me through.

I bit my lip, smoothed my shirt and stepped onto the playground. Before my eyes even adjusted to the sunlight, an out-of-breath, sweaty boy named Mike Bowen blurted out an invitation. Batman, Superman and Aqua Man were over at the eagle's nest kicking butt and fighting crime. They needed a Wonder Woman.

They needed me.

They didn't care that I couldn't skip. They'd seen me climb to the top of the monkey bars like a pro. They needed an Amazon Princess who could pilot their invisible monkey bar plane with aplomb. In one fluid, coordinated motion, I grabbed the first monkey bar, hoisted myself up, through and onto the top of my invisible jet, and turned over the ignition.

> *"Walk out onto that playground like it's yours."*

"Skippers, get out of my way," my spirit screamed. "I AM A FIERCE AMAZON WARRIOR. I fight cosmic foes so your playground is safe enough for you to skip."

How perfect. Imaginative, plot-spinning boys taught me to soar. And Miss Lyon taught me to roar.

It's been forty years now, but looking back I realize Miss Lyon knew something I didn't. Hallways at recess are empty. They are echo chambers that bounce our fears and failures back to us.

Oh, for all I know, maybe she really just wanted to get to the teachers' lounge and needed to clear the hallway. But my greater hunch is that she saw an opportunity to pour life and purpose into a lonely young person who was just one kind word away from finding her bravery.

"Walk out onto that playground like it's yours."

As a high school senior, I landed the lead role in *Oklahoma!* Even though other girls in my class had sturdier, steadier soprano voices than me, I learned my lines, practiced with a voice coach and walked onto that stage like it was mine.

At my first real newspaper job interview — which I flubbed in almost every conceivable way — I walked into the boardroom like it was mine. And I got the job.

A couple of years into my journalism career, my city editor told me to grab my notepad because I needed to head over to a United Way event for an interview. "Who am I interviewing?" I asked.

"First Lady Laura Bush," he said, waiting for a reaction. He didn't get one. I had learned years earlier to walk into any room like it was mine.

At my first-ever public-speaking engagement last year, I walked up onto the stage with that same confidence. I got tongue-twisted a few times. But the audience responded with laughter and attentiveness, and a line a dozen-deep when I was done talking.

At my church, where I lead a D-group — our churchy hip term for discipleship group — I walk weekly into a room filled with high school students. I try to understand what makes them tick. I hope that I'm helping. I don't always wear the latest fashion, but I walk into the room like it's mine.

And you know what one of the girls said to me a few weeks back? "How do you do it? You have such confidence, but it doesn't come off as arrogance. Someday, I hope I'll carry myself that way."

"You want to know the trick?" I asked her.

"You bet," she said.

"Just walk out onto the playground like it's yours," I said, telling her a story about a hallway, a teacher and a little girl who had ninja-level monkey bar skills. We walked out arm-in-arm and enjoyed a good laugh. And she promised me she would never forget the words.

— Laurie Davies —

How Losing My Home Improved My Life

*Coming out of your comfort zone is tough
in the beginning, chaotic in the middle,
and awesome in the end... because in
the end, it shows you a whole new world.*
~Manoj Arora

"I'm sorry, Lisa, but Debbie and I are going to move back into the house. You're going to have to find another place to live."

I couldn't quite believe what Neil, my landlord, was telling me on that warm April night. *I'm going to have to move? But I want to stay right here where I am. This is my home!*

I had tears in my eyes, and so did he. I had lived on the first floor of his Staten Island two-family house for more than twelve years — longer than I had lived in any place since my childhood home. Ever since I moved back to the New York City area in 2000, Neil, a butcher in his fifties, had been like family to me.

Originally, Neil lived on the second floor of the house. But a few years ago, he had moved a few miles away into his girlfriend Debbie's house. He renovated his old apartment and the attic, and rented out that space to some young members of the Coast Guard. But after a torn rotator cuff had ended his grocery career, he and Debbie had decided to sell her house and move back here.

Neil had never raised my rent, which was $750 a month, dirt-cheap for New York City. This was a big comfort when I was laid off from my newspaper job during the height of the recession and couldn't find more than piecemeal work for two years. He promised me that I would always have a home, even if I had a hard time making the rent. However, I always made sure that I paid the rent before any other bill.

Now, I was still recovering from the recession, and I was going to have to find a new apartment and pay more. *A lot more,* I thought.

That was part of the problem. Neil was making a lot more money from the new tenants upstairs, so it made sense for him to keep those tenants and move into my apartment. He was very nice about it, and gave me six months to find a new place. Nevertheless, I was devastated and worried. I was so upset that I got into bed, pulled the covers over my head and cried. It was only 8:30 p.m., but I just wanted to go to sleep and forget this was happening.

Around 12:30 a.m., my upstairs neighbors had a few friends over, and they were making some noise. I stormed out of bed, opened my front door, and yelled up toward their apartment: "Can you keep it down already? I have to get up in five hours to go to work!"

I was so wound up afterward that I couldn't sleep. So I called Jon, my best friend, to bemoan my bad fate. But Jon surprised — and annoyed — me.

"Look on the bright side," he said. "Maybe you will find a place you like better. Let's face it. Your apartment isn't exactly the Taj Mahal. And you complain all the time about that crowded bus to and from the ferry. Why don't you find a place where you don't have to take that bus?"

"How can you say that?" I snapped at him. "This is way out of my comfort zone!"

"C'mon, Lisa. Did it ever occur to you that change could be good?"

"No!" I screamed, and hung up on him.

I fumed for the next few days about our argument. But what if Jon was right? Why was I so afraid of change? Why did I assume that every change would be bad? Why was I so negative all the time? Yes, I had a bad break losing my job, but why couldn't change be good sometimes? Maybe my life needed to be shaken up. Maybe I was in a rut.

The fact was I had let myself go in too many areas. When was the last time I had tried to do something with my writing skills? Or with my weight, which had gotten out of control in recent years? When was the last time I did anything outside of my routine? When was the last time I felt positive and hopeful about anything?

That summer, as I started looking at apartments, I began to think about new possibilities. Maybe I could get better furniture, be a better housekeeper, and have an apartment I could be proud of again.

It was a good thing Neil had given me six months to find a new place because I needed most of that time to save money and find an apartment, which was frustrating. I loved the view from the first place I looked at, but the landlord had already promised the place to someone else. Other apartments had parking issues, or were too small or expensive. And some of them had landlords who seemed just plain weird, like the woman who asked me four times whether I was planning on having a baby even though I was in my late forties.

But as the leaves started falling that year, I wondered if I was being a little too picky and was in denial about having to move. I prayed that I would find a place that was right for me. When was it going to happen? Time was running out.

Finally, that October, I spotted the apartment of my dreams in a new home in a nice neighborhood. The place had a stainless-steel refrigerator, stove, and microwave oven. Great overhead lighting. A built-in washer and dryer. Central air conditioning and heat. No more having to rely on crummy AC window units. The floor was beautifully tiled, unlike my old apartment's worn-out wood floors. This apartment also had a luxurious bathroom that looked like a spa. My old bathroom looked like a crime scene.

The new place was also close to the train and the express bus. While it was farther from Manhattan than my old place, the public transportation was better and more convenient. Plus, the neighborhood had a pharmacy and grocery store less than two blocks away. I could get along well without a car, something that wasn't the case at my old place.

But the apartment was $200 a month more than my current apartment, and it was more than I wanted to spend. It took me two weeks of agonizing, but I finally decided that it was the place for me. I signed a lease and agreed to move in right after Halloween. Moving was very stressful, but I got through it.

Once I had a new place, I was motivated to have new — and better — furniture. I was able to get a fancy new bed at a great discount thanks to one of our clients at work. I also saved a few pennies and bought some good, gently used furniture. My brother bought me a dresser. And Jon put together a bookcase, TV stand, and coffee table for me.

It took a few weeks to get the place fully in order, but I remember how proud I was to show my new digs to my friends, Jon and Ann, one Saturday night when they came over for dinner.

As time went on, I found myself doing more things out of my comfort zone and feeling more positive about life. I started to address being overweight. I began a regular exercise plan and started making meals in my new kitchen, instead of wolfing down junk food. I became more conscious and mindful, and ran regularly — another thing way out of my comfort zone — which helped me lose eighty pounds. I became so dedicated to running that I completed over 250 road races, including eight marathons.

I also started to get out of my comfort zone professionally. I took a risk and pitched *The Washington Post* website about an article idea. To my surprise, they said "yes." Not only did they run "The Redemption of A-Rod" on the website, but they also ran it in the Outlook section of the Sunday edition, which I consider the most prestigious section of the paper!

As change upon change built up in my life, I felt like I was a different person. My life had improved in so many ways, and it all started when I shed the cocoon of my old apartment, took a risk and found a new place to spread my wings. There's a reason they say that the end of your comfort zone is where the magic happens.

— Lisa Swan —

50

Endings Can Be Beginnings

*Every story has an end but in life
every ending is just a new beginning.*
~Uptown Girls

I still clearly remember the night when my dad gathered our family in the living room. After nearly eleven months of unemployment, we could sense what this meant. Even though my dad usually had a way with words, he skirted around saying what we knew was coming. Finally, he said it: "I accepted a new job." And in turn, I had to accept my fate.

I blurted out the obvious question, "Where?" Before my father could finish saying "Austin, Texas," I had burst into tears, practically inconsolable. I would have to completely start over, which was less than ideal for a sophomore in high school. My crying continued well into the night.

After that I was done. Not another tear fell.

Following that December night I became numb, withdrawing into myself in an attempt to make leaving seem painless. While my dad commuted back and forth between California and Texas, my sister and I were allowed to finish out the school year, leaving me with six months to sabotage my relationships with people who cared about me. As a result I felt detached, almost as though I was living a double life while I kept this secret from my friends and others around me. I was consumed with self-pity, questioning the purpose of engaging in the world around me since I knew I was leaving. However, somewhere along the way of counting down the days in anticipation of the end, I found myself counting down the days in anticipation of the beginning.

Suddenly I stopped feeling sorry for myself. I decided to take charge of my life and add some certainty to my unclear future. I diligently researched high schools and neighborhoods, and in return my parents gave me a say in where we would begin the search for our new home in the Austin area. Once we purchased our new house, I could see my future unfolding before me. With knowledge comes power. I did not have to become a victim of my circumstance, but instead a victor. I could take this clean slate and use it as an opportunity for self-improvement.

My self-improvement began by emulating confidence. My end goal was to become proactive and independent, which at the time seemed overwhelming. I knew the only way to achieve this was by taking baby steps, so I e-mailed the tennis coach at my new high school and inquired about trying out for the team. The seemingly simple e-mail soon turned into a conversation as he put my mind at ease, reassuring me that I was "coming to a great school and tennis community," and my prospective team was looking forward to having me.

The interaction could not have gone better. Little did I know that would set the course for my "new and improved" life. My coach had gone on to inform the team of my arrival. Within the week, I was communicating with a redheaded girl on the varsity team named Danielle who had reached out to me via Twitter. It dawned on me that the only things she knew about me came from an Instagram account and a horribly outdated Facebook profile. This was my chance to put my clean slate to use. I could assume the role of the confident girl I wanted to be. For the first time I felt like I was in control, because for so long I had let other people, whether friends or unacquainted peers, control me. This was my time.

More than six months after my family packed up our cars and drove to what I had come to view as my promised land, I have never felt more "me." I successfully threw myself into everything I possibly could, enjoying the process of uncovering what I truly did and didn't like, not what my peers dictated I *should* like.

At my old school I would have never given math club a second thought, even though I was fairly skilled in the subject. However, it was a new school, a new me, and I decided to challenge myself and join Mu Alpha Theta, a mathematics honor society. Shocking as it may be, I actually enjoyed being a "mathlete," but even more shocking to me was the fact that no one teased me for my decision. It seemed as though everyone around me had already realized that they should "live and let live."

It was then that I realized the judgments I perceived from others were, in actuality, nonexistent. The perceived ridicule was purely something I allowed myself to fear, and moving gave me the freedom to see that I decide what shapes me. The courage and confidence I had sought had been there all along, simply waiting beneath my insecurities to finally surface when the time was right.

The night I learned I was going to move, the person I used to be evaporated with my last tears. The debilitating dread of what I thought was the end was replaced by anticipation for a new beginning. While every new beginning contains an element of fear, it also contains an element of promise.

— Brianna Mears —

Chapter 6

Make Me Time

What You'll Find in This Chapter

f there's anything we learned during the pandemic, it's that life is unpredictable, and nothing is guaranteed. You've got to live it with joy while you can. That means carving out time for yourself and for seeing your favorite people.

This chapter focuses on how you can live your life more joyfully, by deliberately creating time for yourself — "me time" — and time with your most important loved ones — "we time." Self-care, work/life balance, and decluttering your calendar are all eminently doable. You just have to realize what you're missing and then develop a strategy for solving the problem.

Intellectually, you know you need to carve out that important time. That's why I've chosen stories for this chapter that will provide you with great role models and usable tips so you can reorganize your calendar and create some R&R time every day, or at least every week.

Betsy Franz writes about how overly busy she was in her story, "Life in the Slow Lane." This was a woman who was always running late and doing too many things. So, when her car ran out of gas one morning on the way to work, Betsy was frustrated. She was going to miss an important meeting.

But then Betsy got out of her car, looked east, and saw the sun rising. It was casting a beautiful light onto the river she was parked by; there were ducks swimming, and there was a magical fog over the water. She was awestruck and couldn't believe she'd been driving by this glorious scene every morning without noticing it.

Betsy says everything changed for her that day — the day that her car, and her life, ran out of gas. After that, she spent more time talking to people at work. She took long walks and listened to the sounds of nature. And she even started getting to work late on occasion, on purpose!

Kristine Byron was another woman who spent way too much time working, to the detriment of her family and herself. That was until her mentor told her to put some "lily pads" on her calendar. What were those? They were times she blocked out with fake appointments so that she would actually have time for her personal life. Like a frog, Kristine would hop onto those lily pads when she needed a little sun and peace. Her story is called "Looking Forward to Those Lily Pads."

Being disciplined about carving out time is important. And that's why I've included Rebecca Hill's story for you, called "My Mondays." Five days a week, from Tuesday to Saturday, Rebecca dedicated all her time and attention to her customers. Her two jobs — as a fitness instructor and a combination innkeeper and concierge — kept her on her toes. Sundays were devoted to "pajama day" with her husband. And then, on Mondays, Rebecca took time to pamper her most important customer: herself. Mondays were her "My-days," and she made sure she spent them doing things that made her feel great. My-days gave Rebecca the positive boost and recharge she needed to approach the rest of the week with energy and enthusiasm.

51

Dinner with Kay

I know what I bring to the table, so trust me when I
say I'm not afraid to eat alone.
~Author Unknown

Being a parent is hard enough, but being a single parent is overwhelming. After twenty years of marriage and two kids, I found myself a single mother. When my husband left, I was all the kids had. I had no family to help me where I lived, so I did what any mother would do. I rose to the occasion and worked my fingers to the bone to provide for them.

At times, I was working sixty-plus hours a week. I had as many as three jobs at a time. It wasn't easy, but my kids never went without. I never missed a bill, never had a late payment, and all without child support. The only problem was that I was working myself to death.

One Easter weekend, I worked thirty hours from Friday to Sunday, with little to no sleep. On Sunday night, I fell into bed exhausted. My next memory was waking up in an ambulance with two paramedics holding me down. I had no memory of how I got there, and I had a splitting headache. They kept asking me what kind of drugs I was on. Seriously? I'd never taken drugs in my life. All I remember is being angry and confused.

They took me to the hospital, and over the course of a couple of days, they deduced that I had simply collapsed from exhaustion. Apparently, I'd gotten up in the middle of the night and had a seizure. I had bitten my tongue and hit my head on the doorknob of my bedroom closet. The saddest part was, I didn't even know my own children. My daughter said I looked right at her but didn't recognize her. Yet, I kept telling the paramedics to call another employee to open the business because I couldn't get there. That's ridiculous, don't you think?

When I was released from the hospital, I began to rethink everything. As a single parent, I had to provide, but I was going to have to find a better way to do it. I needed to be home more for my kids, work fewer hours, and still make ends meet. The only way was to find a better-paying job, which wouldn't be easy.

In time, I did find a better job, and I was able to once again think about taking care of me. I had been taking care of everyone else for so long that I'd forgotten about myself. Growing up, my mother was always sick, and I had to take care of her. After I got married at eighteen, I soon had the two children and a husband to take care of. I had never been a priority, and the thought of doing something I enjoyed seemed foreign.

> *I had been taking care of everyone else for so long that I'd forgotten about myself.*

The first thing I did was take up jogging. It helped me get back into shape and forced me to eat right. I then began teaching aerobics classes so I could help other women get their lives back. I did everything I could to talk with other single moms about taking care of themselves so they'd be better equipped to take care of their children. However, my favorite thing to do was to go out to dinner with Kay.

Every two weeks, Kay and I would go out to dinner. My children were old enough to stay home alone for a couple of hours, and I always made sure they had their favorite dinner to eat while I was gone. Kay and I just relaxed, forgot our troubles, and enjoyed the time out. We never went anyplace expensive. My daughter always asked why she never got to meet Kay. I just told her, "Someday."

Time passed quickly, and my children grew up and moved on with their lives. One day, my daughter asked me again about Kay. "Who was she?" she asked. Finally, I explained that Kay was my middle name, and those nights I went out I was alone. It was a time to just be me and treat myself. It was my me time. She was shocked to find out that Kay wasn't a real person. However, Kay was a real person. She was the part of me who needed to feel special once in a while.

It's easy to get lost as a mother because we love our kids dearly. Sometimes, we just need to find ourselves. Kay is still one of my favorite dinner companions.

— Brenda Beattie —

52

Career Magic

More men are killed by overwork than the importance
of this world justifies.
~Rudyard Kipling

T he gift I'd been striving for — working day and night to achieve — had finally arrived in the form of a phone call. My heart raced as I listened to the words I'd been waiting to hear: "We'd like to offer you the position of District Conservationist in Mifflin County."

I accepted my first supervisory role, determined to take on any new challenge life threw my way. Already blessed with a position as a trainee in resource protection, the promotion was a real honor. I reported to my new office in Lewistown, Pennsylvania with eagerness and resolve. Ready to save the world!

Applying for the job in Mifflin County took a pole vault of faith. I grew up outside of Pittsburgh, far from the rural countryside where my career had now taken me. The differences in culture and surroundings were astonishing. I soon realized a major traffic jam in Mifflin County consisted of being the third car behind an Amish buggy.

The shopping centers and subdivisions of my old world were replaced by flourishing farm fields, stretching from forested ridge to forested ridge. It felt like I'd found heaven on earth. The community welcomed me with open hearts and genuine delight. Smiles and joy proved to be the norm, beaming from every corner of the county. Living in this tranquil paradise was beyond my wildest dreams and life seemed to be filled with limitless opportunities.

I decided to be the best District Conservationist in the history of the world. No demand too great. No obstacle insurmountable. With a new staff, my major duty was to be a great supervisor. So, even though fieldwork was the responsibility of the staff, I figured the best way to be that great supervisor was to engage in as much of it as possible. I wanted to prove to them I didn't expect them to do anything I wouldn't.

I raced out of the starting blocks and sprinted towards a mountain of new goals. A mountain which grew higher and higher, while I took on more and more projects.

Meanwhile, while I was out in the field doing their work, the staff spent their days lounging in the air-conditioned office complaining about life. Worse, the paperwork involved with being a supervisor continued to pile up.

And on top of my mounting tasks, I wanted to learn all there was to know about farming and conservation. Using every moment I could spare, I devoured textbooks to learn about crops, cows, and everything rural.

Pretty soon life became a tornado, spinning wildly out of control. I was doing fieldwork during the day and working late into the evening trying to catch up on my paperwork.

In a crushing moment, it hit me: this wasn't the way I pictured my dream job.

My stress snowballed. Life's balance disappeared. No matter how hard I worked, I slipped further and further behind. The dreams of grandeur I had when I took the position dwindled... fading into oblivion.

Time off, even on weekends, became a pipe dream. I lost sleep worrying about the work accumulating on my desk and the countless unfinished tasks cluttering my mind.

Finally, after eight months in the position, I requested a meeting with my supervisor, George. Making the call to him consumed me with dread. It was the ultimate admission of defeat. But I realized it was time to fess up and let him know how far behind I was.

I felt dejected, burned out, and exasperated.

On the drive to George's office a week later, my mind played movies of George's rage and anger. I could already hear his disappointment. My pride would be bruised, my honor tarnished — even destroyed. I readied myself for the bitter pill I was about to swallow.

When I arrived, I feigned a smile at his assistant, and entered his office. I took a seat across from George and exhaled.

"I'm sorry George. I've worked so hard and poured my heart and soul into my job. But I'm feeling like a miserable failure. The more hours I put in, the more I get behind. I need help." I could barely look him in the eyes when I added, "I'm truly sorry to disappoint you."

The tourniquet in my stomach tightened as I readied myself for the worst. Then, to my surprise, George smiled.

He kicked back in his chair and said, "Relax. Enjoy yourself. Life's too short to waste with worry. There's one little word you need to learn. That word is no. You don't need to take on every project. You don't need to juggle every ball. You don't need to waste time with worry. You need to enjoy life and focus on all the good. You'll be far more productive with far less anguish."

> *There's one little word you need to learn. That word is no.*

At that moment, it felt like a two-ton weight was lifted from my shoulders. Then George reached into his desk drawer and pulled out a book, *How to Stop Worrying and Start Living* by Dale Carnegie. He handed it to me.

With a relaxed smile, George said, "Read this and learn to love your life."

I studied the book in my hands, feeling as if I'd been given a gift from heaven.

George continued, "Larry you are a darn good employee and supervisor. You make me proud. Keep up the great work and dedicated spirit and enjoy every moment."

The remaining weight on my shoulders lifted. A smile drifted back to my face and into my soul. I knew I'd just been handed one of those rare change-your-life-forever moments.

And then George dispensed some advice I'll never forget. He said, "A supervisor is someone who you look up to and respect, who wants the best for his people, and who guides with kindness. Be a fabulous supervisor and lead with a loving heart."

What a revelation! And delivered by one of the most amazing supervisors I've ever had.

I left the office a new man. I devoured the book. The words empowered me with a whole new perspective and respect for the rare gift of living a happy and fulfilled life.

From that day forward, when my mind would clutter with negative thoughts of worry and lead me down the path to despair, I became aware how hopelessness crowded out all the good. But positive thoughts made room for creativity, productivity, love, and happiness.

Now, after nearly thirty years, thanks to one man's wisdom and encouragement, there's an opening in my life for everything that is good and magnificent in this world. It's a treasure I cherish every day as I celebrate the magic in every moment!

— Larry Schardt —

53

Recharge Rental

The sea, once it casts its spell,
holds one in its net of wonder forever.
~Jacques Cousteau

I hit a wall. I am the girl who rarely says "no," the one my friends say is the busiest person they know. A sometimes demanding career, chairing a local professional group, helping to found an international professional group, becoming a condominium association board member, participating in writing and Bible classes, caring for a parent's affairs, providing stateside assistance to a deployed Army brother, and caring for two dogs had burned me out. I needed a vacation.

I scheduled a week off from work and searched for beach rentals. At first, the search was futile. Most properties were too expensive, some would not allow dogs, and some were too far away from the beach. At the last minute, I found a property for the right price, with a dog-friendly fenced yard, across the street from the beach. Was this property too good to be true?

I took off for the rental with my dogs in tow. Finding the condo was easy. Inspecting the premises, the first thing I noticed was the same throw rug in their kitchen as in my own. It felt like a good sign. I let the dogs loose to run and roll in the yard and continued my inspection. The condo was very clean, the bed and sofas were all comfortable, and there were plenty of pots, pans and dishes for a week of meals. Settling into this strange place felt like taking a deep breath.

We went on unleashed walks and runs on the beach. Schools of playful dolphins offshore kept pace with my walks. Sitting under the pier in the shade, I traded technical manuals for fiction for the first time in years. Fresh air and sunshine, surfers, cooperative birds and interesting flowers growing in the sand inspired creativity with my digital camera.

I now refer to this place as my recharge rental, and it has become the one calendar entry each year written in stone. Each trip yields a new adventure. One year, I took a boat tour around Cumberland Island, where John F. Kennedy, Jr. was married, and saw wild horses. That trip was especially eventful because such a bad storm hit us on the way back that you could see nothing but torrential rain and wind from the boat windows. Comforting the terrified woman sitting next to me, I learned she too was visiting from Atlanta. When the storm finally subsided, we saw the actual lifeboat from which Navy SEALs rescued Captain Phillips, bullet holes and all.

Every visit, I meet nice people. A man on the beach told me how to recognize shark teeth in the sand. I never found any teeth, but I collected lots of beach glass and unusual shells. Another year, during a beach walk, a woman stopped me because she thought she knew me. It turned out we have a friend in common in Atlanta. One year, I met a local author. Last year, I met the owners of the condo upstairs, joining them for wine and pizza. That's how I found out about and witnessed a turtle hatching where they count the hatched eggs of endangered sea turtles.

Enjoying an annual visit to the beach has allowed me to step out of life's hamster wheel and replenish my energy. An added benefit is that it is the perfect halfway point for my mother's trip home. When my mom visits Atlanta from South Florida, I meet her halfway and drive her in, or travel with her halfway back. This year was the first time she joined me at the condo on her way home. The night before she left, we ate dinner at a wonderful beachside restaurant with live music. The evening was one of the best that either of us could remember. It was the perfect end for her visit to Atlanta, and the perfect beginning of my annual retreat.

—Bonnie L. Beuth—

54

My Mondays

The best days are unplanned,
random and spontaneous.
~Author Unknown

Six days a week, I devote my days to others. One day a week, I assert my independence by making sure I am responsible only to myself. I believe that time is the most valuable currency we have, which is why I am committed to giving myself time each week that's all my own.

Tuesday through Saturday, I work. I have two part-time jobs and they are both social and customer service-oriented. One job is as a circuit trainer at Curves where my priority is making sure our members get a fantastic workout while having fun. This often means entertaining them while coaching, compelling (and sometimes outright cajoling) them into "working harder and really feeling the burn!" My other job is as an innkeeper at Channel Road Inn. There, in addition to baking homemade goodies, I greet the hotel guests and help them make plans for their time in Los Angeles.

> *Six days a week,*
> *I devote my days*
> *to others.*

That is time-intensive because it requires taking their individual desires and interests into account. Guests rarely tell me up front what they're interested in. I don't think they're being evasive — I just think we all run at such frenetic speed in today's modern world that we lose touch with who we are and what we like to do. Even when I ask what their interests are they often say, "I don't know; we just want to do 'California things' and have fun." But I know each person is an individual and there are hundreds of "California things" to do.

Through the course of conversation I hear patterns emerge. It becomes clear that some guests are the outdoorsy types, so I steer them toward surf lessons, horseback riding and hiking through the Santa Monica Mountains. Some guests need to be pampered and have calming experiences, so I steer them toward botanical gardens, day spas, yoga classes and meditation centers. Some people love amusement parks, so Universal Studios and Disneyland are the obvious recommendations. Others are intrigued by art and find fulfillment by going from museum to museum. To create a meaningful experience, it's important to help the guests slow down and think about who they are and what activities they would really enjoy doing. I always remind them, "You can't do everything, so it's important to find the activities that would make you happiest."

My Sundays are devoted to spending time with my husband. We are both homebodies so we love to pad around the apartment in our pajamas and do NOTHING for the entire day. We call Sundays "Pajama Days" because more often than not, we never even get out of our pajamas. Sometimes he wanders in and out of his music studio if he gets a song idea. Sometimes I sit at my computer if I get a writing idea. But for the most part we lie in bed, watch movies, read books, and order food to be delivered. Sundays provide a sanctuary of time for us to reconnect as a couple after a busy workweek.

And then there's Monday! Monday is my day. For this one day, I am neither a circuit trainer nor an innkeeper. I am, of course, still a wife but, barring an emergency, I only consider my wants and desires on this one day. I assert my independence by doing whatever I want, whenever I want, from the time I wake up to the time I go to sleep.

Most Mondays I'll spend writing, but sometimes I just wander aimlessly through department stores, browsing and looking at all the beautiful dresses, shoes, jewelry and furniture the world has to offer. Such reverie! I love the way the various patterns and textures look and feel. Whether they're in my size or not, I delight in running my hands through racks of dresses just to see all the beautiful colors whoosh by. I love to touch the zippers and buttons on the shoes and purses. I like to peruse jewelry, especially pearl jewelry. I can get lost for hours looking at furniture and imagining which pieces I'd buy if I ever won the lottery and could build my dream home.

Sometimes I'll go out to eat by myself and sometimes I'll meet a friend for lunch. Either way, it has to be a restaurant that offers vegetarian options because this is my day and I don't want to have to struggle with the menu.

Sometimes I'll stay home and play with my cat, Anaïs — or if she's not in the mood, then sometimes I'll go by an animal shelter and play with their cats. I have my favorites!

If I've gotten a coupon or a Groupon-type deal, I'll go get a mani/pedi. I love getting manicures and pedicures. The massage aspect is fantastic, and the end result looks great, but my favorite part is choosing which polish I want. Even though I almost always pick a neutral color for my toes and clear on my fingernails, some days I'm feeling sassy and have my toenails painted red!

Sometimes I'll have a second "Pajama Day," but this one all by myself. When I have a "Pajama Day" by myself, I sleep in the middle of the bed, use all the pillows and set the air conditioner to exactly the temperature I like.

Mondays (or My-days as I like to think of them) are important to me. I anticipate and plan them throughout the week and bring particular focus to them as I go to bed on Sunday. Just like with the hotel guests at Channel Road Inn, I know that to create a meaningful experience, it's important for me to slow down, clear my mind, reorient my thinking to putting my needs and desires first, and to think about who I am and what activities I'd really enjoy doing the next day. I try to get re-centered, so come Monday morning I will be able to honor myself as an independent person with individual tastes and desires.

Not everyone likes to window shop or play with cats all day, but these activities relax me. Some people might not like to spend their day in front of the computer trying to write a story, but that's often what I'm drawn to. Some people don't like to eat alone at a restaurant, but

I do — so I do. As I plan my Mondays, I always remind myself what I tell the hotel guests, "You can't do everything, so it's important to find the activities that would make you happiest."

I know we can't all have an entire day to ourselves each week. My friends who are parents tell me that it is an incredible luxury. Even so, I hope we can all find at least a few hours each week to assert our independence and do whatever we feel like doing. It is unbelievably freeing and empowering to re-remember that. Even if you are a mother, a grandmother, a daughter, or a spouse — you are also an independent, free-spirited, unique individual with idiosyncratic wants and desires that deserve to be listened to and honored.

— Rebecca Hill —

55

Just Burn It

Cherish your yesterdays, dream your
tomorrows and live your todays.
~Author Unknown

"Why don't you just burn the stupid candle?" My best friend, Wynter, and I were thirteen years old and had a close enough friendship that she could provide little gems of unsolicited advice like this without making me feel too annoyed or offended.

On this particular day, we were in my bedroom trying to decide what to do for the next couple of hours until her parents came to pick her up. She had wandered over to my dresser to examine my rather impressive candle collection. I had a candle shaped like a cup of coffee, one that looked like an ice-cream sundae, one that looked like a fishbowl, and various other oddities.

Wynter picked up a large, round, dark blue candle. Unlike most of my other candles, it wasn't shaped like any particular object. A subtle swirl of colors reminded me of a sky at twilight. The candle had tiny holes poked into the side so that, when lit, it would presumably cast a luminescent glow. I say "presumably" because I had never actually tried it.

"It's part of my candle collection," I explained. "If I burn my candle collection, then I won't have a collection anymore!"

Wynter was undeterred. "But it's a candle! It's meant to be burned! Let's just see what it looks like when it's lit. I bet it's really pretty."

"Maybe someday."

Wynter rolled her eyes at me, but I would not be persuaded. The candle remained unlit that day—and for years afterward until, at some point, my mom cleaned out my old room and got rid of most of the junk cluttering it up, including the candle collection that had been too precious to burn.

My friend didn't realize it that day, but she had provided me with a piece of advice that I've continued to follow years later: "Burn the stupid candle."

As an adult, this phrase has popped into my head many times and in various situations. Debating whether to use my "fancy lotion" or save it for later because I don't want it to run out? *Burn the stupid candle.* Wondering whether I should get out the china my grandmother gave me as a wedding present or keep it shelved until a more impressive occasion comes along? *Burn the stupid candle.* Considering whether to use a restaurant gift card to surprise my husband with an impromptu date or hang onto it until we have something meaningful to celebrate? *Burn the stupid candle.* It's such a simple piece of advice, but I think that's the reason it's meant so much to me. It's something I've been able to joyfully put into practice over and over again.

After all, restaurant gift cards get lost; china gets broken; fancy lotion gets poured onto the carpet by the three-year-old. And candle collections get unceremoniously dumped in the trash when we go off to college. None of the material things matter, but memories do.

Life is short, and "someday" is today. Now I burn all the stupid candles—and relish every luminous moment.

—Jayna Richardson—

56

Looking Forward to Those Lily Pads

Love yourself enough to set boundaries.
Your time and energy are precious.
~Anna Taylor

n my twenties, I began my career in Tupperware. I was looking to supplement my husband's paycheck and still be home with our growing family. I earned my Tupperware sample kit and bought a datebook, ready to fill in all the Tupperware parties I was going to hold. There was no doubt in my mind I was going to be successful!

As my datebook began to fill, I found that I was able to encourage other women to join me in this fun and lucrative career. Soon, I became a Tupperware manager, still holding parties and now training the girls on my team — eventually totaling fifty of them.

As my success grew and my datebook filled up, I found I had no time for myself. I was missing events with my children because I was so booked up with Tupperware parties and trainings. If I saw an empty time slot, I filled it, as any successful person would do.

My personal life was suffering, though. When I booked a party on my daughter's birthday, I knew I had to do something fast.

I was ready to quit. I met with my mentor/trainer, and the first thing she asked was to see my datebook. "Well, no wonder," she said. "You have no lily pads."

"What is a lily pad?" I asked.

"They are me-time spaces you block out in your day or week. Spaces in your week that you leap to one after the other for relief from your busy schedule."

I thought a full datebook made me look successful, and that people want to do business with successful people. My lily pads were my children's events, birthdays, manicures, and lunch with my mom or a friend. Even an occasional bubble bath with Calgon bath-oil beads! I started adding entries to my datebook that simply read "Lily P." and the time.

I learned to put everything in my book in code. I had been so afraid to turn down a party or training opportunity with one of my Tupperware dealers, but I found that when they saw that the time they wanted was already booked, they were fine with switching to another time that I offered them. My lily pads were my secret me time and they were easy to protect.

I realized it was up to me to safeguard those special times for me and my family. I learned to schedule my week and stick

> *My lily pads were my secret me time.*

to my schedule, with lily pads to help me leap through my week with a smile on my face.

— Kristine Byron —

57

Me First Beats Martyrdom

*As you grow older, you will discover that you
have two hands, one for helping yourself,
the other for helping others.*
~Maya Angelou

We all hear, all the time, that we need to take care of ourselves first — because that's how you're the most helpful to everyone else in your life, namely your children, aging parents, neighbors, or any loved one nearby. Yet, how often does that me-first mandate translate to everyday life?

For me, it's not often, and I suspect I am the norm, not the exception. For some reason, we women are wired differently. I can barely recall an incident where my own needs trumped someone else's. Even as a child, I can remember not wanting my little brother or sister to do without, hence I did. Whether it was a Christmas celebration where the children outnumbered the gifts, a birthday party where the take-home prizes fell one short, or a family dessert where there were two cupcakes for three children, I was always the one who did without while smiling.

Such behavior followed me to the workplace. I found myself assuming similar roles: the big sister, the peacemaker, the appeaser. A pressing Friday deadline? No worries, I'll stay late. No coffee in the office kitchen? No problem, I'll make a Starbucks run. An unexpected Sunday meeting? No big deal, I'll cover it. And that routine continued for years — until the day that it didn't.

Looking back, I am at a loss to identify what significant event triggered such a change. Truth be told, I don't think there was a single event. Rather, it was a years-in-the-making build-up. But I do recall the day I just said, "No!" My boss at the time was packing up early on a summer Friday afternoon, expecting me to cover an unexpected deadline. I recall marching into his office and simply stating that I had to leave by 5:00 p.m. He hadn't asked me to stay late. Rather, he just assumed that I would and, with all due respect, had no reason to think that I would not since I had stayed late for years without being asked.

Truth be told, I guess he must have been a bit surprised — incredulous perhaps — but I did not linger to discuss it. I merely returned to my cubicle, feeling rather giddy, and packed up my things by 4:55 p.m. I was prepared to enjoy a summer weekend.

That day marked a turning point in my life and a new chapter in self-care. I wish I could say that the change was dramatic, but it was not. That self-care muscle had to be developed and then exercised regularly. That summer weekend did turn a new page, but it would take years for that book to be finished.

My journey to self-care started with leaving my job on time. Well, almost on time — old habits die hard. And some days, I was still there after 5:00. But most days, I arrived home when there was still daylight. That was a new phenomenon, and my first reaction was guilt. *The sun is just setting… I should be at work,* I told myself.

Years ago, I learned that the quickest way to silence that nagging voice in my head was exercise. So, I laced up my sneakers and started to walk every evening upon arriving home. A creature of habit, those twilight walks became a ritual, and I looked forward to the alone time these walks provided. Before long, I was completing three miles within an hour.

One good habit seemed to beget another, and soon I was sleeping better and eating healthier. My energy level was at an all-time high. Feeling so much better about myself, I visited a new hair salon and had my "crowning glory" cut, re-styled, and highlighted. That week, I received so many compliments on my appearance that I decided to incorporate a weekly visit to the salon into my budget.

Ironically, every employee received a cost-of-living increase the following week, and mine was exactly the cost of a salon visit. For someone who had religiously banked every increase, I felt almost giddy earmarking the money for a weekly indulgence. But I also felt that the Universe was applauding me. Phrases like "Yes, you are worth it!" suddenly started to challenge that nagging voice.

While routine visits to the local hair and nail salon can be outward signs of self-care, I also felt an internal, seismic shift within myself. Ironically, while I now had more me time and downtime, I found myself becoming more possessive of that time. It was difficult to articulate, but I didn't want to just "fill time."

Perhaps I sensed somehow that time is a limited and precious commodity. While I may have had more hours each day, I knew that there were symbolically more grains of sand in the bottom of the hourglass than were at the top. And what a wake-up call that realization proved to be.

In the coming weeks, I thought a lot about what makes me happy, gives me pleasure, and provides me with purpose. I started spending more time in nature, treasuring conversations with friends and loved ones, and enjoying cultural pursuits.

An avid reader my entire life, I made a pact with myself concerning all the time I devoted to reading. If I didn't thoroughly enjoy a book by the third chapter, I stopped reading it. That may sound like a minor tweaking to most, but for someone like me, who on occasion portrays some OCD traits, it felt like freedom. A self-confessed people pleaser, I then promised myself that if certain friendships had run their course, I didn't have to continue to nurture them. And while I continued to eat healthy, I gave myself a lifetime pass to never eat turnips, Brussels sprouts, or broccoli again!

It's been close to ten years now since I began my self-care regimen. Looking back, I cringe when I think about how negligent I was in regard to caring for my younger self. Back then, I measured my worth by how much I gave, how much I sacrificed, or even how much I had suffered for some greater good, which I still have trouble defining. Truth be told, by taking better care of myself, I find that I have become a better, more accepting and authentic person than the martyr I had been so proud to emulate in my misguided youth.

— Barbara Davey —

Life in the Slow Lane

The moment one gives close attention to any thing,
even a blade of grass, it becomes a mysterious,
awesome, indescribably magnificent world in itself.
~Henry Miller

I always seemed to be running late. I'd wake up in the morning early enough to have plenty of time to get to where I wanted to go. But by the time I found myself on the road headed for my destination, it was obvious that I was going to be late. So I'd strap on my seatbelt, put the car in gear, and slam the accelerator to the floor in an attempt to make up for the five or ten minutes that I'd somehow lost. The scenery became nothing but a blur as I played chicken with the traffic lights and kept my mental radar on the alert for the men in blue.

This constant rushing also extended into other aspects of my life. When I went grocery shopping, I looked much like the winner of an all-you-can-spend-in-five-minutes shopping spree. I'd race up and down the aisles throwing in items right and left. My cart would take the corners on two wheels as I yelled out my deli order to the startled lady behind the counter.

Or, at the mall, I'd race through the stores like an entrant in the hundred-yard dash. There was no window shopping for me. I'd plan my route before I even walked through the doors and then neither rain nor sleet nor an unexpected sale at JCPenney could keep me from making my rounds.

I had to rush around like that. There just weren't enough hours in the day and I was afraid I might miss something if I didn't hurry up.

And then one day, as fate would have it, I ran out of gas. I had been running behind as usual so I hadn't noticed my gas gauge. As my car coasted off the road, I looked at my watch and slammed the steering wheel in frustration. I had a meeting in fifteen minutes and I hadn't even finished preparing for it.

But as I got out of my car, an amazing thing happened. I looked out towards the east, and the sun was just beginning to blaze over the horizon. There was a low misty fog hanging over the river and some ducks were cutting thick, smooth trails across the otherwise glass-like surface of the water. A few sailboats sat at anchor, their mirror images extending out before them. And as the sun inched up through tiny trails of clouds that stretched across the sky, it extended beacons of glorious, wondrous light that shouted with all its beauty and strength, "Behold world! I have risen, again, for another day!"

I was awestruck. This glorious scene had been going on right outside my car every morning and I had never taken the time to see it. I had been rushing around in such a hurry to not miss anything that I had been missing everything!

I turned toward the road. Traffic was whizzing by at breakneck speed. I wanted to shout at the drivers, "Stop! Look what's happening over here! You're missing it!" But instead, I climbed up and had a seat on the hood of my car. And I quietly, joyfully, patiently watched as the sun painted a brand new day: a day of ducks and sailboats and silvery reflections on a mirrored sea.

When a co-worker finally recognized my car and stopped for me, I had somehow been transformed. My heart, my mind and my soul were all lighter. I went into work but was jealous that my car got to stay behind for a few more hours and watch the transformation of morning into afternoon, as the ducks and the river and the sailors all woke up and moved into their day.

It was as if I had been switched from 78 down to 33 rpm that day. Life went from a fast jitterbug into a slow, fluid waltz. I slowed down enough to see the people I worked with. To talk to them about things other than work. To notice if they were particularly happy or troubled and to see it they needed to tell me why.

I began taking long, slow walks around my yard and neighborhood, noticing for the first time all the mysteries and wonders that were right there for me to see all the time, patiently waiting for me to slow down enough to notice. Not only were there sights that I had been missing, but I began to hear entire symphonies all around me: birds singing, wind blowing, leaves rustling. And as I continued to practice my newfound peace, I discovered, to my amazement, another sound: a still, small voice deep inside my soul. And this voice had incredible things to say, images of intense beauty to point out, flashes of great insight, pearls of deep wisdom and constant words of inspiration, encouragement and guidance.

Life is different now. For years I had been like a hamster in an exercise wheel, running and running and running and never realizing that the destination I was racing to... was exactly the place that I already was. In fact, I've traded in my exercise wheel for a hammock, and this lazy hamster is sometimes quite content to just lie on my back and spend an entire afternoon trying to make clouds disappear. And incredibly enough, the world is still turning. It didn't need my hamster wheel for momentum after all.

I'll admit that I am a few minutes late to work sometimes now. And I take forever in the grocery store. And window shopping and people watching in the mall can take an entire afternoon. But life is no longer passing me by. I am here, fully present, in every moment of life as it unfolds before me. Joyfully, peacefully, patiently traveling this life in the slow lane... and enjoying every precious moment of it.

— Betsy S. Franz —

59

Three Choices

*As I am sure you know, when people say,
"It's my pleasure," they usually mean something
along the lines of, "There's nothing on Earth
I would rather do less."*
~Lemony Snicket, The Penultimate Peril

"It all comes down to three choices." These were the wise words I heard one day while watching a daytime talk show. At the time of this "light bulb moment" I was consumed by a very busy vocation that involved pleasing a lot of people and I was also a single mom of three teenagers. Any given day contained more requests for my time than I could count, and I usually felt I needed to give an answer right away. That answer was usually "yes." Consequently I felt overwhelmed.

Then, on a rare day when I was home in the afternoon, one of my favorite talk show hosts talked about the "three choices." She had been prone to saying yes more than she should, and she talked about how overwhelmed she felt. However, she had learned that she didn't have to answer a request right away. If she didn't feel ready to say yes or no, she discovered that there was a third option she'd not previously employed: "Let me get back to you." She related that by giving herself time to think about how she wanted to respond, she often declined requests that she might have previously — and prematurely — said yes to. Now she was giving herself breathing room to consider her schedule, and more importantly, her desires and priorities. And she noted that it was important to have the integrity to follow up with your answer later.

It was a great idea, and in the many years since, this has been my practice. It has brought me great peace, as well as the feeling of greater control over my schedule. If you want to simplify your life, this is a beautiful tool to use. The next time someone asks something of you, remember that you have three choices. You can say yes. You can say no. Or you can say, "Let me get back to you." Consider your priorities and your desires. And then, with integrity, give your answer.

— Kimberly Ross —

60

The Lunch Hour

Time is an illusion, lunchtime doubly so.
~Douglas Adams

I clutched a yogurt in one hand as I tried to eat and catch up on customer e-mail during the noon hour. Even fifteen minutes in the employee lunchroom seemed too much of a luxury. My company, like many companies, had cut costs by not replacing people as they left. The survivors were expected to take up the slack.

For me, this meant no lunch hour, plus taking work home in the evening or on the weekends. I didn't feel I worked at a job; I felt I was my job. I wanted to quit, but given the economy, I felt I couldn't until I had another job in hand. Nice in theory, but given how cranky all the extra hours made me feel, it was difficult to convince potential employers to hire me. I felt trapped. Then a chance conversation with a stranger's six-year-old daughter changed my outlook. The young girl was positively bouncy, standing in line with her mom at the grocery store.

"Good day at school?" I asked.

A nod.

"What's your favorite subject?"

"Lunch."

I smiled at the answer. I remembered when that had been my answer. At lunch, there were no adults to tell you what to do and when to do it. You could sit and talk with your friends or play an exuberant game of four-square. You could draw pictures or swing on the monkey bars. The time was yours to do whatever you wanted. Sometimes we planned our time, bringing stickers to trade or Chinese jacks for a weeklong tournament. Sometimes we were more spontaneous, only deciding what to do while we were eating our peanut butter and jelly sandwiches and slurping our little paper cartons of milk.

That brief encounter left me wondering: What had happened to lunch?

I knew that by law I was entitled to a lunch break at work. So I decided to simply start taking it. The office was located in the downtown area of a small town and I set out to explore it. A few blocks away was a local art museum with free admission. At the end of another street, I was startled to discover some horses grazing in a field. A cute gift boutique made for pleasant and sometimes humorous browsing, particularly looking through the leftover holiday items and laughing at the sometimes funny things, like jack-o'-lantern sunglasses and temporary Santa tattoos that no one had the foresight to buy.

When the weather turned cold, I visited the used bookstore or public library. Near the library was a small man-made pond that attracted ducks and small children with their parents, all of whom provided much amusement as they demanded to be fed. Even running errands at lunch to the bank or the post office brought me a small measure of joy. Doing those errands during the week freed up some time on the weekends for fun activities.

When I decided to take back my lunch hour, I braced myself for catty remarks or stares from my co-workers, but they never materialized. In fact, I watched in amazement as some of my co-workers started to drift away occasionally from their own desks during lunch. We started inviting each other out for walks during good weather and discovered that we had other topics of conversation beyond the now common complaints about work.

I'm still looking for a new position, but with less stressed-out urgency than before. You can't always change your circumstances, but you can always change your perspective.

— Michelle Mach —

Chapter
7

Step Outside Your Comfort Zone

What You'll Find in This Chapter

When I turned fifty, my husband and I started forcing ourselves to have new experiences, whether they were simple things, like shopping at a new grocery store, or challenging things, like paragliding off a cliff over the Persian Gulf. That's when I decided to make stepping outside your comfort zone an important theme in *Chicken Soup for the Soul* books.

It turned out that our contributors had plenty to say on this topic. They were challenging themselves to face their fears and try new things, and they reported how that changed them for the better and led to more new things and a broader, more meaningful life.

Whether it's the little things, like new foods, or the big things, like flying to a faraway country, we feel empowered when we do something that challenges us. I talk about that in my story, "Run," in this chapter, about paragliding. I was terrified, but it changed me. Now I know: If I can run off a cliff in Oman, anything is possible.

You'll undoubtedly be motivated to try more new experiences after you read this chapter. There are role models galore in these pages. Victoria Otto Franzese for example, decided to have a policy — she would just say yes to everything. That way she didn't even have to think about it. In her story, "A Year of New Things," she talks about doing something new every day for an entire year, activities as small as doing a sudoku puzzle and as big as dog sledding.

Sometimes trying new, scary things involves reaching out and making connections with other people. In the story "Becoming the

Glue" Kate Lemery tells us that she was a stay-at-home mom with three kids under the age of five, and she was lonely. She decided to become a room parent in her oldest child's kindergarten class. She also signed him up for soccer. But she still wasn't making any friends in her new town. Then an old friend suggested she throw a party for all those moms she didn't know. Kate was hesitant, but she sent out the invitations, and now she has hosted several of these "mommy mixers" and finds herself the "glue" that brings the mothers in her community together.

My favorite quote of all time is from John A. Shedd: "A ship in harbor is safe, but that is not what ships are built for." You'll find Rachel Dunstan Muller sailing away in "Leaving Harbour." It wasn't until her mother died of breast cancer that Rachel decided to shake up her life. She says, "For most of my adult life, I'd chosen to stay safely anchored in a series of sheltered harbours, both literally and metaphorically."

It was time for Rachel to break out of that comfort zone where she always chose security over risk. She made a resolution to live by the word "fierce" for an entire year and say yes to all the things that she would normally turn down. That meant taking a dance improv class, going caving, and in this story, going halibut fishing in open water. Rachel was terrified about the boat trip, but using her new open-minded perspective, she pushed aside her worries and focused on the sea, the sky, and the wind in her hair. She says, "I've come to believe that we're not fully alive if we're not at least a little frightened on a regular basis."

61

Run

Continuity gives us roots; change gives us branches,
letting us stretch and grow and reach new heights.
~Pauline R. Kezer

Okay, so I would never jump out of an airplane. How could I ever trust that a piece of fabric with a million strings coming out of it wouldn't get tangled up and fail to work? I have plenty of friends who have done it, but I won't.

But I'm all for doing new and scary things, especially as I get older, because I recognize the value of saying "yes" and ensuring that my world doesn't get narrower and narrower. And I've been inspired by all the Chicken Soup for the Soul stories that I've read by people who were advancing in years and made a special effort to try new things. So last year, when I was facing the prospect of turning sixty, a truly surprising development, I renewed my commitment to trying new things, including the *scary* ones.

And that's how I found myself standing at the top of a 1,000-foot cliff in Oman, on my way to a beautiful beach resort on the Persian Gulf.

You might think that taking a beach vacation on the Persian Gulf was enough of a "step outside your comfort zone" experience, but *that* was easy. It was gorgeous and luxurious and they picked us up at the airport in Dubai and took care of getting us across the border into Oman. Oman is a beautiful country on the Arabian Peninsula, known for its craggy sandstone mountains that plummet right down to the sea. It's very dramatic to see those tall mountains with sheer cliffs right next to the water, occasionally with beaches running along the edge of the sea.

The challenging part was the approach to the resort, which is so remote that you have three choices for the last part of the trip: 1) arrive by speedboat; 2) drive down a narrow, winding mountain road with hairpin turns and no guardrails; or, 3) jump off that 1,000-foot-high mountain cliff and paraglide down to the beach. According to tripadvisor.com, the really cool guests paraglide in.

I decided, that as a very cool fifty-nine-year-old, I would paraglide down to the beach. I imagined some kind of fixed-wing thing, like bird wings. That made aerodynamic sense to me. Wings that were already in place would be guaranteed to work — not like parachuting out of an airplane where the fabric might somehow *not* get itself organized into the right shape, or the strings might get tangled up.

So I was shocked when they were putting the harness on me and I turned around and saw a flimsy piece of fabric lying on the ground behind me — with lots of strings attached to it. That was when I realized that *para*gliding is *called* that because you use a *para*chute. For someone who specializes in words and clear language, I had truly been off my game!

But I didn't have much time to think about it because they were already strapping me in. Then they stuck a helmet on me. I don't know *what* they said this was for, but whatever they were saying, what I *heard* was: *to identify the body*. And then they told me that it was critically important that I run toward the cliff and absolutely not stop under any circumstances. Because if I didn't run right off the cliff, the flimsy piece of fabric with the one million strings wouldn't catch the air and I would plummet to my death.

Before I could change my mind the guide and I were running toward the edge of the cliff. And then, miraculously, that parachute filled with air and we were soaring, riding the air currents and flying even higher than where we had started. The guide was thrilled that the air currents were so strong, and that we could stay up an extra long time. Of course, I was only half enjoying it, because the other half of my brain was trying to remember what "wind shear" was and whether that was relevant. If the winds changed, could we just drop like a rock?

Nevertheless, we soared for fifteen minutes and then, finally, we flew lower and lower until we put our legs out and ran to a stop on the beach. *Mission accomplished, time for a stiff drink, and I never have to do that again!*

But it was empowering, and I'm so glad that I did it. I've tried plenty of other less scary things since then, because now I compare everything to paragliding. If I can run off a cliff in Oman, I can certainly ride a roller coaster back here in the States, or be a keynote speaker at a conference, or try a new kind of food. Everything seems possible now. And sixty doesn't feel quite as old as I feared.

— Amy Newmark —

62

No More White Walls

Our home tells a story about us, so we may as well take
the opportunity to make it a stylish one.
~Deborah Needleman, The Perfectly Imperfect Home

A small bell chimed to announce my presence as I pushed open the shop door. There went my hope of entering unnoticed. A salesman hurried to meet me with a broad smile. "How can I help you today?"

I resisted the urge to make a hasty exit and forced myself to greet him instead. "I'd like to see some paint swatches."

Our home was more than ten years old and way overdue for a fresh coat of paint. The past ten years had been good to us, too, as we developed special friendships. It was because of those friends that I found myself in the paint store.

It started innocently enough with visits to each of their homes. Then I invited them to ours. Two friends, Jan and Linda, graciously admired our home, but were curious about one thing. I steeled myself for what I knew was coming. Jan was the first to ask. "Beautiful... but, um, can I ask why all the walls are white?"

It was a natural question. Their homes included color-coordinated rooms, accent walls, and color-themed bathrooms. Every room proclaimed their confident decorating abilities. On the other hand, every wall in our home was stark white. The label on the paint can may have had a fancy name such as "Pearl Onion" or "Ice Cube," but I had to face facts: It was still white.

How could I explain my reasons for all white walls? It's not because I don't enjoy color. I had admired their homes. I watched HGTV, and I'm a fan of home makeover shows. I read *Better Homes and Gardens*. I learned to differentiate between "warm" and "cool" colors. I even knew the difference between saturation and intensity. And still my walls were all... white. When it came to actually selecting colors, I became paralyzed with indecision.

I learned the colors of the rainbow in grade school by memorizing the acronym ROYGBIV. Red, orange, yellow, green, blue, indigo, violet — so pretty when they form a bow in the sky. Or adorn wildflower petals. Or when they paint the clouds in glorious sunsets. I've always enjoyed splashes of color... as long as they stayed outside.

When it comes to painting my walls, I panic. Too many choices. *What if it doesn't look good when I'm finished?* Of course, I know I can repaint, but I barely have enough time to paint it once, let alone redo it. So in looking back at more than thirty years of marriage and four different homes, every wall in every home has sported a boring shade of white.

Not anymore. I was ready for a change. I *needed* a change. So I smiled at the salesperson and followed him to the rack of paint chips.

"What colors did you have in mind?"

It was a simple enough question. With my friends' encouragement echoing in my thoughts, I said I was thinking about starting with blue for the dining room. And perhaps gold for an accent wall in the living room. He nodded approvingly and pointed to groups of cards. Perhaps this wouldn't be so hard after all.

"What shade of blue were you considering?"

It was then the colors betrayed me. The wall of paint chips induced a familiar feeling of panic. We had moved way beyond ROYGBIV. Later, I learned this one store offered 231 shades of green, 152 variations of red, 188 shades of blue, and 154 variations of yellow. Even my old friend, white, was disloyal — with 184 different shades. Honestly!

Blue? No such thing. Too easy. Instead I read names such as Adriatic Sea, Oceanside, and Poseidon. Next to them were Gulfstream, Côte d'Azur, and Amalfi. *Amalfi? Really?*

I didn't fare any better searching for the right shade of gold. Auric, Nugget, and Alchemy were nestled next to Overjoy, Midday, and Nankeen. *Seriously?*

Giving in to curiosity, I glanced through the reds. Habanero Chile, Fireworks, and Heartthrob joined Valentine and Heartfelt as options. The green family also sported its own creative labels, including Julep, Argyle, and Picnic. I shook my head when I noticed one paint chip labeled Gecko. I may live in Florida, but not in a million years would I put a lizard on my walls.

Still, I was determined to do this. So I grabbed a handful of blue and gold paint cards that seemed to be the right hues, thanked the salesperson, and left. Back home, we held the various chips against our walls, compared them to our furniture and window treatments, and tried to imagine how the rooms would appear. The graduated intensity of color on each card made it even more difficult to choose. On some cards, it was almost impossible to discern the difference between the shades.

We finally settled on two choices. I called them blue and gold, but their official names are Caspian Tide and Mushroom Bisque.

Once we chose the colors, the next step was the prep work. Covering the furniture, taping the edges of the walls, and laying a drop cloth took almost as much time as the actual painting. The job lasted four days from start to finish — one day to prep, one day to paint, and one day to remove miles of blue painter's tape from the walls and ceiling. The last day was reserved for scraping permanent paint flecks from our hair and skin. With every drop that had landed on me, I marveled at how the decorators on television makeover shows can finish an entire room in one afternoon and not get a speck of paint on themselves.

I do have to admit, the final product looked terrific. Color really does make a difference. It even made me feel different. And I was thrilled to invite those same friends back to see the result.

In fact, the dining room and living room look so good that I've been eyeing our bathrooms. There may be a place in our home for Habanero Chili after all.

— Ava Pennington —

63

A Year of New Things

*Happiness is achieved when you stop waiting
for your life to begin and start making
the most of the moment you are in.*
~Germany Kent

The year I turned fifty, I resolved to do something new every day. When I tell people this, they always want to know what my favorite "new thing" was. They assume that I did something really different and amazing, like moving my family to an exotic place or learning to fly a helicopter. And they are inevitably disappointed when I say that my favorite thing was doing something new. Every. Single. Day. For a year.

Balancing 365 new things with work and family, while still managing to do the laundry and get dinner on the table every night, was not always easy. In the early weeks of the project, I often found myself at 11:45 p.m. wracking my brain for something new that I could actually accomplish in fifteen minutes. Thankfully, it turned out there were lots of things I had never done before that I could complete in a short period of time. I finished my first sudoku puzzle. I signed up for an online class to learn Italian. I smoked a cigar. I curled my eyelashes.

As time went by, I found it was easier to just keep my eyes open to the possibilities that surrounded me. It turns out there were new things everywhere, and all I had to do was make a little effort to enjoy them. And so, on a bitterly cold Saturday when I would normally have stayed home curled up with a book, I bundled up and set off to attend an Ice Festival. I got up crazy early one weekday morning to see a Blood Moon. I celebrated National Dog Day with my pup.

It wasn't long before my friends learned that I was open to almost anything I could consider a new thing, and the invitations began pouring in — not just from friends, but friends of friends. As a result, I went dog sledding, enjoyed stargazing on New York City's High Line, had lunch with Antonia Lofaso, who has appeared on *Top Chef*, attended a Fashion Week fashion show, and met Pulitzer Prize-winning author Gilbert King. I went to numerous lectures on all kinds of topics that I never would have previously considered useful or interesting and found something to appreciate in every single one.

Whenever I learned about something that seemed remarkable, I compelled myself to pursue it. Instead of "Why?" I began to ask "Why not?" I made my default response "Yes." When I learned about a local group trying to get into the *Guinness Book of World Records* by having the most people jumping on mini trampolines at once, I signed up immediately. The designated morning was cold and rainy. None of my friends or family members wanted to join me on my quest, but when I got to the field where the event was being held I found hundreds of like-minded folks. Together, we jumped for more than an hour, exhilarated by the exercise and the joy of accomplishing something slightly weird but totally wonderful.

A fair amount of my new things involved food. I tried wild boar. I ate nettles. I sampled gooseberries. I drank Limoncello. I made home-made pesto and hummus for the first time. I made pizza from scratch. I discovered that Thai eggplants don't look like any other eggplant I've ever seen; they are green and round, but the flesh cooks up soft like a regular oblong aubergine. I found out that I don't like radishes roasted any more than I like them raw, but that I love passionfruit in all forms.

As I look back on the year, it doesn't matter to me that many of my "new things" weren't exactly meaningful. What mattered is that I discovered there is an endless number of new things for me to try. It seemed to me an obvious sign that at fifty, my life was lush and full of promise. I could continue to grow, stretch my wings, and learn more every day for the rest of my life. I enjoyed the idea of changing my

> *I discovered there is an endless number of new things for me to try.*

mindset, making a mental stretch, and getting out of my comfort zone. If nothing else, it gave me a reason to welcome each day as an opportunity to experience the world a little differently, to counteract all that's easy, predictable, or monotonous.

I can't fly a helicopter yet. But I *am* in a *Guinness World Records* book!

— Victoria Otto Franzese —

64

The Big, Dead Rat

There is only one proof of ability — action.
~Marie von Ebner-Eschenbach

L ast winter, we had rain for two straight weeks. It rained almost every single day. I would think, *Geez, if I wanted to live in Portland, I'd move to Portland. God knows I'd save money on rent.* It wasn't so bad; I caught up on writing and movies as the rain came down. Nothing could prepare me, though, for what I found one day in my back yard.

I went outside to put birdseed in the bird feeder. On my way back to the house, I noticed a tail. The tail did not look like one of my cats' tails. It was right behind my miniature tree, which I'd named Brooklyn. I took a deep breath, and then looked behind Brooklyn. It was a rat. A big, dead rat. Like many a woman before me, I yelled, "Eeek!" and ran back in the house. Why I did this, I don't know. The rat was dead. It would not harm me. I figured out the rat might've been killed by my cats, Ida B. or Opal. This was good; they were earning their keep. Or it died from the extreme weather. Either way, I had a big-assed, dead rat in my yard. I had to deal with it.

But I didn't want to. I had plenty to do around my house, work and life. I kept thinking about a Bailey White essay I had read years ago. Something had died under her house. Mrs. White (Bailey's mother) called an exterminator to get rid of the dead animal. He said, "Don't you have something like a husband to take care of that for you?" Bailey had to crawl under the house and get the dead animal herself.

Although I don't mind being alone, this was one of those times I wanted something like a husband.

The next day, I procrastinated. Got work done. Wrote a tribute to Elizabeth Taylor, who had died recently. I was hoping maybe the rat's family had carried him off for a Viking funeral. Finally, I went outside. He (or she) was still there. I sighed. He looked like Templeton the rat in *Charlotte's Web*. He definitely had Templeton's tummy when he ate too much at the fair.

I went back inside. I washed my hands and then grabbed some newspapers. Put on rubber gloves. Walked outside again. Did the sign of the cross. *Dear rat, I hope you had a good life.* I covered the rat's body with the newspaper, and then put it in a plastic bag. I ran outside and dumped it in the trashcan.

I went back inside, removed my gloves and washed my hands again. Afterward, I realized that maybe I didn't have something like a husband, but I had myself. And there are times when "yourself" is all we need—even when it comes to dead, big rats. Things have to get done, and if we wait around for someone else to do it, we'll be waiting for a long time.

—Jennifer Kathleen Gibbons—

One Brave Thing

The biggest rewards in life are found outside
your comfort zone. Live with it. Fear and risk
are prerequisites if you want to enjoy
a life of success and adventure.
~Jack Canfield

After separating from my husband in 2004, I descended into a dark hole of depression. I was living in the little box my husband's words and actions had built around me. I was not a brave soul, and at that point in my life I had no idea what was to come. Even though my second book had just been accepted for publication, I was stuck. I didn't know how to move forward with my life.

A good friend who had helped me grow strong enough to leave my husband took me out to lunch one day. After we placed our orders, she folded her hands together on the table and leaned in as if about to impart a tremendous secret.

"You're stuck," she said.

I blinked and nodded as tears began to fill my eyes. "Stuck and scared and not sure how to fix myself enough to get unstuck."

My friend smiled and nodded. "Been there, done that, burned the T-shirt. You need to do one brave thing."

For some reason, whenever the word "need" comes out of someone's mouth in relation to my life, I immediately start thinking of reasons why I can't do whatever the "You need to…" is.

Even as I began to shake my head, my friend leaned closer. "Stop. Right now. Just hear me out, okay?"

I nodded and leaned in, too.

"One brave thing a day. That's all you have to do. Just one small thing every day, and you'll be able to change your world forever."

As I sat and contemplated her words, she took a sip of her iced tea.

After nearly a minute, I asked, "But what is the one brave thing I should be doing?"

She smiled in a way that made me think of Yoda. "Whatever it is you're not doing now because you're afraid. You could make that phone call to the coffee shop asking to do a book signing, call the library and set up an appearance, submit another book, or just go next door and introduce yourself to the neighbors. All it takes is a minute of courage to start and then a deep breath to follow through. Just one thing. One brave thing. Every day. Think you can do that?"

At that moment, the waitress arrived with our lunches, so I had a minute to process.

One thing.

Just one thing.

That shouldn't be too hard, I thought. And I had hundreds of things to choose from. My want-need-should list filled a dozen pages in a notebook I kept on my desk. I'd started the lists ages ago, and pulled out the notebook every couple of months to add to the lists or reprioritize the numerous entries. Rarely did I actually cross something off the list.

> *One brave thing.*
> *Every day.*

As I mixed my Cobb salad together and assured the waitress that everything looked fine, I gave serious thought to my never-ending to-do list.

One brave thing a day.

"I like it," I said finally. "And I think I can do it."

My friend smiled. "You might surprise yourself. Now, can you commit to me here and now that you will do one brave thing every day for the next month?"

A month? Thirty brave things. All at once the fear that had been my constant companion for most of my life kicked in once more. "I don't know," I stammered.

Her smile widened as compassion and understanding shined from her like a porch light in the night, somehow dispelling my trepidation. "Okay, how about doing it for just a week? And really, all you have to do is one brave thing a day. Don't look at the whole week ahead; just look at today. All I ask is that you try for the next seven days to do one thing every day that takes you out of your comfort zone. Some of them may work; some may not. All I ask is that you try. Then, once you've done that one thing, I want you to call me and tell me what you did and how it turned out."

A week sounded more reasonable. And like she said, all I had to think about was today.

"Okay, I'll do it," I said, feeling happier already.

"Good," my friend said with a grin and nod of approval.

After she dropped me off at my apartment that afternoon, I pulled out my book of lists. Flipping through the pages, I found myself growing overwhelmed. I closed the book again, laid both hands on it and said aloud, "Help me, angels. I need to do just one brave thing. What should it be? One thing. Just one thing."

Immediately, the words "book signing" came to mind. The one thing I had been dreading most was putting myself out there as an author. Not giving myself time to think too much about what I was doing, I flipped to the page of possible book-signing locations. The list was complete with phone numbers. I grabbed my cell phone and dialed the local library.

Five minutes later, I hung up. My smile could not be contained. I had a date to speak to the library's teen reading group about my young-adult novel and my life as a writer.

I felt so excited about knocking that out of the park that I made three more calls and booked two more signing dates. Then I called my friend and thanked her.

Even now, thirteen years later, when I find myself stuck, I remind myself of what I now refer to as OBTAD. One. Brave. Thing. A. Day.

— Susan Walker —

66

Chicken Soup for the Soul

Becoming the Glue

*Since there is nothing so well worth having as friends,
never lose a chance to make them.*
~Francesco Guicciardini

O ur three kids were all under age five, we'd recently moved to the suburbs, and I'd stopped working to be a stay-at-home mom. Most of our friends lived outside our immediate community and didn't have children. This all added up to a nonexistent social life for my husband and me.

I needed to fix this, so I became a room parent in my son's kindergarten class, partly to spend time with him, but also to make more friends within the school community. I also signed my son up for weekend soccer. While those activities gave me the opportunity to socialize with other moms, it was challenging to cultivate friendships. I only saw my fellow room parents a few times a year, usually amid the gleeful chaos of class parties. On the soccer sidelines, I found it impossible to simultaneously watch the game, keep track of my young children, and maintain conversations with other parents.

I craved deeper interactions with the smart, interesting moms I saw around school. But we all led busy lives. How could I make this happen?

"You should throw a party," suggested a friend who happened to be a professional event planner.

"I can't do that. I don't really know these women," I replied quickly. I hardly even had my closest friends over to my house. The thought of hosting an adult party terrified me to my introvert core.

"Just invite a few people that you've talked to and ask them to bring along a friend. You'll meet even more people that way. It will be fun," my event-planner friend said.

I ran this idea by my husband, certain he'd agree it wouldn't work. "Great idea," he said. "I'll stay upstairs with the kids, and the party can take place on the main floor. Can you serve chicken wings?"

Chicken wings were not going to make the menu. However, channeling some of my husband's enthusiasm, I picked a date and set up an electronic invitation, cobbling together a guest list of moms from my son's soccer team, my fellow room moms, and a few other moms I'd started saying "hi" to at school pick-up.

But I didn't hit Send.

I started to talk myself out of it. There were so many reasons this wouldn't work. With five mess-makers in my household, what if I couldn't get my house "party-ready" in time? What if guests noticed the stains on my carpet, or the outdated window treatments that I'd always disliked? What if someone asked to tour my basement, the general dumping ground for every orphaned object my family possessed? What if no one showed up? What if everyone showed up and had an awful time?

"None of that will happen," my event-planner friend assured me. "People will be glad to have a chance to get out and recharge their own batteries."

I wasn't so sure, but I sent out the invitations anyway. Then I waited, checking the online RSVP status approximately 2,000 times a day.

Replies began trickling in. Before long, I was expecting thirty-eight women at my house. Thirty-eight!

I cleaned a lot during the week leading up to the party. This helped distract me from my anxiety. On the designated night, I kissed my husband and kids as they trekked upstairs toward bedtime. I set out an assortment of beverages and tried-and-true appetizers, none of which were chicken wings. I queued up my specially chosen "fun" music program on my iPad. And I nearly bit my nails down to bloody nubs.

But you know what? Everyone showed up. They even seemed

glad to be there, just as my friend had predicted. Soon after the guests arrived, I had to turn up the music because it couldn't be heard over the chatter. Fifteen minutes later, I had to turn it up a second time. Before long, I had the music on maximum volume, and it still couldn't be heard because people were talking and laughing that much. It didn't seem to matter whether my refreshments or living room were Martha Stewart–approved.

I was euphoric. Throughout the evening, I had a number of great conversations. Several ladies even stayed longer than the suggested end time on the invitation, and we made plans to get together again.

I've hosted more of these "mommy mixers" since then. Guests sometimes bring beverages or appetizers to share, which makes far less work and cost for me. I've stopped biting my fingernails now that I've got my routine in place.

The more I do it, the easier it becomes. My friend network has grown and deepened, and I've met people I wouldn't have otherwise. It feels very good to be in control of having more fun.

One new friend I made through these parties recently said to me, "Every social group needs some sort of glue to keep everyone together. You're that glue!"

— Kate Lemery —

67

Thunder Thighs and All

I might have a little bit of cellulite. I might not be toned
everywhere. I might struggle in this area or that.
But accepting that just empowers me.
~Kim Kardashian, Harper's Bazaar

"You want me to present myself half-naked to a bunch of strangers?" I asked my husband, Wayne, when he suggested I join his master's swim team.

"All body types are there," he said, knowing how self-conscious I was about my size. "And all ages and skill levels," he added, anticipating my next argument. "It's not about what you look like or how fast you swim. It's about getting in the water and enjoying some exercise."

Enjoy? When was the last time I enjoyed being in a bathing suit? Probably the last time I was thin, which was around age ten.

And when was the last time I swam laps? Had I ever? No.

My husband was the fish in our family. Growing up he'd spent summers at his neighborhood pool, competing on the community swim team, and in high school he was a lifeguard. As a kid, I was more the show-up, splash-around-when-I-got-hot, and then go-eat-snacks-on-my-towel type.

I'm not sure how he finally convinced me to go. I think it was the promise of the social aspect. I had just moved from Phoenix to Jacksonville to join him — he'd moved earlier for work — and I hadn't started working or making any friends yet.

"The team is great," he said. "They get together and have parties from time to time. They go out to eat after practices. Trust me. You'll like it."

It was something for us to do together as a couple. Sort of. He'd swim in a faster lane than I would, but we could talk driving to and from the pool. It might be fun.

If it weren't for the fact that I had to put on a bathing suit.

Which in and of itself, wasn't that bad. On the occasions we did something that called for a bathing suit, I kept my thighs covered with a sarong or shorts. That's what I was most embarrassed about — my thick, jiggly, cottage-cheese-stuffed, stretch mark-scarred thighs. All of me was chunky, but my thighs were the worst. They were hideous and I knew it. I was doing the world a public service concealing them.

Now my husband was asking me to expose them for public viewing. It made my stomach churn.

"Give it a try one time," he said. "That's all I'm asking. If you're miserable, I'll never ask you to go again."

I gave in, because my heart knew how lucky I was to have a husband who wanted to spend time with me. Thunder thighs and all.

My stomach was in knots all the way to that first practice. To my relief, a lot of people were already in the pool swimming warm-up laps when we arrived. Wayne introduced me to the coach, Walter.

"I've never done this before," I confessed. "I'm afraid I'll be slow."

"No problem," said Walter. "We've got a lane for all speeds. Let's try this one for starters. See how it fits."

He led me to the first lane. A lady in her seventies was at the wall adjusting her goggles. "Joan, this is Courtney. She's a newbie. Show her the ropes, will you?"

"Be glad to," said Joan. "Grab a kickboard and hop on in. I'll explain how we work things around here!"

The moment of truth had arrived. I walked back to the bleachers, set my towel down next to Wayne's, and stripped down to my swimsuit. Then I dashed back to the lane and quickly got in.

Joan explained the drills and how we shared the lane; then we started swimming.

It was tiring, but invigorating. Joan couldn't have been nicer. Before I knew it, practice was over and everyone was getting out. Wayne came over to check on me.

"How'd you do? It looks like you survived."

"I'm still afloat," I reassured him.

"You hungry? Some of the team is grabbing a bite after. Want to join them?"

"I don't know…"

"You should go," Joan encouraged. "I have to get home. But I think they're going to Pizza Palace. Have you been yet?"

I shook my head.

"It's really good Italian food. You'd have fun. Great way to get to know everyone," she said.

"If you want to go, I guess that'd be fine," I said to Wayne.

"Great!" he said. "But… that means you'll have to get out of the water."

I looked toward my towel, A.K.A. my Thigh Shield. It was blocked by a gaggle of swimmers.

Wayne was right. There were all ages and body types present. The swim team wasn't comprised of the *Baywatch* hard body studs and beauties I had imagined. They were regular folks, some more toned than others, who were currently drying off and talking about everything from work and kids to swim strokes and current events.

How I envied them their casualness; they were in no hurry to hide their bodies.

The fact still remained that I was embarrassed about my body and I was about to expose it for all to see.

Hesitantly, I climbed out of the water and tried to rush to my towel as inconspicuously as possible. Before I got to it, someone shouted, "Hey, Wayne! Is that your wife?"

Suddenly, I was living a nightmare. Me. Dripping wet. Thighs totally exposed. The center of attention.

My safety blanket (towel) was a few feet away, but it might as well have been miles. There have been few times in life I have felt so exposed or vulnerable.

But everyone was so nice and welcoming. No one stared at my legs. No one gagged or threw up at the sight of them.

I look back on that now and laugh. Swim team was the best thing that ever happened to my body image. I never got ripped or lean from swimming. But I learned new skills, like flip turns and the butterfly stroke. And by the end of that summer I was standing around after practice talking and laughing without rushing to cover myself up anymore.

Because that was the best part of all—I made friends. Ones who accepted me as I am, warts and all. Or, in my case, cellulite thunder thighs and all.

— Courtney Lynn Mroch —

68

A New Prescription

When it comes to staying young, a mind-lift beats a face-lift any day.
~Marty Bucella

There are three little words that seem to precede any sort of advice I get these days. "At your age," my son says that I should not jog or I could break bones. "At your age," his girlfriend says I can "get away" with wearing anything but mini-skirts. Frankly, I never really cared to jog or wear mini-skirts at any age, but especially at my age, I don't like to be told what I can or can't do.

So imagine my dismay when my optometrist told me that at my age, I should update my eyeglass prescription to trifocals. "At your age," he told me, "it is fairly common."

I don't know if I want clearer vision. Maybe it's a tool of denial, but at my age a little bit of nearsightedness can be kind when I look in the mirror. I don't see the deepening wrinkles and increasing gray. My backside isn't sagging. I just need some new underwear.

Pointing out personal safety, my optometrist prevailed. The vision technician helped me choose some new frames. I am sorely out of sync with today's fashion because I leaned toward thin, wire-rimmed granny glasses. They were cheaper. The girl frowned and handed me some thick, dark angular frames. I slipped them on and she beamed.

"Those eyeglasses make you look twenty years younger," she said seriously. I peered closely into the mirror. She was right! I barely recognized myself. I straightened my back, feeling confident and, well, youthful. Why is it that I suddenly felt twenty years younger? I was taught that what was inside counts. External effects shouldn't matter. But by golly, these eyeglasses had a strange and positive effect on me.

"What you wear really does affect how you see yourself," she said, grinning at her own optometric pun. On the way home, I decided to shop for a new outfit to go with my new glasses. My usual style did not go with these contemporary frames and I chose summer capris in sunny colors. I found myself trying on open-toed sandals instead of practical flats. Since my toes were going to be displayed to the public, I got a pedicure for the first time in years.

Why had I quietly aged into dreary-looking clothing? I went through my closet and saw that an old woman had slowly moved in. There's nothing wrong with comfortable clothes, sweatpants, elastic banded jeans, thick holiday sweaters and easy slip-on shoes in brown and black. But wearing them made me feel like I was cocooning. Maybe, like a butterfly, it was time to emerge for my second life. I reminded myself that I didn't have to skimp on my own clothing budget now that there were no more school clothes to buy for the kids, no prom dresses or graduation suits. Maybe it was time for me to dress for a successful second half of my life.

Today, alongside the comfy clothes, there are pretty silk dresses, linen suits, colorful skirts and fun shoes. And because I need a good reason to wear these outfits, I go out to new restaurants, concerts and social gatherings. In the past, I'd decline partly because I never had anything to wear. I used to say, "Why buy anything? I never go anywhere."

My favorite new outfits include zippy new exercise clothes. Hiking shorts. Yoga pants. Swimsuits. At my age, Lycra is more like a medical prescription. New clothes in general help you feel youthful inside and out. They are more important than we know. After all, Mark Twain once said, "Clothes make the man. Naked people have little or no influence on society."

"Aren't you glad you updated your prescription?" my son asked. "You're getting out more." He's right. I love my new vision on life and new clothes.

And at my age, I just might go jogging in a mini-skirt with my new eyeglasses. Okay, maybe I won't. But I can if I want to. I just happen to have a more suitable outfit that matches this fabulous new prescription.

— Lori Phillips —

69

The Year of Exploration

You can't be brave if you've only had
wonderful things happen to you.
~Mary Tyler Moore

Touretta Lynn's School of Hard Knocks was no joke. My hands trembled as I double-knotted the laces on my white roller skates and tightened the throatlatch on my helmet. I raised my eyes to the dozen or so heavily-inked women gliding around the cement track. Though no two women were dressed exactly the same, there was a semblance of a uniform — ripped T-shirts, black fishnet stockings, and spandex shorts so tiny they'd make marathon runners blush. The women's expressions were also uniformly grim as they deftly crossed their skates on the turns, then pumped their arms to speed down the straightaways.

A heavy metal door slammed behind me, and Naptown Roller Girls Coach Sin Lizzie entered the Warehouse Lair. She wore blue nursing scrubs, and the blood-stain resistant fabric wasn't lost on me. At least she probably knew CPR and how to stitch up an open head wound. In a sport where the athletes adopt pseudonyms like Sandra Day O'Clobber and Nancy Drewblood, her medical training would be in high demand.

I peeled myself off the bench and took a moment to get my balance. Then I wobbled across the cavernous warehouse to join the check-in line. Stapled to the plywood wall to my right was a poster from the movie *Whip It*. Actress Ellen Page leapt over a fallen skater with a look of fierce determination on her face. My stomach flip-flopped, and I gulped.

The girl in front of me in line pivoted on fluorescent wheels that matched the hot pink streaks in her hair.

"Last week was brutal," she said, and I forced my gaze from the full sleeve tattoo on her arm to her freckled face. "I heard three girls puked."

"It's my first day," I admitted, fidgeting with my elbow pads.

The girl studied my 105-pound beanpole frame, gaunt arms, and sunken cheeks. She wished me luck and turned away.

I didn't tell her I used to be a kickboxer. I didn't tell her I used to have another fifteen pounds of pure muscle from jumping rope, working the heavy bag, shadow boxing, and cranking out pushups, sit-ups, and squats by the hundreds. I didn't tell her how I used to relish pushing my body to the brink of exhaustion, high on the thrill of hitting and getting hit. I didn't tell her, but I wanted to. Not like she'd have believed me anyway. I barely believed it myself anymore.

When I reached the front of the line, Sin Lizzie peered at me over her clipboard.

"Name?" she said.

Dogs can smell fear. Dogs and this woman. I forced myself to meet her gaze.

"Brass Nicoles," I said. "Reporting for duty." I was tempted to salute.

She handed me a waiver, which I signed without reading. Then I joined the rest of the trainees on the track and braced myself for the unknown, ready to conquer my fear.

It'd been four years since I'd graduated from a top-ten business school and landed a marketing job with "upward mobility." By twenty-five, I was my company's go-to creative powerhouse and had been accepted to a prestigious evening master's degree program. In whatever time remained, I laced up my gloves and transformed into a 120-pound, hard-ass Muay Thai kickboxer. For a while, I'd been able to do it all. I was promoted, got straight A's, and excelled at the gym. The more I juggled, the prouder I was.

Then, one morning, I walked into a coffee shop and was blindsided by my first panic attack. The experience was terrifying and left me profoundly shaken. The attacks grew more frequent, overtaking me anywhere, anytime, with no warning. It would be months before I received a definitive diagnosis: Acute Anxiety Disorder.

With the news came shame and self-loathing more debilitating than the attacks themselves. From the moment I rolled out of bed in the morning to the time I curled back under my covers at night, my only goal was to keep the panic attacks at bay. I lost my appetite and survived on protein shakes and dried fruit. I almost dropped out of grad school and nearly resigned my job. After months of steady decline, I made the heartbreaking decision to quit kickboxing. Emotionally and physically exhausted, I was in self-preservation mode.

I spent the next year getting back to basics. No more skipped meals, appetite or not. No more late nights at the office or doubling my grad school course load. No more skimping on sleep. But as the year drew to a close, I couldn't think of a single adventure or accomplishment that made me proud. Granted, I was slightly healthier and more functional. But I didn't recognize this girl either. She wasn't the least bit interesting. And if my own life didn't interest me, what progress had I really made?

So the next day, I did something drastic. I formed a steering committee of five close friends to help me confront my anxiety and rebuild my shattered psyche. I tasked them with issuing me monthly challenges that would test me in every way—challenges entirely outside my control that I vowed to complete no matter what. I called my experiment The Year of Exploration and started a blog so friends could follow along.

> *I called my experiment The Year of Exploration.*

During the twelve months that followed, I tackled more than twenty committee-mandated challenges, as well as several of my own. I endured the Naptown Roller Girl's brutal training camp and learned the art of curling, sailing, and fantasy football. I visited new churches and begrudgingly took up running. I closed down my first bar and created a piece of abstract art with Tombi, a 10,000-pound

African elephant. I even agreed to a series of committee-mandated blind dates (and nearly broke up with my steering committee in the process). I learned to redefine success and unearthed my will to live in the strangest of places.

It wasn't easy. I considered quitting every day, but I didn't. I still suffered brutal panic attacks, but I lived. I got frustrated, tired, and overwhelmed. But I persevered. No matter what my committee — and my life — threw at me, I didn't break. Maybe I wasn't a weak, worthless failure after all. Maybe I was a survivor.

When the year came to a close, I stood in front of sixty friends and family to complete my final challenge — a live reading from the memoir I'd been writing about my experiences. I've never been prouder of myself than I was that night.

Shortly thereafter, my friend Sarah invited me to a yoga retreat in Costa Rica. I felt a familiar pang of panic. What if I had an anxiety attack on the plane or in a foreign country? What if my disorder ruined my vacation and hers? Not to mention, I didn't know anyone else going on the trip, and I'd never done yoga. Then I thought about how far I'd come. I thought about all the times I'd been nearly paralyzed with fear, but pushed through it. I'd survived The Year of Exploration and emerged a stronger woman. I could do this. I took a deep breath.

"I'd love to," I said. "When do we leave?"

— Nicole K. Ross —

70

Leaving Harbour

Scared is what you're feeling;
brave is what you're doing.
~Emma Donoghue, Room

t's still dark as my husband, brother-in-law, nephew and I walk down a forested road to the wharf where our chartered boat is waiting. We're on an extended family holiday on the west coast of Canada, and the four of us have booked a halibut-fishing trip with a local guide.

This is my first open-water fishing trip, and I'm nervous. More than nervous—pretty much terrified. The boat is small, with only two seats at the front and no below-deck shelter. We'll be heading out for deep water, maybe even beyond sight of land. But I keep my anxiety to myself. Only my husband knows how much the effort is costing me.

To ensure that I don't wreck anyone else's trip, I've planned a number of strategies to help me cope once we're out on the water. I've taken medication to prevent seasickness. I've been praying, meditating, and practicing relaxation techniques. I've got my phone loaded with soothing music.

We reach the boat, and our skipper welcomes us aboard. There's a brief orientation, and then we cast off from the dock and motor toward the mouth of the inlet. I watch the sky lighten, reflecting on the decision that brought me to this moment.

***

For most of my adult life, I'd chosen to stay safely anchored in a series of sheltered harbours, both literally and metaphorically. It took my mother's death from breast cancer at age sixty-five to wake me. My mother lived with courage and intention right to the end of her journey. On the other hand, I had let anxiety play far too big a role in my life. I'd done some courageous things in the two decades following university, but too many of my decisions — big and small — had been influenced by fear.

Consciously or unconsciously, my default was to choose security over risk, to stay safely in my comfort zone whenever possible. As I reflected on where I'd been and how I wanted to spend my remaining years, I knew I had to make some big changes.

And so, in 2016, I made a resolution to turn my relationship with fear upside down. I resolved to live by the word "fierce" for an entire year, which in practice meant two things: I would not allow myself to make anxiety-based decisions, and I would deliberately put myself in challenging situations. Reasonable fear was acceptable, however — there would be no skydiving in my immediate future.

***

Now, I am living with my decision to be brave. The water gets choppier as our small boat leaves the shelter of the inlet heading for open water. My husband squeezes my hand. "I'm okay," I mouth. And it's true — at least for the moment.

By this point, I'm five months into my resolution to live fiercely, and I've already forced myself into a number of courage-building experiences. I've signed up for a dance improv workshop that culminated in a public performance — even though at forty-five I had no previous dance or improv experience. I've faced my fear of heights, climbing a series of almost perpendicular ladders on the rugged West Coast Trail. I've donned coveralls and a helmet to go caving at a nearby provincial park. And with each successful new experience, my confidence has grown. I can do this.

The wind whips my face as the shoreline recedes behind our boat. I say a grateful prayer for the good weather. The water isn't glass, but it's calmer than it could be, and the medicine I've taken is keeping motion sickness at bay.

If my recent adventures have taught me anything, it's to stay in the moment—no borrowing trouble from a hypothetical future, no ruminating on past experiences. To keep myself grounded in this moment, I focus on my seven-year-old nephew. He's beaming, thrilled to be out on the water on this brisk morning. His excitement is unexpectedly contagious. I begin to think that this fishing trip might actually become more than an endurance test. I might enjoy my time at sea.

With this epiphany, everything changes. I stop monitoring myself for the first signs of panic. I forget about my phone and its playlist of soothing songs. I take in the sea, the sky, the forested islands to our north, and the snow-capped mountains behind them. There's salt on my lips and wind in my hair. I'm alive!

We're on the water for over four hours, and panic never does rear its head. I return to land with my dignity intact, a new adventure under my belt—and a fifty-pound halibut in the cooler. My fishing companions have been equally successful. We'll be eating well for days!

***

Leaving harbour that morning was just the beginning. I continued to push the boundaries of my comfort zone for the remainder of that year—and every year since. With each new experience, I gained more confidence. Courage, I've learned, is a muscle that gets stronger with use.

It's been four years since I caught my first off-shore fish. Since that time, I've tackled phobias, started my own business, and launched a career as a professional storyteller. I leave the comfort and security of a safe harbour almost every day on my quest for new opportunities. It's scary sometimes, but that's the point. I've come to believe that we're not fully alive if we're not at least a little frightened on a regular basis. Here's to living life fully!

—Rachel Dunstan Muller—

Chapter 8

Be Yourself

What You'll Find in This Chapter

"**N**o one is you, and that is your superpower." Those wise words come from life coach Elyse Santilli, and they sum up what you'll find in this chapter, stories that will help you feel comfortable in your own skin.

So many of us, myself included, are down on ourselves about a variety of things: our weight, our hair, our careers, our parenting skills, our messy lives. Whatever it is, we find fault with how we're doing it.

But in actuality, when we have goals — getting fit, raising children well, getting promoted at work, finding love, being adventurous — they should not involve a wholesale change in who we are. They should just involve being more of who we *already* are and knowing that we *are enough*.

Aleksandra Slijepcevic had to discover that for herself. In her story, "What Breaks You," she tells us that her boyfriend broke up with her, advising her to figure out who she was. Six years later, she realized he was right. She had been putting *his* needs first, adopting *his* likes and dislikes as her own. She says, "He never lost sight of himself." But she had.

Through yoga practice and a lot of introspection, Aleksandra says, "I shed massive layers of the shy, reserved, afraid, and dependent girl I was at twenty-one. I took back the power I had ceded to men. And it was like coming home!" Now Aleksandra's ready for love again, but this time with full knowledge of who she is and what she wants and deserves.

Most of us have some kind of body image problem, especially women, who are often unwilling to be seen in a bathing suit or even in exercise gear. Tonya Abari, a large but fit woman, felt like that. She always avoided the Zumba classes at the gyms she joined, even though that was what she really wanted to do. And thus she kept abandoning her fitness goals and quitting the gyms.

Finally, Tonya says, "I thought long and hard about my reticence." She forced herself to take a Zumba class, and she loved it. She became a regular and made a new group of friends, and then, when the instructor quit, she stepped in and was hired to teach the class! Tonya says, "I'd not only empower other women, but I'd be able to fuel my own confidence." Her story is called "Have Fun. Be Silly. Dance Crazy." Because isn't that what we should all be doing?

How about embracing whatever it is that makes you different? Jody Fuller did just that, as he relates in his story, "A Lifetime of Stuttering." Instead of hiding his difference, he chose to put it out there front and center, volunteering to read aloud to his eighth-grade class. Now he's a comic, a motivational speaker, and a soldier with three tours of duty in Iraq. He found his superpower for sure.

The stories in this chapter will help you find your own truth. After you read them, think about what makes you unique. And embrace that power. You'll find plenty of role models and advice in these pages to help you make the most of it.

What Breaks You

My willingness to be intimate with my own deep feelings
creates the space for intimacy with another.
~Shakti Gawain

When I was twenty-one, I met a guy who I thought was "the one." Our relationship took off. We spent weekends together, attended parties from sunup to sundown, and exchanged cheesy text messages and phone calls when we were apart.

I put his needs first. I believed that pleasing him was my way of keeping him around. When he showed up — handsome, charming, confident, and open hearted — I couldn't believe that he would like someone like me. Soon enough, his likes, dislikes, and opinions became my own. It was unhealthy, and no matter how distanced I became from friends and family, I truly believed that it was love and these were the sacrifices that girlfriends needed to make.

One day, after not hearing from him all weekend, he called me at work and broke up with me. Just like that. He said he was bored and that I needed to figure out who I was. To say that I was crushed was an understatement. I felt like someone had just unplugged me, and I was slowly dying. I wondered what I had done wrong. It took many years to learn that asking that question was the root of the problem.

Fast-forward six years, and I am writing this from the headspace of a woman I never dreamed I would become. After the breakup, I found solace in yoga and meditation. It became a practice — a *sadhana* — that would pull me out of my self-sabotaging darkness and into the very lesson my ex-boyfriend was trying to teach me all along: be selfish. What angered me most in our relationship was the fact that he was always putting himself first. It made me feel unwanted, unseen, and unwelcomed, like I wasn't a part of his life plan. What he and the Universe were trying to teach me was that I wasn't a part of his life because I had never made it a point to be a part of my own.

> *I wasn't a part of his life because I had never made it a point to be a part of my own.*

He never lost sight of himself, and he was right. At the time, I didn't realize that he was giving me back a gift I had so easily tossed to the wind: myself.

During my time being single, I turned inward. In yoga, we call this *pratyahara*. Once all the distractions of the world fall away, and once you're rejected by someone, there's nowhere else to go. It's time to face yourself. I faced all of my demons, triggers, traumas, and dark corners that had never seen the light of day.

In 2014, I started my yoga teacher training, and then I taught my very first yoga class. I still get goose bumps and teary eyes reflecting back on a class full of my peers, cheering me on as I taught.

Yoga gave me not only a desire to get back to my own self-care and love, but it gave me my voice! Today, I teach, write, travel, and live my life with purpose, authenticity, and passion. Finally, I know who I am. And I know I would have never arrived at such a gift without the pain of being rejected in that relationship. For this, I am grateful.

I shed massive layers of the shy, reserved, afraid, and dependent girl I was at twenty-one. I took back the power I had ceded to men. And it was like coming home! The voice I used to teach yoga was the same voice I used to say "no" more often than I said "yes" now that I wasn't worried about being liked.

Somewhere out there, a like-hearted man will believe in the same for himself, and our paths will cross when each of us is ready. Gabrielle Bernstein, renowned speaker and author, always says, "The Universe has your back." And it does, steering us toward something bigger and better. Every single person we meet is our guide and teacher, especially the ones who bring us pain and trauma.

I'm a firm believer that the loves lost are our mirrors, showing us who we really are. Allow yourself to stand tall in that reflection and find gratitude for what breaks you, because what breaks you is also what rebuilds you.

— Aleksandra Slijepcevic —

72

Openly Gray

*You cannot swim for new horizons until you
have courage to lose sight of the shore.*
~William Faulkner

was not happy with my reflection in the mirror. My normally clear skin displayed age spots. Wrinkles surrounded my eyes. Large pores appeared on top of my nose. Rogue hairs sprouted out of my chin like *Three Billy Goats Gruff*. My eyebrow hairs progressively turned white. My long and lush eyelashes from yesteryear had diminished. My normally pouty lips had grown thin. Another loss was the pink flush from my rosy cheeks.

Age was an unapologetic thief, slowly stealing my self-confidence and what was left of my beauty. Applying moisturizing creams, serums, and facial masks became my ritual. I never left the house without wearing bullet-proof eyebrow pencil, voluminous mascara, and plumping lip gloss.

After menopause, my body began to change. My hourglass figure contained a little more sand than usual. My waist grew larger, and calling that new feature a muffin top didn't make it any sweeter. Aging changes your body in ways you could never imagine. High heels became a thing of the past because arthritis pain invaded my previously perfect joints… no more beautiful stilettos or strappy sandals.

Dyeing my naturally brunette hair a light auburn every six weeks was becoming a burden. The bathroom linen closet always had a box of L'Oréal do-it-yourself hair color on the shelf. There were no gray hairs on my watch. But lately, I'd had to color my hair more often. Every time I looked into a mirror, the silver roots were shining like a beacon. I began, parting my hair in a zigzag. It was an ingenious disguise for the silver scoundrels. It gave my short hairstyle a little sass and served a purpose at the same time. I suddenly felt like a magician using smoke and mirrors with a little sleight of hand.

It got worse, and to cover those annoying roots, I was forced to dye my hair more often. Now I was coloring every three weeks. I began to ponder giving up the fight. Gray was becoming a trend among the younger generation. Celebrities were suddenly coloring their hair gray by choice. If Pink, Katy Perry, and Adam Levine could do it, so could I.

But I didn't want to grow my hair out slowly. It would take entirely too long. What if I got the color stripped out? Then no one would be the wiser. My daughters knew a master hair colorist whom they trusted. Nicole's naturally soft brunette locks sported golden highlights, and Laura's naturally auburn tresses were tinted a bright fiery red reminiscent of the Disney princess Ariel. Their hair turned out spectacular, so maybe she could help me.

I weighed the pros and cons for several weeks. If I hated it, I could just recolor it again…. right? Would I look stylishly trendy? Or would I look old and tired? Not buying hair dye would save tons of money. It would also save valuable time. I definitely wouldn't miss cleaning messy stains off the bathroom sink and ruining white towels. This was a difficult decision. Finally, I built up enough courage to book the appointment and for the next few weeks, I stopped dyeing my hair. I let the color fade to make it easier to remove.

The half-hour drive to the salon was nerve-wracking. For moral support, my girls accompanied me. I was anxious but excited at the same time. I sat tentatively in the chair as Sara, my tattoo-covered stylist, applied the stripping compound to my auburn hair with what looked like an ordinary paintbrush. She wrapped my head in foil and plastic and left me to "cook." I felt like a baked potato. As I waited, my mind raced. She checked my progress every fifteen minutes to see if the color was lifting. After about an hour, she announced it was reveal time. She rinsed out all the gooey mess. I stepped back into the chair and looked in the mirror. My hair was completely and totally white. The sudden shock sucked all the breath out of my lungs. She saw the frightened look on my face and asked if everything was okay. At that moment, I wasn't sure if I liked it. In fact, I hated it… and I was trying to remember if I had a coupon for another box of hair color.

She continued to razor my hair into the cute style I had pointed out on Pinterest. Then she rinsed my hair again and applied toner along with a purple conditioner to remove any brassiness. She confidently wielded curling irons and hairspray like magic wands. The woman in the mirror who was looking back at me was a totally different person. Was it shocking? Yes. Did I like it? Absolutely! My hair was a lovely, rich silver tone.

On the drive home, I worried what my husband was going to say. Would he love it or hate it? When I walked into the house, he loved my new look and gave me a much-needed, stress-relieving hug.

The first thing I did was post a selfie on Facebook. I bravely announced that I had officially quit dying my hair. I was "openly gray." I wasn't sure how everyone was going to react to the transformation. Comments on social media could be brutally honest at times, so I sat back and nervously waited. My phone kept dinging with dozens of comments. They were all genuinely positive. Everyone loved the change. Reading all the kind and uplifting comments just reinforced the decision I made.

The next few weeks were interesting. Everywhere I went, the compliments followed. People would approach me completely out of the blue… in the freezer section of the grocery store… in line at the bank… at the accountant's office… and even while I was pumping gas. My husband would just shake his head and laugh because we couldn't go anywhere without someone telling me how beautiful my hair color was. It was crazy. If it had been friends or family being polite, I could understand it. But these wonderful folks were total strangers.

For me, the unspoken assumption that gray hair automatically means unattractive is shattered. I get more compliments now than I did for the entire thirty-five years I colored my hair. It has been almost two years since I made the decision to succumb to my God-given hair color. I have never regretted my decision or looked back. My gleaming sterling-silver hair will forever be my signature. Now I smile when I see my reflection in a mirror because, according to the kindness of strangers, I am beautiful at any age.

—Robin Howard Will—

73

Hit by Lightning

Be who you are and say what you feel,
because those who mind don't matter,
and those who matter don't mind.
~Bernard M. Baruch

My son stared stoically out the window of the car. Looking closely, I saw the tracks of earlier tears on his cheeks. What had happened? He'd been fine when I dropped him off at school. What could have gone so wrong in the past seven hours? How could he possibly look so sad when he should be so happy?

Two weeks previously, my son had been selected for a scholarship to attend the college of his choice because of his academic accomplishments and community service. Our entire family had been in a celebratory mode. We were so grateful for the news. It was such a wonderful achievement and relief to know we would get financial assistance for his college education.

So what had gone wrong? Why such a sad face and downcast eyes?

I finally got the answer after a few hours of probing. I learned that my son's scholarship news had generated jealousy among his friends. Not only were these classmates unsupportive, but their comments reflected resentment that he was thinking about "going away" to college. Since he was "a nerd" and "so rich" now, they said he might as well go away, because he wasn't welcome with them anymore.

As his mother, I felt I should know how to make everything

better, but I didn't. The mocking and bullying didn't make sense to me. I kept wondering how something so positive had been twisted into something so negative. I searched for words of comfort, but nothing I said helped my son.

When the scholarship had first been announced, my son's school was as excited and proud as we were. The award reflected positively on the curriculum, teachers, and staff. The school had held a ceremony for the announcement. The news had been printed in the school paper, and a news release was sent to the media. I felt it must have been that publicity that triggered the recent comments — and, in the ensuing days, the negative rhetoric just kept coming.

For the first time in his life, my son did not want to go to school. He began saying he was not even sure he wanted to go to college. Nothing I said or did made any difference. Every day, he seemed more dispirited and downhearted. His sadness hung like a gray cloud over our whole family.

Nothing his teachers said had much impact either. Both his counselor and his principal offered words of encouragement, but there was not any change. The slump in his shoulders and the sadness in his eyes remained.

The taunts from his peers also kept coming.

After a few weeks, I felt my son was becoming seriously depressed. His world was crumbling. When he announced that he wanted to give up the scholarship, I knew something had to be done.

I decided to go up one more rung on the academic ladder and take him to visit the superintendent of schools. I didn't know the superintendent, having encountered him only at a few academic functions and community events, but no one else in the school system had been able to change my son's outlook. I was desperate.

The superintendent's office was in a separate administrative building, removed from the high-school campus. When we arrived, it was hard not to be impressed by the imposing and impressive surroundings. It was a very professional, successful atmosphere, and I felt fortunate this busy man had agreed to see us.

Our initial interaction centered around introductions, school activities, and congratulations on my son's scholarship. The superintendent, however, seemed to sense what was wrong and why we were there. He began to address my son directly and maintain eye contact only with him. They talked about the merits of education, how it was hard to change one's surroundings, and the benefits of new challenges. I can't recall his exact words, but it was something along the lines of the following:

"Whenever you decide to grow a little and extend yourself above the norm, there is always a danger you won't be the same. It's like the trees in the forest. When one tree decides to grow taller than all the rest, that tree is most likely to get hit by lightning. It's a chance you take. When people are different, it seems like they're more likely to be attacked for those differences. I know this because when I was a teacher, I had no problems. I fit in with all the other teachers with whom I worked. I was surrounded by colleagues and friends. I wanted to be a principal, however, and when I achieved that goal, I found some of my colleagues and friends resented my advancement."

I remember wondering where he was going with this, but I noticed my son was sitting up in his chair and listening intently. He was obviously interested in this man's perspective, so the superintendent went on.

"When I decided to become the superintendent of all the schools in the system, it was even worse. I remember the resentment... the lack of encouragement. I know what you're feeling, but you can't let those feelings keep you from your goals — because I'll tell you a secret. You know those trees I mentioned, well, when you do grow taller, and you rise above all the other trees in the forest, you realize there is so much more to see. Your view is better than ever. You can see the sky, the stars, and everything else beyond your little local forest. Once you see what's out there, you realize you can't go back. You've seen it, and you're not the same. You want to grow taller and extend yourself even further because you want to see more. You want to do more. Don't be afraid to grow, son. In the long run, you won't regret it. I never have."

Well, I don't know if it was him, his words, the office, or the trees in the forest, but my son finally smiled. He shook hands with the superintendent, stood up a little taller, and, within a few days, returned to the bright, smiling, effervescent boy we'd always known.

In the weeks that followed, I tried to figure out what the difference was and why this man's advice had resonated. I believe my error was in downplaying the problem and telling my son that what other people said didn't matter. The superintendent knew that those words did matter to my son. He understood because he'd been there.

Years have passed, and my son is now a respected physician. I'm very proud of him, and I remain very grateful that one man took the time out of his busy day to give my son some personal and heartfelt advice that made all the difference.

—Billie Holladay Skelley—

74

Self-Discovery

*I was always looking outside myself for strength and
confidence but it comes from within.*
~Author Unknown

was sitting poolside at my birthday party, dangling my feet in the
water, when I suddenly felt old. All that seemed to be missing to
complete my spinster persona was a houseful of cats. This was
not what I had pictured for myself at thirty. In the midst of all
my friends' wedding ceremonies and baby making, I felt lost — sad,
single and hopeless.

With all my fruitless soul mate searching, an entire decade of
personal opportunity had passed me by. Sitting there, scouring my
memory bank, I couldn't think of a single unique or significant moment
from my twenties. Aside from the typical college graduation and start
of my career, I had done nothing that I considered important.

How did I allow myself to end up there? I didn't have photos of
exotic locales, tales of adventure, or anything that would indicate I
was doing more than breathing and occupying space. That moment
served as my epiphany, and I recognized that my decade-long pity
party must come to a screeching halt. Right there, in the midst of my
"celebration," I made a decision to accept my life as it was and start
living it from that point forward.

I realized I should have spent far more time building my experience
catalog and far less time scouring Austin, Texas for Mr. Right. Only
to be sorely disappointed, I might add, when he didn't materialize.

Waiting around for what I thought would make me happy only made me miserable, and if my twenties could evaporate so quickly, I reasoned it wouldn't be long until I was a blue-haired old lady sitting on my sofa lamenting about that whole bunch of nothing I did in my youth.

When I finally quit searching for the man of my dreams, I took my first step toward self-discovery. I purchased a guitar and learned to play it. It wasn't long until I'd written some songs, and before I knew it, I'd stepped further out of my comfort zone and bought that first home I'd convinced myself had to be a joint purchase.

With these two notches in my belt, I went on to audition for *Nashville Star*. I traveled by railroad. I walked sixty miles for breast cancer, stood atop the Empire State Building, mastered roller coasters, witnessed a whale breaching in the bay, landed in a helicopter on a glacier, deep-sea fished, grew my own vegetables, ran a half marathon, dog mushed, delivered a speech in my community, and played sand volleyball on a league. I met my childhood hero, Dolly Parton. I ziplined in a rain forest. I donated my hair to cancer patients.

When I let go of what I thought I was supposed to become — a wife and mother — and embraced what I actually was — a strong single woman — I discovered my value. With every activity I attempted, my confidence soared until I had a firm grip on who I was and what I could do. Today, I'm a highly driven, creative and adventurous person, because I made a conscious decision to scare myself as much as possible.

And, sure, I had my doubts from time to time. I wasn't positive I could actually play volleyball, for example, but when game day finally arrived, I forced myself to attend. It was awkward since I hadn't even seen the courts since junior high, but there I was in the midst of total strangers, playing my heart out. It turned out that I wasn't half bad. A mouthful of sand here and there, but some solid passes and serves, too.

It was horrifying to climb a forty-foot pole before jumping off a platform and sailing 200 feet above a canyon. But I soldiered through the nausea, and afterwards, I felt as though I could master any challenge. At last I was strong, single, and hopeful!

Those victories of my thirties built the resilient woman of my forties. My newfound confidence came in handy when I was diagnosed with breast cancer. I refused to let my diagnosis boss me around. Two years later, I'm still breathing and occupying space, but now, unlike that first forgotten decade, it's with a purpose. In fact, I think it's safe to say that had I continued on the former stagnant path of my twenties, I would not have possessed the confidence or determination to face that breast cancer challenge.

Today, as a middle school English teacher, I share the lessons I've learned with my classes in hopes of inspiring them to be more. While it's obviously my educational responsibility to teach them how to be better readers and writers, it's also my personal responsibility to lead them toward their own paths of self-discovery. As recently as last week, I suggested that they invest in a small journal, not to write diary entries, but to record the special events and activities of their lives. I wish I'd started seeking growth opportunities earlier, but I remind myself that it's better to have lost ten years than twenty or thirty.

And by the way, while I was out living life, Mr. Right found his way to me.

— Val Jones —

75

Seventeen Words

*Always remember: You have a right to say no
without having to explain yourself.
Be at peace with your decisions.*
~Stephanie Lahart

I never thought that something shared on Facebook would have the power to change my life. I was wrong. Seventeen words were all I needed.

Pictures of my grandbaby's latest exploits. Humorous cat memes and kitten shots. Pictures of what my friends ate for lunch. Video clips of people acting foolish. Oh, and don't forget all the scrumptious recipes that I'll save yet never make. These are the things that I thought Facebook was for. And maybe a farm game or two... or five. For years, that's how I spent too much time on this popular social-media site.

I can tell you the date I saw the words that had such a profound effect on my life — March 16, 2011. They're recorded in my journal.

I was journaling almost daily during this period of time. Five months earlier, I'd experienced sudden cardiac arrest and lived. I was on an airplane on the way to a conference, about thirty minutes from landing in San Francisco. Luckily for me, there were three doctors on board — one sitting immediately behind me. In less than a minute, I had medical care, oxygen, and a defibrillator.

I survived, but months later I was still trying to come to terms with what had happened. Hence the daily journaling with my musings about life, its meaning, my purpose, and how I survived this incident.

This particular March morning, I scrolled through my Facebook feed and saw a friend's post. She wrote: "Let go of anything inauthentic and all activities that do not mirror your brightest intentions for yourself."

The words resonated in my soul. I jotted them down on a small scrap of paper lying by the computer, and then logged off and went about my business.

> "Let go of anything inauthentic and all activities that do not mirror your brightest intentions for yourself."

That post kept haunting me throughout the day. I knew my life at that point in time was not authentic. My activities did not mirror my brightest intentions. After several days of looking at these words and reflecting on them, I re-wrote them on a clean piece of paper and taped it on my laptop.

Curious as to the source of the words, I messaged my friend to ask where she'd gotten them. She didn't remember.

This was at the height of my farm-game obsession. I, along with many of our friends, played FarmVille. But one little farm game was not enough for me. Oh my goodness, no. I needed more. More farms, more crops, more livestock. All in virtual form, of course. I had five different farms in five different games.

I even scheduled my crops around my other activities. If we were meeting friends for dinner, I'd set it for grapes, which would ripen in four hours. While at dinner, I'd be checking my watch because I needed to get home in time to harvest those grapes. I didn't want them withering and dying. That would be horrid. I'd have to delete the whole crop and start over.

On a workday, I'd spend at least two hours farming my little acres of paradise. On a day off, I'd dive deep into the farms, sometimes spending four hours or more working the soil, harvesting crops to gain coins so I could plant more crops. I added buildings and roads. I built fences to keep my llamas contained — all with my little wireless mouse.

One afternoon, I glanced down at the words taped on my keyboard. Then I looked up, and my eyes strayed to the backyard view outside the window. Here I was tapping away at the computer, planting and harvesting virtual crops for hours every day while a half-acre lot outside the window lay fallow and untouched.

How was that living an authentic life? How was this an activity that mirrored bright intentions?

It wasn't.

I stopped cold turkey that day. FarmVille and the other four farms were left to wither away, leaving chickens and llamas to fend for themselves.

The computer games weren't the only tasks to come under my newly awakened scrutiny.

A birthday party for a friend? Absolutely. I was there in a flash. Spending time with friends was an authentic activity that I wanted to cultivate.

A baby shower on a Sunday afternoon for a co-worker from a different department? Nope. That got nixed. Since we all worked most Saturdays, Sundays were family time. Although I liked the co-worker whom the shower was for, I barely knew her.

Time spent walking the dogs around the block? Working in my newly claimed garden space? Spending time creating a special gift for a longtime, treasured friend? Those all passed the test; they were activities that mirrored my intentions and values.

Spending hours writing Christmas cards to people we never interacted with during the year? A New Year's Eve party with acquaintances we hardly knew? Meeting someone I didn't really enjoy for coffee? These failed. They didn't measure up to how I wanted to spend my limited available time.

That phrase I'd copied from a Facebook post became a mirror I used to examine how I spent my time and energy. Seventeen words. That's all it took. One little, easy-to-use tool was all I needed to become a woman living a more authentic life filled with activities and people that enrich and fulfill me.

— Trisha Faye —

76

A Flowering

An angel can illuminate the thought and mind of man
by strengthening the power of vision.
~St. Thomas Aquinas

I grew up during a time when shopping for what we now call "plus-size clothing" was torture. I had to go to the "misses" or teen department even though I was only eight years old.

I was always the youngest person shopping in the stores that carried clothing my mom felt was appropriate for me. The clothes were more middle-aged church lady than high school student. Feeling I had no choice, I accepted that those were indeed the clothes for me.

Eventually, I came to believe that "invisible" was the way I should dress. I shouldn't seek out clothing that hugged my curves; instead, I should seek to have a big swath of black cloth swallow me up.

This was how I bought my clothes until I was in my twenties. And then, a few years ago, I was exchanging an ill-fitting swath of dark cloth I had bought a week earlier for a wedding. When I presented the outfit to the young saleslady at the cash register, she looked confused.

"Are these clothes for you?" she asked.

I was completely flustered. Why was she asking me this?

"Um... yes," I admitted.

"No way," she said, shaking her head. "I am not selling these clothes to you. You are too young for these!"

I was in shock, but before I could protest, she came around the counter, took me by the hand, and showed me several beautiful pieces that had color, patterns and shape. She showed me clothes that I always figured were not for me — I had been told as much, and unfortunately, had believed it.

Before I left the store, my sales angel gave me some advice: "Those clothes you were planning to buy — don't buy clothes like that ever again. Don't hide yourself."

I nodded and smiled. For the rest of the day, I couldn't stop thinking about her advice. An amazing thing had happened. A seed was planted, not only in my mind but also in my heart. Something in me had shifted when I bought a coral-colored blouse for the wedding! It was a life affirming purchase. It's pretty difficult to hide while wearing coral.

Each time I bought clothes after that crucial day, I looked for items I liked, not items that someone else might think were acceptable for my body. I chose colors that complemented my skin tone and made my heart smile. I bought clothes in my actual size — not ones that would swallow me up and hide me!

Each of those decisions watered the seeds planted that day, and gradually, I began to bloom.

There have been a few times in my life when someone has encouraged and guided me. These encounters have ultimately led to new ways of thinking and living for me. I remember how significant and empowered I felt that someone took the time to assure and mentor me, simply because they cared. Girls need to know that no matter their size they are important, and so are their ideas and choices. They need to know that their worth has nothing to do with their dress size and we are all valid and valuable.

That is what I felt that day the saleslady refused to sell me an outfit. I didn't know it then, but it was one of the best things that could have ever happened to me.

A few years ago I saw my sales angel again. I told her how she had changed my life. I was able to thank her and encourage her to continue planting those beneficial seeds, because once they take root and blossom, the fruit produced is shared with others, so they too can blossom.

— Maxine Young —

77

Not Your Average Joe

*It takes courage to grow up and
become who you really are.*
~e.e. cummings

The burden of my secret was weighing me down. It was like a
ticking time bomb, waiting to explode.

"Why don't you go hang yourself?"

"People like you should shoot themselves."

"You should be burned to death."

"God looks down on people like you."

It's hard to believe that by the age of sixteen I'd heard every single
one of these phrases and hundreds more. Some came from the mouths
of my peers, but what's even scarier is that some came from the mouths
of adults, the people who we respect and look up to the most.

I had always been asked if I was gay. Most of the time people
would just assume I was and tease me about it. I never came out and
said I was, because I wasn't sure, and I was also afraid of the reaction
I would get.

In middle school most of my days were spent observing how I
was "supposed" to act and who I was "supposed" to like. I spent a lot
of time arguing with myself as I tried to figure it out. By high school I
had a clear understanding of who I was. It had finally clicked. I knew
I was gay, it was something I would never be able to change, and I
accepted that. I was not a mistake, and my confidence and acceptance
of myself grew every day. I knew that my family loved me, my friends

loved me, but most importantly, I loved myself.

I knew my very close friends wouldn't have a problem with my sexuality, so I decided to tell them first. I still had to do the biggest thing of all—tell my parents.

I have a dad who's as conservative as it gets, and a mom who, god bless her, is the complete opposite. I was raised in an open-minded household. This taught me to be myself, show emotion, and listen to both sides. I had an amazing family unit, which made it even harder to tell them because I didn't want to risk losing that. I knew when I told my friends, I could risk losing them and make new ones, but I couldn't make a new family. I waited half a year for the right time to tell them, but it didn't happen the way I planned.

It was a Saturday night and I had just gotten home from a friend's house. The news was on. Surprisingly, it was about gay people serving in the military. My parents asked me why I looked confused.

"Gay people can't serve in the military? What kind of crap is that?" I said.

"Yeah," my dad said, "it has been that way for a while."

The questions started, and then as usual, a debate erupted. I was very curious about this, not understanding why someone's sexuality should be a factor in determining whether or not they could serve their country. I had many questions and my dad was getting angry because I didn't think it was right.

"Why is this so important to you? Are you gay or something?" he asked red-faced.

My heart skipped a beat and time slowed. This was not how I had planned to tell them.

"Yes," I said firmly.

The room quieted. My dad started to say something but nothing came out. Eventually he took a deep breath and said, "Well, that's fine with me."

I was shocked and a little upset. It didn't sound sincere. I had heard all those horror stories about parents making their kids move out. I eventually walked out of the room, leaving my dad in there to grasp the situation, to look for my mom so I could tell her too. The words came out easier when I told her, probably in part because she had gay friends and was completely fine with them. She was shocked; she said she had no idea, but that she would love me until the day she died. My dad eventually came and hugged me. He said he was in shock but didn't want me to think he would ever not love me because of the person I loved. This put all my worries to rest, but I knew I still had a long road ahead of me.

The support that I had from my parents and my friends was unbelievably satisfying. I finally felt like I had nothing to hide, and I could be myself. My sexuality does not define me. I am not a stereotype — I am a human being. My journey is not over, but the hard part is. Yes, I want to get married, and yes, it's to a person of the same sex, but why does that matter? Love is love. I'm truly happy with who I am.

Hi, my name is Ian and yes, I'm gay.

— Ian McCammon —

78

A Lifetime of Stuttering

Awakening is the process of overcoming your false self
and discovering your True Self. It begins when you
decide to grab the tiger by the tail and ends with the
tiger tenderly licking the sweat off your brow and face.
~Steve Baxter

For the first decade or so of my life, my older brother and I were the only two kids I knew who suffered from the speech disorder known as stuttering. Miraculously, around the age of twelve, my brother's stuttering stopped. I was very happy for him and equally excited for my future. I was thinking "two more years." Thirty years later, my stutter is still going strong and I wouldn't want it any other way.

If I had a nickel for every time I was made fun of, I could have potentially retired at twelve. It's not easy being a kid, and it's especially difficult when you're different.

The biggest fear for most Americans is public speaking, so imagine being a stuttering child having to read aloud a paragraph from *Charlotte's Web* as the entire class looks, listens, and laughs. It's not easy. Imagine sitting at your desk with your palms sweating, pulse racing, and heart pounding as if you're about to testify against the Mafia, when, in fact, you're simply sitting there waiting to read a paragraph from *Where the Red Fern Grows*.

That all changed for me in the eighth grade when I decided to ease my anxiety by volunteering to read each and every time. My hand was always the first to go up and stayed up for most of the class. I chose to be in complete control of what and when to read. If kids laughed, they laughed. I'd usually have a witty one-liner to shoot back at them, which would ultimately shut them up. From that point on, I never again looked at my stuttering as a significant challenge.

Fast forward to 2012 and I'm a comic, a speaker, and a soldier with three tours of duty in Iraq. I currently hold the rank of Captain in the Alabama National Guard.

When I started out in comedy, my goal was simply to make the audience laugh. After each show or online video, I'd get feedback on how my comedy helped educate them with respect to their family and friends who also suffered from this speech disorder. I was blown away. Until seeing my routine, they'd never considered the challenges a person who stutters faces on a daily basis. Imagine the fear of talking on a telephone. Imagine the fear of ordering food at a restaurant. Imagine the fear of not being able to say your child's name.

I also get random messages from young men and women who aspire to serve in the military but feel they are not qualified due to their speech disorder. Being able to inspire them to follow their dreams might be the highlight of what I do. Stuttering is no joke but having the ability to inspire and create awareness of stuttering through humor has truly been a gift from God.

Stuttering is still one of the great unknowns. I've been stuttering for forty years and still can't explain it. I can probably do a better job of explaining the Pythagorean theorem. I do know, however, that four out of five people who stutter are male and that only around one percent of the world's population will ever know what it's like to get "stuck" on the simplest of sounds. I, just like any person who stutters, have my good days and bad days and everything in between. Additionally, we don't always get hung up on the same sounds, words, or sentences. And finally, the number one pet peeve for most of us is having people finish our words or sentences. We have something to say, so let us say it.

I've had the great fortune of attending the last two National Stuttering Association (NSA) annual conventions. The convention is not a pity party. It's a fun and inspiring celebration filled with education, awareness, acceptance and empowerment.

Because of my upbringing and military service, I've always been an adapt-and-overcome kind of guy, but attending the NSA convention has even opened my eyes to the difficulty many of my fellow stutterers face each and every day. I've even met people who stutter when they sing.

The NSA convention is a four-day conference. In 2011, we had the writer for the Academy Award winning film *The King's Speech* as the keynote speaker. I may be the only person who stutters who has not seen the film. Another great film featuring a person who stutters is *Star Wars*. James Earl Jones, the voice of Darth Vader, endured severe stuttering during his childhood but has gone on to have one of the greatest voices of our time. He truly beat the odds. Of course he did have one slight advantage; he was a Jedi.

There are days when I, too, wish I was a Jedi, but that has nothing to do with my speech.

Whether it's a big nose, ugly toes, or a run in your pantyhose, we all have perceived flaws that each of us should embrace, because if we don't embrace them ourselves, how can we possibly expect it from others?

— Jody Fuller —

79

Have Fun. Be Silly. Dance Crazy.

What the new year brings to you will depend a great deal on what you bring to the new year.
~Vern McLellan

I was a serial New Year's resolutioner. I'd show up at the gym each year on January 1st with a newfound enthusiasm to tone up and shed the pounds. And then I would quit. Every year. It was an endless cycle that lasted most of my adult life — post-undergrad through my late twenties — until the year of my thirtieth trip around the sun.

After an impromptu move to a new city on my thirtieth birthday, I joined a nearby gym. It was July, not even New Year's, but this time I meant it!

I'd always wanted to join the Zumba classes at my previous gyms. I would hear the music from the main floor and dream about sneaking into the back of the class to let loose. I'd press "Play" at home and, in my twenties, I even participated in filming a dance fitness DVD. All of this led to obtaining a Zumba teaching certification. But there was no way I was going to walk into a dance class. Everyone in the classes always looked like professional background dancers — smooth, fluid, and on the beat. Certainly, most were nowhere near my own size — well over 200 pounds and 5'9". And if they were, they stood awkwardly in the back of the room as if they wanted to remain invisible.

Just a few weeks after joining the gym, I thought long and hard about my reticence. The fate of my commitment to this new gym relied on mustering up the courage to take the Zumba class — and that courage really paid off. Not only did I find the strength to take the class, but I knocked down an existing no-new-friends wall in order to connect with four other amazing women (resolutioners who found love in dancing, too). We were front-row Zumba fanatics.

The four of us were regulars. Accountability partners. Friends. Each week, we texted each other and made sure we were en route to our favorite weeknight dance party. All of us, unique in our own rights, let down our hair and danced like there was no tomorrow. Personally, I was really proud of myself for finally having a regular routine. Almost a year later, I was still holding strong.

After seven months, our Zumba instructor quit without notice. Apparently, she left to open a dance studio in her hometown. The fitness manager alerted our class that Zumba would be cancelled indefinitely until she could find a replacement, which could take a few months. A few months with no classes?

Knowing that I had a certification collecting dust, I told my dance crew in jest that I'd be willing to teach the class so we could continue our weeknight parties. "We can't wait a few months!" I joked, but the ladies were serious in their support for me teaching the class. *Me? Teach the class?* Yes, I had the certification, but was I ready to actually teach an entire class? *I don't look like a fitness instructor. Will anyone even come to class?*

Reluctantly, and with convincing from my tribe, I submitted an application to the manager. She'll probably never admit it, but in response to my application, her eyes said, "Are you sure you're applying to be the instructor?" But the words that came from her mouth were, "Great, Tonya. I've scheduled an audition for you next Tuesday. By the way, you'll be auditioning in front of a live class."

I walked into my audition with confidence in the routine, but I still wasn't confident about my physical appearance. I'd never seen (in the flesh) an instructor who was a size 16. I loved to move my body to music, but I had a loose tummy and thighs that jiggled. Against my better judgment, I wore Spanx underneath and all-black compression leggings — an attempt to appear a smaller size. I was slightly discouraged when I heard a woman whisper from the back of the class, "Is she teaching the class today?"

The manager handed me a headset and turned on the music, but no one was prepared for what happened next. I froze. Not because I was nervous, but because I couldn't breathe from all the shapewear I had on. "Can I have a minute?" I ran into the bathroom where I stripped off all the uncomfortable clothes. The little voice — the same one that consistently popped up during resolution time — whispered again, "Be the exception to the rule this year. Just have fun, be silly, and dance like crazy."

Jiggly thighs and all, I went back into that room and showed the manager (and the class) why she couldn't pass up the opportunity to hire me as a Zumba instructor. I knew there were other women who felt like I once did — too afraid to walk into a fitness class because of insecurities or feeling too shy to dance their pain away. By teaching the class, I could show women how to have fun during the process of getting fit, and I'd be able to give an hour of hope to someone who needed it. I'd not only empower other women, but I'd be able to fuel my own confidence.

Needless to say, I got the Zumba instructor job on the spot. The same woman who was hesitant about attending class would now be teaching others. Strong, influential, and leaving it all on the dance floor. Now that's a resolution to be proud of.

— Tonya Abari —

80

Naturally, Powerfully Me

*It was when I realized I need to stop trying
to be somebody else and be myself,
I actually started to own,
accept and love what I had.*
~Tracee Ellis Ross

Oh. My. Goodness. They are right. I AM beautiful. These words rang through my head one sunny day in June as I looked in the mirror after successfully styling my curly hair. It was 2013, and at this point I'd had natural hair for about six months.

I always felt a sense of dread when looking in the mirror, so I usually approached the task tentatively. I have many less than fond memories of sitting in a chair as my mom wrestled and tugged my coarse, thick hair into four neat braids with barrettes. That style seemed to follow me throughout grade school, until the sixth grade. The struggle of maintaining my natural hair weighed heavily on me, and my mom's hands, and always made me feel that something about me was... off.

Shortly before getting my sixth-grade class picture taken, my uncle walked in the house and said to my mom, "One of my friends is a hair stylist; she said she can do her hair." I watched as she sat in silence for a few moments, looking both relieved and concerned.

After what seemed like hours, my mom said, "Okay, let's go ahead and try it." She turned to me and said, "Cassie, you're going to get a relaxer. Remember when I used to get my hair straightened? That's what we're going to do for you. This will make your hair a lot easier to manage!" Easier to manage? That sounded more than good to me! My mom proceeded to tell me more about what to expect, and we set an appointment to see my uncle's friend at the salon.

After sitting in that salon chair, my hair was no longer a hassle, unless you count having to make appointments every few weeks to maintain the relaxer before, God forbid my hair got "nappy" again. Taking care of my hair did get a bit easier; however, having a new look did not change how I felt about myself. It did nothing to build my confidence. I was still the same self-conscious little girl, now with straight hair (and bangs, ugh). My lack of self-confidence stuck with me as I transitioned into adolescence and young adulthood.

After ten years, I decided I had enough of "the creamy crack," keeping up with hair appointments, and finding someone I could trust to relax my hair. I wondered what it would be like to let my hair be... free. I sat at my desk in my college dorm thinking about how I would look with natural hair. Would I be able to pull it off? Could I commit to learning a whole new way of doing my hair from YouTube?

I wondered what it would be like to let my hair be... free.

I graduated from college in May 2011 — and that was also the last month I got my hair relaxed, as attempting to go natural right before my graduation day felt a bit risky. I transitioned back to my natural curls slowly instead of doing the "big chop." After about thirteen months of transitioning — buying hair products I didn't know how to use and wrestling with my combination of straight and curly hair, I started to feel that I made the wrong decision. I almost went to get my hair relaxed again, but decided to stick it out. It all made sense when I finally cut the relaxed ends off my new curly hair.

After I unraveled the two-strand twists in my natural hair that day in June, I watched the curls frame my chubby cheeks and felt like I was meeting someone new for the first time. Before that fateful moment, I never saw this young woman who looked like she had just experienced the best day of her life. Indeed, I was witnessing the birth of a new version of myself in front of that mirror.

I stood there for another ten minutes, turning my head from left to right, up and down. Years of doubt and low self-esteem melted away as I looked in that mirror. I had felt more confidence in those ten minutes than I had in all my twenty-three years of life. I lifted my head high, stuck my chest out, and walked out of my graduate dorm room like a goddess floating on a cloud.

Returning to my natural hair texture helped me get more acquainted with my personal power and strengths. Making the decision to go natural may not be a big deal to some, but it has been a monumental change for me; it changed my view of how I fit in this world. After that summer day, I found myself speaking up a little louder. I stood a little taller. I smiled a little wider. I really started to believe in myself.

Since that day, I have continued to build my confidence and encourage myself to live in my truth, and I continue using my natural hair as an outlet for self-expression and creativity as unapologetically as possible. I've become more creative with my natural hair; I experiment with hairstyles I never thought I would wear.

In that moment in the mirror, I found who I wanted to be, twenty-four hours a day, seven days a week. I am incredibly grateful that I had the opportunity to welcome my true self into the world that day.

— Cassandra L. Tavaras —

Pursue Your Passion

What You'll Find in This Chapter

The American author Joseph Campbell said, "Follow your bliss and the universe will open doors where there were only walls." That's something that I've learned from our stories—the value of pursuing our passions in our quest for happiness.

If you have a job that you only do to pay the bills, then that is your job, but it doesn't have to be what you *do*. Find some time to do what you actually love doing.

I've heard that you should think back to your favorite activities when you were ten years old and try to do those now. For me, it was two things: reading, and hiking in the woods behind our house. And now I do just that—I read for work, I read for pleasure, and when weather and time permit, my husband and I go hiking on the trails in the nature preserve in our neighborhood.

Happiness is not a mysterious, elusive lottery ticket meant for only a lucky, random few. It is a jackpot within everyone's grasp once we remove the obstacles we put in our own paths and give ourselves permission to do the things we love.

Your long-buried passion can give you purpose, or it can just give you a way to hand yourself some much deserved "me time" each week. That was the case for Jayne Thurber-Smith, whose story "Not Available" shares how she pursues her passion for horseback-riding religiously, every Saturday, no matter what else is going on. Family birthday party? Special occasion? Not till after 2 p.m. Everyone knows that Saturdays until 2 are sacred for Jayne. As she says, "Sometimes, I'm joined by a friend and other times I ride solo, but it's always a reset and recharge of my batteries for another week in the real world."

Pursuing your passion can be life changing. In Doug Sletten's case, it was. He had always wanted to be a lawyer but had become a teacher instead, sacrificing his dream for a steady job so he could support his family. Finally, when he was twenty-nine, he talked to his wife about it. She was supportive. Then, he spoke to his father, saying he was worried about how old he would be by the time he finished law school. Doug says, "He put down his newspaper and said simply, 'How old would you be in four years if you *didn't* follow your dream?'" Done. Doug was off to law school, and he tells us, in his story "Three Years," that he happily practiced law for twenty-five years.

Pursuing your passion can send you in the other direction, too. Martin Walters was a banking and finance guy for his whole career, not that he enjoyed it. He said that he was always searching for happiness. When he got downsized out of the job that he didn't like anyway, his wife pointed out that the only job he always talked about was the one he had when he was young, working at a grocery store. Now Martin is happily working as the produce department manager at the new supermarket near him.

As you embark on your journey to happiness, make sure you jettison what doesn't matter to you and analyze what truly makes you smile. After you've cleared the debris out of the road ahead, your passion in life may be right there in front of you.

81

Ripe for a Change

Find a job you like and you add five days
to every week.
~H. Jackson Browne

For my fortieth birthday, my daughter gave me an empty glass jar on which she had written the word Happiness. "When you find what makes you happy, you can put it in here so you don't lose it!" she explained.

The gift nicely summed up the vast majority of my life: a search for happiness. I certainly was happy as a boy; I can't tell you how many times I've relived boyhood games in my mind. I reminisced about childhood so much that my wife even called me "Peter Pan." Even young adulthood was fun: I loved working at the grocery store, setting up the produce stand, helping customers select the perfect level of ripeness. It was relaxing and I loved interacting with the people I helped. If the real world hadn't beckoned, I could have worked there forever.

But when I became an adult, it seemed that everyone around me had found their correct life, and more importantly, had found happiness in that life. I always felt like I was still searching. I took a job in banking to support my family, but what really made me happy were my two young daughters. When they started growing up, however, I felt lonely and pointless again. My job and the long commute seemed absurd. Pushing papers and meeting deadlines without interacting with clients felt pointless; I'd come home and the girls would be at their friends' or at practice or rehearsal. And I wasn't there to see it.

Thinking about my job consumed more and more of my free time. Over the years, the banking industry had been heartless, and various mergers and acquisitions always left me questioning — and sometimes losing — my job security.

"Just leave work at work," my wife advised. "Come home, find something that makes you happy, and get absorbed in it."

Easy for her to say. She finds happiness in anything — reading, gardening, talking, cooking. In fact, there isn't much she doesn't find joy in — except for watching me mope around the house, miserable.

When the girls moved out, a new bank acquisition sent me away from the stress of New York City into the quiet cities of the South. At first we thought it was a blessing — and it was. My wife and I were now closer to where our daughters had moved. I had a shorter commute. And for a few weeks, I was happy.

But soon the doldrums came again, and my wife declared with frustration, "As long as you're working, you're never going to be happy, Peter Pan!"

A blessing in disguise closed the office, and the company offered to move us back to New York. My wife was horrified that I might accept the offer and frightened about what might happen if I didn't. We considered it carefully, and we decided we didn't need a lot of money anymore: our home was nearly paid off and our girls were out on their own. We could settle for a modest salary, health insurance, and proximity to our daughters.

I declined the offer.

I loved the first few months of being jobless. It was everything I ever thought I wanted. I repaired every problem with the house. I pruned the trees. I created built-in shelves in all the basement storage areas. Crown molding, recessed lighting… I did it all.

Once the adrenaline wore off, however, that tiny seed of worry sprouted in my soul. Why hadn't I gotten any calls from sending out my résumé? I knew the economy was bad, but I expected a handful of interviews by now.

"All the jobs are in New York," my wife sighed one night.

"I won't move back there," I insisted.

My wife understood, and she was glad for the decision, but she was starting to worry. She watched our checkbook carefully. She started cutting corners at the grocery store, buying store brands and skimping on her favorite treats.

Two years went by, and although my wife wouldn't say it, I knew what she was thinking: she wondered whether finally, now that I didn't have to work a job I hated, I was happy. I saw the anger growing in her face as she left for work each day and glared at me as I sat on the couch sipping coffee and watching television. I wanted to tell her that the joy of it had worn off after a matter of months. That I only continued repairing our home so that I'd have something to do. That now I felt useless and old. I had run out of job prospects and home-improvement projects, and the days blended together.

I wanted to work.

I wanted to be happy.

It took two years of résumé revisions, of unemployment workshops, of promising interviews that for one reason or another just "didn't pan out." My cover letters were lackluster. I realized the drive that had helped me through my early career had been my desire to provide for my family. Now, they were provided for. My epiphany came when I realized that, for the first time in my life since childhood, I could worry about ME.

One day at breakfast, my wife eyed me over her coffee. "You know," she said, "when we were younger, you always used to tell me that your favorite job was working at that grocery store, stocking produce. A few times you even mentioned that, money aside, that would be the only job that would make you happy. Do you remember?"

> *"Your favorite job was working at that grocery store, stocking produce."*

I smiled. "Of course I do. I can still see those lettuce heads, those glistening apples. I still remember the particular weight of a cantaloupe just begging to be sliced and enjoyed, the feel of a tomato that will be ripe in time for dinner. Helping people instead of pushing paper…"

My wife smiled. It was a relaxed smile, a smile I hadn't seen in a few years.

"What made you remember that?" I asked.

"I saw they're opening up a new supermarket in the next town over. It just made me think of — well," she said, trying not to be too blunt, "I saw an advertisement for a produce department manager. I just thought — "

But she was too late. I had already retrieved a cover letter and résumé from the kitchen desk. "I sent this in three weeks ago," I said. "I've already had a phone interview with the store manager, and he says there are a few positions he'd like to see me fill. My interview is next Tuesday."

Weeks later, happily in my new position, I gazed at the "happiness" jar on my dresser. It was now filled with all my favorite snapshots from my life, from the birth of our daughters to their graduations and weddings.

I may have lost it, but I found it once again. "The love of family," I think to myself each night before bed. "That is what my happiness has always been."

And tomatoes.

— Martin Walters —

82

Not Available

*If you're lucky enough to find anything in life that gives
you five seconds, let alone an hour of relief from life,
you should try to do it forever.*
~Jack Antonoff

've always loved horses, but for years my riding took a back seat
to my four kids' soccer games, hockey practices, dance recitals,
karate classes, and golf tournaments. As my children became
more independent, I decided it was time to put myself on the
calendar. After twenty years of being at the beck and call of my family, there's now a standing rule that I will be available to no one on
Saturdays until after 2:00 p.m. That's now my barn time, and it's
sacred to me.

> **I will be available
> to no one on
> Saturdays until
> after 2:00 p.m.**

Since Saturday afternoons are the only time
in the entire week that works best for all
six of us Smiths to get together, we now
schedule luncheons for birthdays and other
special occasions at 2:30 p.m. instead of
noon. No one complains about a late lunch,
though. If Mama's not happy, no one's happy, and this mama is always
very happy when she shows up for lunch after her barn shift—happier
than after any massage, pedicure, or facial.

I have a work-to-ride lease at a nearby stable and it's the best of
all worlds. As soon as I arrive at the stables, I always pause to take a
deep cleansing breath or two, inhaling the sweetness of freshly mown

hay and the beautiful wild roses growing beside the shower stall.

I get in a little exercise mucking and hauling hay bales for a couple of hours while chatting with other stable hands or listening to a favorite podcast. Then in return for my chores, I get to walk out to the pasture, get my leased horse Tara, saddle her up and go for a joyride. Sometimes, I'm joined by a friend and other times I ride solo, but it's always a reset and recharge of my batteries for another week in the real world.

When I returned from my most recent vacation with my faraway siblings, it felt too short, as always. Feeling homesick for them, I got to the stables bright and early the next Saturday to cheer myself up.

"Did you hear about Heather?" my friend Mary asked with sad eyes as I wiped off my bridle. "It was so unexpected…. She lost her son last week."

Heather's son? I had just met her grandson and granddaughter last month at the stables. They were the same age as my kids, so her son must have been around my age.

"No, how awful," I murmured. "Poor Heather."

"Yes, it's tragic," she said. "I talked to her yesterday. She seemed okay despite everything."

"Yesterday? She was out here?"

"She and her grandkids went for a trail ride. This is the best place to be when you need to get away from real life," Mary commented knowingly.

I nodded silently. Mary's husband had just been through a horrible health scare, and whenever she wasn't taking care of him, she was running out here to take care of herself. We all suffer from various levels of heart-hurt on a daily basis. Our barn is pure escapism — from worry, frustration, hurt, even unimaginable loss.

Relief from real life. We all need it, somewhere, somehow, because life is rough. I'm so glad I've found that horse time can make the hardest landings a little softer. I plan to do this riding thing forever.

— Jayne Thurber-Smith —

83

Three Years

*We must be willing to get rid of the life
we've planned, so as to have the life
that is waiting for us. The old skin has
to be shed before the new one can come.*
~Joseph Campbell

had been out of college for eight years. I finally had all my school loans paid off and I liked my job teaching in a junior high school and coaching football. In my spare time, I had a hobby/semi-vocation refereeing high school football games in the fall and basketball games in the winter. My wife worked as a nurse at the local hospital, and we had two children — a boy in the second grade and a girl about to start kindergarten. All in all, I was relatively comfortable and satisfied.

But since I was a boy, I had had an interest in the law. I watched every lawyer show on TV and liked the movies that showed the parrying and mental sparring of the courtroom. It was always a dream of mine to call myself an attorney. When an older cousin of mine, whom I had always admired, finished law school and became a successful attorney, I knew more than ever that's what I wanted to do.

We were so comfortable, though, and this would be a major disruption, not just for me but for my whole family. Was I willing to sell the first house that my wife and I had ever owned? Was I willing to pull my kids out of school and away from their friends, and my wife out of her job, just to chase my dream? I knew that the "washout" rate at most law schools was about half, and I didn't know if I had the smarts or the study skills to go back to school and make it all the way through. I had heard about the Socratic method that they used as a teaching tool in law school, and it truly scared me.

I needed some advice, and I knew where I needed to go. I was part of the "protest about nearly anything," hippie generation, and my dad and I butted heads for a long time about his "old school" traditions. However, like the old saying goes, my dad got awfully smart when I went to college and learned a few things. So I started going to my dad for advice. He was what the old-timers called a "soapbox philosopher," but he always had sage advice for me. He would seldom tell me what to do, but his little lessons always guided me and led me to do the right thing.

I came into his home one day as he was reading his Sunday paper, one of his favorite things to do. I asked if I could interrupt him for a moment and told him I needed some advice. I explained that it was my dream to become a lawyer, but I was twenty-nine. If I went now, I wouldn't get out until I was well into my thirties. I half expected him to talk me out of it and tell me that I should be happy with the life I had. But he put down his newspaper and said simply, "How old would you be in four years if you *didn't* follow your dream?" I started doing the math so I could answer, and then I realized: That *was* the answer.

So we sold our house and moved into a mobile home in the campus trailer park. My kids started the year in a brand new school, and my wife got a different job.

> "How old would you be in four years if you didn't follow your dream?"

Those were three of the most grueling years of my life, but I loved the study of law. I was never so robbed of sleep or never spent less time with my family, and I made the library my second home. But I made it through. Two of the proudest moments in my life were when I walked across that stage to get my law degree and my swearing-in as a new attorney-at-law.

I practiced law for twenty-five years, and I was always grateful that my father and my family supported my decision to uproot our lives and try something completely different.

— Doug Sletten —

84

You Got This

*The future belongs to those who believe
in the beauty of their dreams.*
~Eleanor Roosevelt

When I was sixteen, I went on vacation to Yellowstone National Park. I remember telling my mom when I returned home that I wanted to be a park ranger there. It was an amazing place.

When I took a career aptitude test my senior year of high school, everything pointed toward the recreation/resource-management field. But my guidance counselor told me, from what he saw, the only thing I'd ever be good at was being a housewife and having babies.

That same year, my mom and I went to visit a college in northern Minnesota. This college was known for its great resource-management program. We traveled six hours to reach the campus. It checked all the boxes, and I had decided it was the college for me.

I met counselor number two. We sat down in his office and made small talk. He asked me what I wanted to be when I graduated from college, and I told him I wanted to be a park ranger. He sat quietly behind his desk and then leaned forward. He looked at me over his glasses and said, "Women can't be park rangers." I was stunned, to say the least. This man did not even know me, yet he was telling me that I couldn't be a park ranger?

I looked at my mom and said, "Well, I guess we are done here." We got up and left his office after only ten minutes. We drove six hours back home.

The next campus visit was just down the road. I met counselor number three, and he also asked me what I wanted to be. I told him I wanted to be a park ranger. He looked at me and said, "Nancy, you can be anything you want to be." I looked over at my mom with a big smile and said, "This is where I want to go to college."

I graduated with a bachelor's degree in Park and Recreation Management with a double emphasis on municipal and resource management. In 1986, I was hired as a seasonal park ranger in Yellowstone National Park. After working seasonally for five years in the Park Service, I became a permanent law-enforcement park ranger and got married to my best friend, Duane.

Shortly after starting my permanent career in my dream job, I was told by the Assistant Law Enforcement Specialist that I had no business being in law enforcement. That was my introduction to working in a man's world. This person did not know me or what I was capable of. While living and working in Yellowstone, I became a Contract Guard for the United States Marshals Service, Emergency Medical Technician (EMT), wildland firefighter, Field Training Ranger, Drug Abuse Resistance Education (DARE) instructor, and mother of two wonderful sons, Cody and Blake.

After nineteen years of living and working in Yellowstone, it was time to move to the next level. I was given the opportunity to work at Mount Rushmore National Memorial as a Supervisory Park Ranger.

After three years at Mount Rushmore, I was hired as a Patrol Captain for the United States Forest Service. My supervisory responsibilities included oversight for law enforcement for Nebraska, South Dakota and Wyoming.

Eight years later, I accepted a position that took me back to the National Park Service. I became the Chief Park Ranger at Jewel Cave National Monument in Custer, South Dakota. Being a federal law-enforcement officer, there is a mandatory retirement age of fifty-seven. As retirement loomed, I spent four years at Jewel Cave. I took on several new roles while being the Chief Ranger to include a seven-month detail as the acting Superintendent.

All good things must come to an end, and on December 31, 2019, I reached mandatory retirement age. That Tuesday morning, I completed one of the toughest radio calls that I have ever made. For thirty-one years, I had called in service (ten-eight) and out of service (ten-seven) every day.

This was my final ten-seven. Sitting in my patrol car, I raised the mic to my quivering lips and took a deep breath before I keyed the mic. "Two-eleven, JECA five hundred."

Dispatch answered, "JECA five hundred, go ahead,"

I responded, "After thirty-one years of service, this will be my final ten-seven." After a long pause and fighting back tears, I went on to say, "Thank you for always having my back."

The dispatcher read the following statement: "Ten-four, attention units and stations on behalf of Sheriff Marty Mechaley, Custer County Sheriff's Office, Custer County Communications, citizens and many DARE students through the years. We would like to thank Nancy Martinz for thirty-one years of service and dedication, protecting and serving the citizens of the United States, with the US Park Service, US Forest Service and the US Marshals Service. We wish Nancy many years of relaxation and enjoyment in retirement. JECA five hundred, ten-seven on December 31, 2019, ten hours, forty-six minutes." My voice quivered, and tears ran down my face as I answered dispatch, "JECA five-hundred retired."

When the dream is big enough, opinions don't matter.

— Nancy Martinz —

85

The Promise

It's not the load that breaks you down;
it's the way you carry it.
~Lena Horne

My dad was dying. His cancer had gotten worse. I moved back home to help, but my mother was determined to do everything herself. She woke up early every morning to read a passage from the Bible to my father. He would stroke her arm lovingly as she lay beside him reciting scripture from Psalms or Proverbs, his two favorites. She always made him a special breakfast that included cheese grits. Sometimes, when the pain increased, she would need to feed him.

My mother lived to care for him. But then one day, there was nothing more she could do. My father had to go to hospice. He told my mom that not being able to have her homemade greens and cornbread anymore is what would kill him. They laughed, trying to find a humorous moment in what was happening to their forty-five-year friendship, their marriage, and a love that made even their siblings and friends a little jealous.

As tragic as it seemed, my dad stayed optimistic to the end. He talked about driving to Erie from Pittsburgh to go fishing. He said my mom would make a basket for the trip filled with fried chicken and potato salad. My mom, on the other hand, was sinking into a dark place. She felt lost without him long before he closed his eyes for the last time.

The night before my father died, he took my hand and asked me to look after my mother — as if he had to ask. I promised, and he smiled with a look of contentment on his face. The next day, he took his last breath.

After the funeral, my mom went into her room and shut the door. When I checked on her later, I found her sitting on the bed with the lights out and curtains drawn. That's where she stayed for the next two months. I had never seen my mom so sad, so listless. A vibrant woman who believed in serving others and making a difference in the community, she was depressed. I started to worry about keeping the promise I had made.

I didn't know how to help her until I rode past my Aunt Ruby's house in the Hill District on the way home from work one day. I stopped by just to check in and see if she was alright. Aunt Ruby was the family matriarch, the sister of my father's mom.

I walked to the door and knocked. A ninety-two-year-old lady with eyes like mine peeked out. "Who's there?"

"It's me, Aunt Ruby. It's Debbie."

"I need you," she said feebly. "Bob left and didn't come back."

Bob was her personal caregiver. For years, she had someone living in her home to look after her, but she was alone this particular day. Turned out, Bob had gotten sick, and Aunt Ruby was trying to take care of herself. I went in the house and cooked a meal for Aunt Ruby, got her ready for bed and locked up.

As I drove home, I thought about my mom and how she always made time for anyone in need and how much she and my dad loved Aunt Ruby. I talked to my mom through the bedroom door after delivering her dinner.

"Mom," I said. "Did you know that Aunt Ruby has been over there all by herself? Bob hasn't been there for weeks." My mother, who had only murmured a thank you to me for her meals for weeks, made a familiar sound. "Umm umm umm," she said. I was heartened by it. I knew she was listening and wanted to help. She cracked the door and asked me question after question about Aunt Ruby.

"Is she feeling well?"

"Did she say she needed someone?"

"Yes, and yes," I answered. That's how it all started.

Mom turned on the lights and opened the curtains the next morning. She asked me if I would mind dropping her off at Aunt Ruby's house.

"Not at all," I said.

I couldn't wait to get her out of the house. Aunt Ruby welcomed my mother with open arms. They sat around like old friends while my mother cooked meals, helped Aunt Ruby shower, combed her long, gray hair and twisted it into a bun. They were enjoying their special time together.

My mom, Aunt Ruby and I took several trips from Pittsburgh to Wilmington, Delaware, to see Aunt Gracie, who was in a nursing home recovering from a stroke. She was Aunt Ruby's little sister. We took the train, and Aunt Ruby and my mom would sing, "This train don't carry no loafers, this train." Aunt Ruby used to sing that song as we rode along Route 376. She moved her head from side-to-side and clapped wildly when she reached the chorus. My mother would join in as we rode along.

Mom was feeling alive again. She smiled more. It was good.

From the first time I dropped my mother off until the day that Aunt Ruby died, there was a spirit of sharing and love between them. I thought that maybe loneliness gave them a bond, but the combination of caring and service made the difference. We all long for someone to talk to, communicate with and love. It gives us a reason for living. My father would be pleased.

— Deborah Starling —

86

New Recruits Wanted

Choose a job you love. You will never
have to work a day in your life.
~Author Unknown

"**N**ew Recruits Wanted." The sign caught my eye and revived my dream of becoming a firefighter. But, just as quickly, I reminded myself that I was getting close to sixty and was probably not the picture-book image of a firefighter. Forty years in construction had taken its toll on my body, but the decades spent as a Level 3 First Aid Attendant had built a certain "rescue mentality" in me that gave me the confidence to visit the fire hall and fill out an application.

A few years earlier, on my way to work, I had assisted at a roadside motor-vehicle accident. It was a head-on collision with one vehicle submerged in a water-filled ditch. I helped a police officer rescue the driver, but she was in cardiac arrest. I was able to start her heart with CPR and save her life. This powerful experience forever changed my appreciation for first responders and the role they play. And though I understand that not everyone can do this kind of work, I believe that those of us who can need to step forward.

My dream of becoming a firefighter began when I watched the television show *Rescue 8*, filmed with the cooperation of the Los Angeles Fire Department. Each week, the two specialists on the *Rescue 8* truck performed all manner of daring rescues and medical calls, as well as attended fires with the regular crews. At an early age, I knew what I wanted to do, and the theme song from that show stuck in my head for years.

Unfortunately, life doesn't always follow the dreams of young boys. A career in construction, a family to raise, and many other factors got in the way of volunteering with the local fire department when I was younger. Now, in anticipation of retirement, my wife and I had just relocated to a beautiful village on a lake about four hours north of Seattle, Washington. I was new in town; I had time to give; I knew I could contribute; I filled out the application and introduced myself to the Chief.

To my delight, I was accepted for training. Yes, I was the oldest recruit. Yes, it was tough. There were five of us in that recruit class. Two of us made it through the training and became firefighters. Three dropped out, one by one, over the weeks of training required. I'm not sure if my maturity gave me the stamina required to hang in there when younger guys were dropping out or if it was just the realization that I would never get another chance.

But I almost quit. I remember that day. We were practicing rescue in a darkened structure. We were crawling around with sixty pounds of gear on our backs, searching for victims in the dark. Afterwards, my poor old knees were screaming, my back was aching, and I wasn't sure I had the right stuff to complete my training. I was ready to give up and let the younger guys do it.

When I got home from practice, some friends were over. I cleaned up and was going to let everyone know that I couldn't do it anymore. But it was Christmas, and my friend, who is an author and inspirational speaker, had a small gift for me. It was a book. But not just any book. It was a beautifully illustrated book of firefighters in action by Vancouver photographer Allan de la Plante. And it was signed by the author with a personalized message of inspiration, encouraging me to follow my dream. As I leafed through the pages with tears in my eyes, I marvelled at the courage and dedication of these brave individuals captured on film. It gave me the inspiration and strength I needed to carry on and complete my training. I knew then that my age didn't matter. What mattered was my attitude and perseverance.

Over the next few weeks, the training continued to be intense, but I never lost focus again. I lost twenty pounds, but at last I was certified as a firefighter. It was almost surreal. And when the tones went off and we responded with lights and siren, there was a song playing in my head. It took me a few years to figure out what it was. I finally Googled the old TV show, and I knew as soon as I heard it. The theme song from *Rescue 8* was playing in my head when we responded to calls. It had been buried deep but never went away. And it gave me courage.

I am currently a trainer with the department. I certify drivers to drive fire apparatus and operate fire pumps. I love to drive the big red trucks and serve my community. And, yes, the theme song from *Rescue 8* still plays in my head every time I drive with lights and siren. I found a place where I fit in with the department despite my age. I am a medical first responder, firefighter, driver, pump operator, trainer and member of the Critical Incident Stress Management team. And at a time when most of my friends are retiring, I have found a new career that I love.

My proudest moment with the department came in 2014. Each year, the members of our department fill out secret ballots to choose the firefighter who most exemplifies the highest work standards and dedication to service among us. In 2014, my peers voted me Firefighter of the Year. It was not a gift to the old guy. It was in recognition for the hard work I had put into building our department.

It's been almost ten years since I walked into the fire hall in trepidation, worried and wondering if I was being foolish. Here I am, rapidly approaching seventy, and I now know that you are never too old to redefine your life; never too old to take on new challenges; never too old to follow your dreams. I don't run into burning buildings or climb ladders anymore. But I am still proud to drive the pumper or the rescue truck to the scene. Yes, with the *Rescue 8* theme song playing in my head. And I am very proud to teach the next generation of firefighters the skills they will need to keep our village safe and save lives. Their decision to become a first responder will be one of the most challenging but rewarding decisions they will ever make. I know it has been mine.

— Fred Webber —

87

Escaping Insomnia

If you do what you love, it is the best way to relax.
~Christian Louboutin

I honestly don't know why I set up the painting table. Even as I put out the paints and brushes, I felt foolish. I was a single parent, pedaling fast to take care of my four kids. I had no family nearby to help and little extra time after work and the kids' sports.

Even after I set up the table in our kitchen, we all knew I wasn't going to paint. It just wasn't going to happen. And it didn't.

All my days were the same. I got up, hustled the kids off to school, went to work, and then picked them up, fitting dinner in around their karate, softball and soccer. At the end of the day, I fell into bed exhausted.

Then the insomnia returned. I found myself wandering around the house at three in the morning. With nothing to watch on television, I cleaned the floors, made the kids' lunches, and tried to catch up on chores. By the end of the week, my checkbook was balanced, and the chores were done. That's when the painting table became more than a rectangular object taking up space in the kitchen. It seemed to call out to me.

I tried to ignore it. I told myself there were other things to do. But in those blurry hours when I should have been asleep, painting seemed like as good an idea as any. It was something to occupy my mind until maybe I could go back to sleep.

One night, I sat down, grabbed my brushes and painted. I did the same thing the following night, and then again, until a week had flown by. Most nights, I never went back to sleep, so it was easy to be dressed and ready for work before the kids got up. Every morning, I returned the brushes to their proper places and put my paints away. One morning — I must have been painting for two or three weeks by then — I sat down at the dining-room table and listened to the kids chatter as they finished their breakfast.

One of my girls turned to me. "Hey, Mom, you're nicer when you paint."

Before I could respond, another spoke up. "Yeah. Nicer."

At first, I was surprised that they'd even noticed. The painting table had become just another piece of furniture taking up space. Then my head swirled as I absorbed their words. Nicer? Did that mean I wasn't nice the rest of the time? My stomach flip-flopped as I pondered the implication. I wasn't a good mom — I was mean. My heart sank as I fought back the tears.

Finally, with a shaky voice, I asked, "So, I'm not nice normally?"

A chorus of voices followed, each child offering up his or her thoughts and explaining what they meant. Somehow, they'd noticed that I had been painting regularly, but they'd also noticed a change in me that I was unaware of.

Painting made me happy. They'd seen that and wanted me to know. Trying to ease my insomnia by filling the time with painting, I'd stumbled on a secret to taking care of me — just by letting my creative self come out of hiding.

And now, when days get long, work is too busy, and life wants to swallow me whole again, I can still hear their voices telling me how much nicer I am when I paint. They'd discovered something I might never have recognized: Doing what I like, even in small doses on a regular basis, is important. It makes me happy.

— Debby Johnson —

88

Good, Very Good, Best

*It's never too late to start something new, to do all
those things that you've been longing to do.*
~Dallas Clayton

High school was difficult for me in the mid-1950s. My high school counselor told me that college wasn't in my future. I would graduate in the middle of my class. And we were poor—my widowed mother often stretched a half-pound of hamburger to feed seven kids. He concluded our pre-graduation meeting with, "Benson, I believe the military would be a good fit for you."

I did well in the Army, and my electronics training was a foundation for later things. The counselor's advice was good, but it wasn't the *best* advice I've ever heard.

My work in the Army qualified me for a manufacturing job with a small company in Minnesota. It was a low-paying position, but any job to support my wife and three kids during a Midwest winter was a good job.

The agency I'd been with in the Army recruited me to return to Virginia for an unposted civilian job. The government salary wasn't significantly higher, but health benefits and other perks gave me the incentive to accept the offer. However, I still needed a part-time job to support my family once we settled in.

So I worked evenings and some weekends as a clerk at one of the stores in a rapidly expanding drugstore chain. After less than a year, I was recruited into the company's management program. Compensation in the training program was equal to government employment, so with the expectation of advancement, I changed jobs. Leadership skills I'd learned in the Army were a personal asset in my new occupation.

The day I was promoted from trainee to assistant manager, my district manager said, "You're moving up faster than most, but remember this — while climbing the ladder of success, you might have to climb back down someday. In other words, always treat those you supervise with respect and fairness." His advice was very good, but still not the *best* advice I've ever heard.

We were spending a summer afternoon with friends from church, and our conversation turned to our work and the future. Our friends were preparing to move back to their home state, where they were both certified to teach. My friend Lyle asked about my own work and what might be ahead for me.

I told Lyle that my previous boss, who had recruited and promoted me to manager, was moving up to the corporate office. He told me I was on the fast track for supervising one of the new districts. The increased pay and responsibility seemed like a good incentive to accept the position, but I lamented that the working hours and traveling time would increase.

When Lyle asked what I'd really like to do, I told him, "Teach." I explained that my favorite job had been teaching operation and field maintenance of communications equipment to U.S. embassy personnel when I was in the Army.

He asked if I had a teaching degree, and I told him I had taken only a few college classes. When he suggested that I could enroll and maybe transfer my previously earned credits, I said, "I'm nearly thirty-three, with house payments and a family to support. Do you know how old I'd be if I went to college now?"

He countered, "How old will you be if you don't go?"

That was the best advice I've ever heard.

Three years later, I graduated with a teaching degree and started a satisfying thirty-five-year career as an education professional. I retired from teaching with an advanced degree, and now I can afford hamburger.

My high school counselor's good advice was helpful. My district manager's very good advice was practical. But the best advice I've ever heard, my friend's question, was life-changing.

—John Morris Benson—

A Happiness Throttle

When I get logical, and I don't trust my
instincts — that's when I get into trouble.
~Angelina Jolie

checked the clock on the bottom right corner of my office computer. Only ten minutes longer. I sent another e-mail, then checked the clock again: only nine minutes now. Eight minutes later, as the clock struck 5:29, I closed my office laptop as quickly and quietly as possible, wished my team a good night, and scuttled off the fifth floor.

There should be a survival kit for navigating your twenties. What no one ever tells college students is how little they'll be prepared for the real world once they get out there. Many will not get the job they wanted. The job they do find will be different than the job they dreamed about.

On top of that, friends will be moving to opposite ends of the country, romantic relationships may end, and unless you're in the small minority of twenty-somethings, life will become about surviving paycheck to paycheck, in a world of unpaid internships and night jobs where college degrees mean squat.

Phew. At least I had a job.

The elevator, taking five minutes too long, took me down to the first floor, where the desk attendant tipped his hat goodnight. Trudging two blocks to my car, I shoved my heavy briefcase onto the back seat. I climbed into my Honda CRV and peered at my hair in the rearview mirror. It was frizzing from the humidity as usual. I sighed. Curly hair problems.

I had been one of the lucky ones. After graduating with honors, I'd packed my bags and headed to the big city for a well-paying internship with good job potential upon completion. I hoped this would be my opportunity to expand my professional résumé, enjoy the culture Washington, D.C. had to offer, and figure out what I was supposed to do with my life.

Boy, was I wrong.

Before I knew it, I was swept into the entry-level job world: long hours behind a computer screen, customer service calls from rude clients, horrible commutes, carpal tunnel syndrome, and robotic work I didn't give a darn about.

I had studied the liberal arts: Psychology, English, and Sociology. I was supposed to be working in a job that allowed me to use my passions, not ignore them. This was not at all what I had signed up for.

A dark wave of depression floated over me. This was hell.

Well-meaning opinions from parents and friends did not help. I couldn't help rolling my eyes at their attempts to console me.

"Everyone hates their first job."

"You just need to adjust to the professional world."

"Just give it time."

"You're only twenty-two. You don't know what you want."

But I did know. At least I knew that I didn't want this. Doing what every twenty-something was supposed to do wasn't working for me. Following the path most traveled felt like the fastest path to my self-destruction.

So I decided to turn in my notice.

The next morning, as the alarm shrieked me awake from a peaceful slumber, instead of dragging myself out of bed, I jumped. This was the beginning of the end. As I stepped into my knee-length skirt, black flats, and gray blazer, I was overcome by a sense of calm, the likes of which I hadn't felt for months.

When I arrived at work, I even grinned at the desk attendant.

"Good morning ma'am," he said, a twinkle in his eye.

My smiling co-workers were grinning, too, as they brought fresh toasted bagels and coffee from the kitchen. We made small talk and then settled into our morning tasks. Somehow, the snippy client seemed less angry this morning. The market research less draining. My carpal tunnel syndrome less painful.

As the clock struck 5:29, I approached my supervisor. I calmly shared my action plan.

"Thank you for your hard work," she replied. "Let me know if you ever need anything."

I trudged the familiar path to the parking garage. I paused for a moment and smiled.

Two weeks later I packed my bags and moved back to my college town. I found a job working with kids with special needs and began a part-time freelance writing career. And I found out special needs kids are the greatest and writing is transcendent.

Money is not worth it if you hate your job. The key to happiness may very well be doing what you love. Sometimes all it takes is a spontaneous life decision to bring back your joy. In order to live a truly authentic life, it becomes necessary to throw away the rulebook and answer to one person and one person only: yourself.

— Alli Page —

Movie Critic, MD

Chase down your passion like it's
the last bus of the night.
~Terri Guillemets

"I quit." Those were words I never expected to hear coming from my mouth. I had been raised to persevere in even the direst of situations, but those two little words led me to a new job in a new city with a new home and new patients. I am a family physician, and I had developed the courage to leave a medical practice I felt had stifled my growth as a clinician. I had started over but soon learned I hadn't started over far enough away.

Sitting in my new office during a lunch break, I sighed at the mountain of paper charts sitting on my desk. I had a tendency to skip lunch to tackle all that chart documentation, but something told me to grab a ham sandwich and give my brain a break with a lighthearted Internet search. What I soon discovered made me giddy as a schoolgirl. After a few phone calls, I scampered into the front office and found several pairs of receptionist eyes looking up at me.

"I need to take some time off next week," I said. "Can someone help me adjust my patient schedule?"

Loraine, a receptionist and dear friend, answered, "Sure thing, doc. Anything going on you want to share?" It may have been my happy feet dance that gave me away.

"I am going to go to the movies."

A small giggle escaped the lips of the other staff. "You are going to take time off from work to go to the movies?"

"More than that, I am going to go to a film set in Wisconsin to meet Johnny Depp."

That certainly drew some attention as questions swirled around the room. How did I know about a film shoot? Did I know if the actor would actually be there? How could I know it was not an Internet hoax? Of course, I had answers for all of them. I had confirmed the film shoot with the local Visitor Center in Columbus.

Then came the speculative looks that told me I lost my mind to fly across the country to do such a thing. After all, I was a professional and professionals are serious people; they do proper things and do not pursue obscure adventures. That was what I had always told myself but something shifted in me that day. I had quit a position that made me unhappy, had made all these life adjustments by moving and changing jobs, but I still had not found a way to find that life balance. The stack of papers on my desk told me so.

For me, movies had always been essential escapism. The silver screen could erase every worry and transport me into other worlds for hours at a time. I had dreamed of being a film critic, a female Roger Ebert, since high school and the opportunity to see that magic in action was far too tempting.

But Loraine understood. She smiled a toothy grin and gave me a pat on the back. It seemed she understood that life need not come burdened with conventional trappings.

I completed my chart documentation that day with verve.

A week later, I found myself on a plane to Chicago followed by a three-hour drive in a rental car to Wisconsin. My first stop was the Visitor Center.

"I can't believe you came!" Visitor Center director Kim Bates and I had conversed on the phone several times over the past week. We hugged as if we were long lost friends.

"I wouldn't miss it."

"You must be a big fan then."

I had been a fan of the actor since my high school days, but it was difficult to explain that this trip meant far more than that. I had always done what others expected of me. It was time to step out of that box into what made me happy. Now that I had the means to explore those options it seemed a shame to let it go.

Sadly, the film shoot with Johnny Depp was canceled at the last minute but I did get to watch Christian Bale shoot a scene with Billy Crudup for Michael Mann's *Public Enemies* at the Capitol building in Madison. I also got to tour the downtown Columbus sets and visit a home that had been transformed into a 1930's brothel. My wildest dreams of becoming one with the silver screen had come true.

I went home with an exciting story though I was missing the icing on my fantasy cake. I topped it off a week later when my new Wisconsin friends notified me that Johnny Depp had arrived in town to complete his part of the film shoot. Some would say I was a stalker to hop back on that plane, and I still get picked on to this day, but in my mind what I did was round out the experience.

Columbus was just as I left it, a movie wonderland. As I waited in a crowd that night near the Universal Studios set, a woman whispered, "Did you hear a woman was coming all the way from Connecticut?"

A little embarrassed that I had become a quirky topic of discussion, I answered, "That's me."

A teacher, a hospice nurse, a high school student, they all took me in that night with open arms, and I felt accepted by people who simply yearned for adventure just as I did. No professional roles or social expectations could stymy our enthusiasm. And at four o'clock that morning, Midwestern charm was reciprocated by the bohemian swagger of a famous actor. My heart palpitated when Johnny Depp put his arms around me in a big bear hug. The moment lasted minutes but would be a source of major change in my life.

"Thanks, Johnny."

Back home, central Connecticut regaled my tale through gossip that spreads as it always does through small towns. The patients loved it! In fact, the story had such impact that the town newspaper printed a story on my travels and offered me a position as a film critic that soon expanded to my writing for six local newspapers. I could not believe my good fortune.

A year later, that fortune expanded to the red carpet. Though there were naysayers who told me that my review column was too small or that I had not made enough of a name for myself, my Columbus adventures taught me to always expect more, to keep dreaming. I applied for press credentials to the Los Angeles Film Festival, eager to see the Hollywood premiere of *Public Enemies*. I dashed out of my medical office panting with excitement that I had made it to the big time. "LA just called. I am in!"

A whoop went up through the medical staff and Loraine nodded her approval. Unlike some who stifled others with societal expectations, she knew that you can be whatever you want to be. With her support, my childhood dreams had come to fruition and I could give myself the not so official title of movie doctor.

I completed my chart documentation that day in nirvana.

And yes, the red carpet was amazing.

I learned back then that quitting isn't always quitting. Sometimes it is starting over. By listening to my inner voice, quitting led me to my biggest win, a balanced life doing all the things I loved.

— Tanya Feke, MD —

Chapter
10

Get Outside in Nature

What You'll Find in This Chapter

I love the sense of community I feel when I spend time outside. It makes me very aware that I am but a tiny cog in the gigantic machinery of life on our planet. And every little thing — a fawn playing on the lawn, a chipmunk scurrying by, a bee pollinating a flower — is magical and awe-inspiring, because it is part of a dynamic interlocking natural world that somehow, despite its complexity, works. The great American writer Henry Miller summed it up when he said, "The moment one gives close attention to any thing, even a blade of grass, it becomes a mysterious, awesome, indescribably magnificent world in itself."

Listening to the hustle and bustle of nature puts everything in perspective, too. There are hundreds of species busily conducting their lives all around you. They couldn't care less about the silly things going on in your life because they spend every day hunting for food, raising their young, perpetuating their species, creating their own shelter, and avoiding predators.

Ann Morrow discovered the peace that comes from getting outside, as she tells us in her story, "The Trail to Myself." On the morning of her forty-fifth birthday, she stood at the bathroom mirror and realized that the woman looking back at her was angry, stressed, and unfit. That's when she decided to reclaim control of her life. She grabbed her coat and walked out the front door, even though it was a gray January day. And then she walked. By March, Ann looked different, and more importantly, she felt different. Walking led to a thirty-pound weight loss for Ann, and it set her back on the path to rediscovering her creative side, too.

Winter Desiree Prosapio tells us that she had never liked walking. But when she and her husband adopted a dog that had always lived outside, they had trouble housebreaking him. Winter determined that the best course of action was to walk little Archer frequently. It started with simple strolls down the block, but that puppy was so full of energy that before she knew it Winter had turned into a true walker. And so had Archer. She says, "If I try to skip the walk on any given morning, he looks at me like I've announced that all the bacon in the world has disappeared." And now Winter finds herself walking three miles in a day. She says, "Every now and then, I look at this little dog and think, *Who is walking who?*" Nevertheless, her story is titled "Walking Archer."

In JC Sullivan's story, "Shinrin-yoku Is Good for You," JC tells us that she never went hiking, even though she lived next door to one of the best hiking areas in Los Angeles. Finally, a friend forced her to go for a walk, and JC was hooked, enjoying all the health benefits of what the Japanese call shinrin-yoku, or "forest bathing."

Getting outside means freely moving our bodies, gaining the perspective of being a tiny life inside a much larger world, and breathing the same air as the ancient trees that have seen it all and will still be standing when we're gone. It's the most powerful tool I know to reset your heart and soul. In this chapter, you'll read a lot about the transformative effect of getting outside in nature no matter the season of the year or the season of your life.

91

Shinrin-yoku Is Good for You

Fresh air is as good for the mind as for the body.
Nature always seems trying to talk to us as if she
had some great secret to tell. And so she has.
~John Lubbock

live in Los Angeles, so you'd think I go to the beach all the time. I would if I could, but it can take an hour to get from my lovely, rent-controlled apartment to the closest beach… on a good day. Getting back home? Count on at least two. On the flip side, my place is nestled inland in Los Feliz, home to Griffith Park, which is known for its vistas and hiking and equestrian trails.

Did I take advantage of all those wonderful trails? Nope.

My friend Donna lives very close to the beach, which means that she lives far from me. We both talked about exercising more. And then talked some more. We really talked a good game, but neither of us got any closer to working out.

Being a true friend, Donna didn't point out that I had a gym in my building but failed to use it. My roommate Craig used it daily but even his shining example didn't move me. I went once when it was raining and did a few minutes on the treadmill; once when I locked myself out and needed him to lend me his key; and once when I needed him to take pictures of me (I'm an actor) using the equipment for a role as a gym rat. (That's why we call it acting.)

Donna decided to take action. She volunteered to come to my neighborhood and go for a hike with me. It is a very big deal in LA if someone offers to brave the traffic and come to your neighborhood, so this meant that I had to do it.

The day came, and she found parking easily. To any Angeleno, that is a sign. This time, instead of just talking, we talked and walked, and talked and walked, and talked and walked some more. As we climbed, we felt one with nature. We were rewarded with marvelous city views from the helipad (where they fill helicopters' water tanks during fires).

Donna joked she was probably going to wake up really sore the next day and curse me out. We laughed. The fabulous hike over, we ate fish tacos at my favorite Mexican restaurant nearby. We were proud of ourselves. We had exercised, eaten healthy and had a great time.

At the end of this wonderful afternoon, I told her that I was going to try to hike more often. "The park is so close by, and I don't use it."

"Start small," she suggested. "Try to go twice or maybe three times a week. Otherwise, if you make your goal too big, you won't achieve it and you'll feel worse, which is the exact opposite of self-care."

The next morning, I decided to go for another hike. And, again, it was lovely. Fast forward to a few months later: I now start every day with a hike. I do a small, forty-five-minute hike when my schedule is busy and a monster hike that takes about two-and-a-half hours when I have more time. I almost never bring my phone. It's like my walking meditation. I think about things I'd like to write about, learn lines and appreciate the amazing views.

> *I now start every day with a hike.*

I bump into many of the same people. Sometimes, I see film crews, dog walkers, families and couples. They're enjoying their day. The cyclists are amazing going up those inclines.

Now I'm truly addicted to hiking. When friends come to visit, I invite them to go with me. Many of them don't want to. I mention that no one has ever not enjoyed it, but if they still decline, I don't force the issue. Instead, I go without them. Several of my friends have even started hiking when they're back home. The frugal side of me can't help but point out that it's free.

Daily exercise improves one's life. Ask Jose. I met him hiking. He explained that he had a new workout plan to help him lose 100 pounds. I offered to send him encouraging texts. A few months later, we met for coffee. I would not have recognized him. He had lost sixty-five pounds! He said he has more energy, is more social, and now spends time exercising with his niece and nephew. What a great gift to give his loved ones.

After my monster hike today, I had the energy to sit down and write this piece. I'm calmer and can have an occasional dessert without worry. Turns out, without realizing it, I've been practicing Japanese shinrin-yoku or "forest bathing" (in the sense of soaking in the environment, not skinny-dipping), spending time in the woods, truly appreciating nature. Shinrin-yoku has been proven to have all kinds of health benefits: reducing stress, lowering heart rate and blood pressure, and boosting the immune system. In 1982, Japan even made it part of their national health plan. Because much of my hike goes through wooded areas, I truly believe my daily forest bathing, breathing in the beauty of nature, has made me more creative.

As my super-in-shape (even by L.A. standards) roommate Craig always points out, the secret is to find an activity you enjoy doing. I always thank Donna for her life-altering suggestion that we go hiking. As she listened to me rave about hiking, she vowed to take up her favorite sport again: swimming. Her exercise regimen now includes several trips to the pool every week. A simple hike between friends turned into better self-care for both of us. Who knows? Maybe I'll even start meeting Craig in the gym for a workout.

— JC Sullivan —

92

The Dream We Didn't Know We Had

*When I go out into the countryside and see the sun and
the green and everything flowering, I say to myself
"Yes indeed, all that belongs to me!"*
~Henri Rousseau

f someone had told me five years ago that I would be living happily ever after on a small farm in western Oklahoma, I would have adamantly denied the possibility. Back then, I was a confirmed city girl. I enjoyed the amenities of city life. Then my husband and I decided to move from our longtime home in the city. We looked at houses in several surrounding communities, but nothing suited our needs or our budget.

One day, while we were checking my mother's farm for her, I looked around, liked what I saw and asked my husband, "Why don't we build a house here on the farm?"

To my surprise, he said, "Yes!"

And so began a new and very different chapter in our life story.

From its earliest days, the farm has always been called the Home Place. My great-grandparents, grandparents, mother and uncle all called it home. I spent many happy childhood summers there doing farm chores that were more fun than work for a city girl. No matter my age or the stage of my life, I often returned to the Home Place for peace, quiet and sanity. When my sons were growing up, I would treat them to a day at the farm so they could experience a bit of country life. It was a nice place to visit, but I had no intention of living there.

When we started our new life on the farm, it was far from a magical retreat. It was rugged and unkempt. Cattle had roamed it for over forty years with evidence they had toured the outbuildings.

My husband and I set out to tame the land. We took down dead trees, bulldozed dilapidated outbuildings and planted vegetable and flower gardens and an orchard. We learned new skills as we worked and provided the locals with humorous moments as they answered our naïve questions. We built a home to welcome family and friends, to share the beauty and bounty of the land.

We soon realized the land had played a marvelous joke on us: it had changed and transformed us in our efforts to tame it. We lost weight and gained muscles.

We've learned to recognize and honor nature's cycles and timing instead of clocks, calendars, schedules and to-do lists. With only two clocks in the house, we enjoy the flow of days into nights. Our timeless life allows us to appreciate sunrises and sunsets — each a unique, spectacular event that canvas, camera and words only partially capture.

Living a simple life in the country has led us back to common sense and personal empowerment. We've learned to be creative and resourceful in solving problems. I often consider how my grandparents would handle a situation with fewer resources and conveniences than I have. The nearest large town is thirty minutes away, so we have to think and plan ahead instead of hopping in the car and "running" around the corner for something we forgot. We keep a pantry of staples, preserve much of our garden's abundance and share with family and friends.

In the quietness of the land, we hear and appreciate nature's music — birds, crickets, cicadas, frogs, coyotes, cattle and the ever-present Oklahoma wind. We also listen to the silence. In this silence, we allow the land to guide us to do what needs to be done — where to plant a flower or tree and how to share the blessings of the land with others.

> *In the quietness of the land, we hear and appreciate nature's music.*

Get Outside in Nature |

Nature entertains us with the antics of rabbits and raccoons, and a parade of possums, armadillos and an occasional snake. Coyotes saunter and deer leap across the fields. Migrating pelicans and geese serenade us along their seasonal journeys. Hawks soar in the big sky. Our TV is seldom on as we enjoy nature's big screen, with surround sound, instead.

Walking through the grasses, gazing at the century-old trees and wondering about all the changes and history they have witnessed are relaxing pastimes. My bare feet feel the pulse of the earth and connect me to God and the eternal. I walk down the same country road, noticing the same red anthills in the same places as in my childhood. Some things do not change.

While this picture is idyllic, I have to be truthful: caring for the land is a full-time job — but it's a joyful job. My ancestors left me a rich heritage — not the kind of wealth you can spend, invest or save, but a wealth of spirit, perseverance and love of the land. They taught me to "take care of the land, and the land will take care of you." That's our intention.

As we open our doors to family and friends, we want them to feel that they are at home in the piece of quiet that is the Home Place. Friends who questioned our sanity after our many years as city dwellers feel the magic of the peace and quiet and are reluctant to leave.

Life has brought me full circle to happy, busy retirement days on the land where I spent many happy summer days as a child. We're living the dream we didn't know we had.

—Linda E. Allen—

93

Tiny Sanctuary

I go to nature to be soothed and healed,
and to have my senses put in order.
~John Burroughs

stared at the trailhead knowing exactly what I wanted from my hike before I embarked. I wanted a beautiful challenge, the sort of hiking experience that was brutal on the muscles yet breathtaking in its beauty. I needed steep elevations winding through forested area so canopied by trees that it changed the light of the blazing summer sun. I needed a cold creek to temper the Texas heat, for the humidity to drape itself over me. I needed to sweat out the sadness, worry, stress-eating, secret crying, and sleepless nights that come with mothering a child who is on the autism spectrum.

"Why don't you take a long break for yourself and go on a real hike, like the Appalachian Trail or camp at Big Bend?" a friend asked me when I told her about my plan.

"Because that's not how motherhood works," I said.

I needed a quick dose of peace, a trail that could be hiked in the few hours my son spent in his new autism therapy clinic 16 miles up the road. It was less romantic than sleeping beneath the stars, but healing for both of us would have to be done in smaller increments.

It had been two years since I last hiked the River Place Nature Trail, but it remained my favorite in Austin, a city full of beautiful nature preserves. I considered hiking all of them on my son's therapy days, feeling productive by covering the most territory, but healing doesn't work that way. I needed to be nurtured by the familiar, to walk the same paths each time and get lost in the sort of meditative trance that comes with repetition. Only this trail, an oasis protected and maintained by volunteers from the surrounding neighborhood, would do. Perhaps the love the trail received from its caretakers would soothe me, too.

I knew we couldn't undo the autism, and there are so many beautiful things about his unusual mind that we wouldn't want to. His autism affords him a near-photographic memory, a love of math I cannot comprehend, and an ability to create art with advanced perspective. We do, however, want a life for him with fewer stresses or dangers caused by autism triggers and sensory overstimulation. Like all parents, we want our child to have a life filled with love, independence and self-created happiness.

I looked back down the street and said, "I love you," sending the words out over the wind to my boy on this important day. While he took his first steps toward a different life, I moved forward and took the first steps toward mine.

The first hike was brutal and beautiful. Accidentally, I took the longest part of the trail. It boasted the highest elevation change in the Austin area — 1,700 feet in just a few miles. I needed breaks, several of them. Despite the heat and my dangerously high heart rate from the climb, I felt relief by wading in a stream so clear and cold that I was certain it had been consecrated. I half-expected a vision of a saint to appear.

Instead, I saw a cardinal. It perched for a moment on a large rock facing me, its deep red color a complement to the rich greens that surrounded us. I looked up and saw its partner on a branch, less red but still beautiful. Cardinals are rather common in Austin, but the birds still felt like little guardians along the path, rooting me on as I persevered. They are said to symbolize wisdom and living life with confidence and grace. They were the sort of cheerleaders I needed.

As I approached the end of my hike, I noticed the smooth and heavy rocking chairs that awaited hikers at the end of their journeys. I drank my last drops of water as I allowed the heavy motion of the rocking chairs to soothe my tired body. A breeze picked up from the nearby pond, cooling me off as I rocked back and forth, the trail nurturing me to the very end. Then I took a deep breath and went to pick up my son.

He looked forward to his therapy sessions each week, evolving in a way that gave him visible confidence and happiness. My slivers of time in this tiny sanctuary did the same for me. It wasn't a grandiose journey, but it was ours. At the end of each day, my boy ran toward me, undeterred by my sweat and disheveled hair, with smiles and hugs and some new project to show me. I always waited with my arms open, ready to embrace him with love, joy and the newfound sensation of hope.

— Tanya Estes —

94

Think Like a Dog

*Those who find beauty in all of nature will find
themselves at one with the secrets of life itself.*
~L. Wolfe Gilbert

I was excited to take my rescue Beagle to the river the other day, as it's within walking distance of our new home. Having spent her first six years in a cage, Georgie had never seen a body of water, and I wanted to get there before sunset to watch her experience it.

I was growing increasingly impatient about all the stops her little Beagle nose required. She inspected the grass, dirt, and trees, and licked whatever was stuck to the road. These were all new discoveries for her, and she took her time studying them.

When I accepted that it was fruitless to hurry her along, I whipped out my cell phone and began texting. I thought that I needed something to do while Georgie was slowing us down.

Then, for some reason, I heard the cicadas, and I remembered that the sound of cicadas is my favorite sound in the world. That awakened something buried within me that yearned for the simple pleasures that had been replaced by technology.

I made a conscious decision to be present, and to enjoy the journey to the river, just like Georgie. The journey was just as wonderful as the final destination would be, and it took that little Beagle to remind me.

Now, I admired the intricacy of the flowers and the wonder of the winding ivy on our path. I felt the occasional warm raindrop on my skin from a gray sky threatening to burst at any moment. I smelled the asphalt, the grass and the flowers, and the dirt and the air. I treasured each one equally, as if discovering them for the first time. I took note of the colors everywhere that people would claim I exaggerated if I were to paint them on canvas.

I tripped over my feet and stumbled in some holes, and I was damp with sweat and rain. A few mosquitoes circled my head and landed on my sticky arms. As we neared our destination, I realized something even more important: It didn't matter if we even reached the river. Why must there always be a destination?

Georgie had no idea that we had a destination. She was present for the journey, and she savored every bit of that sweet experience. There was no race and no finish line.

Now I'm not sure who rescued whom.

— Lauren Mosher —

95

The Trail to Myself

*You can't change who you are, but you can change
what you have in your head, you can refresh what
you're thinking about, you can put some
fresh air in your brain.*
~Ernesto Bertarelli

On the morning of my 45th birthday, I stood at the bathroom mirror and stared at a reflection that startled me. "You have a problem," I said to the woman glaring back at me. Resentment and fear showed in her eyes. She was angry with me. And I was disappointed in her.

The past decade had been a whirlwind of work, travel and staggering stress. I had evolved into someone I didn't like very much and allowed myself to veer off-track; it felt like I was living someone else's life. The power to my creative outlets had been shut off and I had stopped writing.

Privately, I was fighting a battle against brain fog and depression. And I feared I'd never be able to end my love/hate relationship with alcohol.

Physically, I was just as broken. An unhealthy lifestyle had padded my body with excess pounds. My knees ached, my back hurt, and I was plagued with insomnia. Mornings were like a bad dream and required large doses of coffee and ibuprofen, an attempt to take the edge off the pulsing headache that resulted from the glasses of wine I'd consumed the night before.

I didn't know myself anymore. Oh, how I missed that adventurous, creative girl who had a passion for words and art and loved the outdoors. I longed to get in touch with her again.

That encounter in the mirror, followed by an argument with my husband, were the push I needed to reclaim control of my life. My husband told me I'd probably feel better if I'd "just get out of the damn house once in a while." So, I did. The argument ended when I grabbed my coat and walked out the front door.

Outside, I stared into the gray January sky. Then, without thinking, I put one foot in front of the other and followed the pavement. I was a mile from home when I realized I hadn't even thought about the argument. The world around me came into focus, and a tiny spark of hope fired in my brain. As I turned toward home, I considered the possibility of making a new start — where pursuing creativity seemed the most logical solution to my troubles.

That first mile began a chain reaction of events that would reshape me — literally — and give me renewed purpose. I enrolled in a program to help me stop drinking, and then purchased a fitness tracker and a new pair of sneakers. It was the beginning of a journey that would eventually lead me to someone I'd been dying to meet — me.

By March, there was a noticeable difference in my outward appearance, but the real changes were happening on the inside. As the weeks passed, I transitioned from sidewalks to walking paths to narrow, winding mountain trails. And by summer, my new addiction was fresh air and altitude.

Something powerful happened on those rocky forest trails. There was shift. My brain started functioning at a higher frequency — as if someone had flipped a switch and turned on the creative energy. The inner critic fell silent, as I let my thoughts wander and explore, the same way I let my eyes explore the landscape. Not only did those steps and miles help me decompress, but they invited a world of new stories and ideas to unfold.

> *Something powerful happened on those rocky forest trails.*

My senses came to life as I learned how to use meditation and mindfulness. As I hiked, I focused on the rhythmic *crunch, crunch, crunch* of the trail under my shoes and the whisper of wind through the pines. I noticed everything. Tiny ants clung to blades of grass, and chattering birds scolded me from the branches overhead. I breathed in the rich scent of loamy earth on north-facing hillsides, where the sun warmed my face, and cool, damp air caressed my arms. I stopped often to take it all in — to breathe, whisper a few words of gratitude, and capture the experience with my camera.

All this led to a physical transformation that resulted in more than 30 pounds of weight loss and eliminated a long list of aches and pains. It also led to a spiritual transformation, where I gave myself permission to stop ignoring my calling. That small, creative voice that used to hide behind excuses was now running down the trail in front of me, waving and shouting, "Come on, follow me!"

The trail saved my life. It made me sane. Made me strong. And helped me find myself again.

What started as a simple "time out" on a cold, winter afternoon led me to the place I was meant to be — which, most days, is spent in front of a computer screen, crafting stories and editing images I hope someone, somewhere will enjoy. But I'm always within calling distance of a trail — that place I go to often to rediscover my joy and reconnect with a world of age-old miracles and new ideas.

— Ann Morrow —

96

The Discipline of Doing Nothing

You cannot pour from an empty cup.
~Author Unknown

can't think of any benefits of this pandemic, but if there was one, it might be how it forced me to slow down. Eventually, I will return to the rat race with all its demands and deadlines. But I hope I never forget the one lesson I learned: to consciously "insert pauses" into my day by developing the discipline of doing nothing.

Many years ago, Coca-Cola ran a brilliant advertising campaign about "The Pause That Refreshes." They were on to something. Pauses refresh us because they allow us to stop, refocus, and rest.

The older I get, the more I've intentionally inserted pauses into my day. Some pauses are only a few minutes long; others are hours. It may be a walk to a faraway copier at work instead of the one in my department. Or driving an alternate route home. Or a day at the beach. The idea is to relax, rejuvenate, and rest by diverting my thoughts from what stresses me to what refreshes me.

Rest replenishes us. And I rest best by, well, doing nothing. I recently read a little book by Sandy Gingras called *How to Live at the Beach*. I love this lighthearted, five-minute read. It's a metaphor that conjures up images of the mentality we have when we're at the beach — and why we need to transport this beach mentality to our non-beach lives.

My son, his wife, and my grandson live near the beach in Santa Barbara, California. Next to Hawaii, it's one of the most beautiful places in the United States. When I head to the ocean with them, I'm awed by the benefits of the beach. It invites us to a state of serenity and calls us to a life of simplicity.

The beach near their home is where I naturally reduce speed and forget about the complexity of the world. The beach may be the only place where I can return to my child-like self by building sandcastles with my grandson or sitting in the surf and letting the waves massage me or float me like a piece of driftwood.

For me, a day at the beach epitomizes the discipline of doing nothing. It's a pause. A prototype of a simpler life. I'm learning how to bring a beach mentality, and all its benefits, back home with me. A beach mentality slows me down, allows me to ponder only what's in front of me, diffuses stress, and allows me to fully appreciate what surrounds me in my nine-to-five world.

During this time of "country closure" (and doing nothing), I've noticed what I typically fail to notice, some of which is in my own back yard: the graceful arc of a hawk; the song of the cardinal, red-winged blackbird, blue jay, robin, or killdeer; the power and precision of the red-headed woodpecker; the wobbly legs of a newborn fawn; the majesty of a doe up close; and the artistic curl of an ocean wave just before it breaks at the shore. Ironically, I notice more when I "invest the time" to do nothing. Who says doing nothing is boring? Doing nothing calms, recalibrates, enlightens, and refuels me.

I've realized that by pausing more, I've seen more, listened more, heard more, and felt more. Yet, pausing is a discipline all its own. It's much more difficult to slow down than speed up.

By developing the discipline of doing nothing, I've learned that a life of clarity, simplicity, and rest awaits.

It's like a day at the beach.

—James C. Magruder—

97

To Kingdom Come

*Running made me feel like a bird let
out of a cage, I loved it that much.*
~Priscilla Welch

The Back Forty, I called it. I claimed it as mine.

Actually, the underdeveloped, underused property was part of the city's parklands and skirted the inside shoreline of the lake that belonged to the Greeley Irrigation Ditch Company. There wasn't even a discernible footpath when I first discovered it nearly three decades ago, but that didn't deter me. I made it my own.

Dodging tobacco-spitting grasshoppers, I pioneered the course and tugged a wagonload of toddlers towards the open arms of spreading cottonwoods and the Promised Land: a damp, deserted beach. Over time, the red Radio Flyer, with its jumble of spindly legs and flapping ponytails, flattened the thigh-high weeds and rutted a trail.

We romped along the lake, the kids and I, flapping our arms like the Canada geese that took umbrage and frantic flight at our intrusion. We waded the shallows; we wandered the shore; we built tea-party castles in the coarse sand. The only running I did was to chase and corral kids for the tiresome trek home.

But civilization encroached in the Back Forty at the same rate as the burgeoning population along Colorado's Front Range. Right before our eyes, a playground sprouted. A soccer field seeded. A sculpture park blossomed. And tendrils of a newly-poured concrete sidewalk wound through it all.

Although school now claimed all four of my children, I still heeded the siren call of the trail, more tempting than ever. I began walking two miles, every day, no matter what.

I walked whenever I could comfortably escape the demanding schedule of an active family. Sometimes, dewy dawn greeted me. On other days, falling dusk settled around my shoulders. The solitary ramblings nourished me and my pace quickened along with my enthusiasm.

I discovered a kingdom nestled against the parapets of the pristine Rockies, and I reigned as queen. I reveled in a bucolic realm of flowering crabapples, fragrant Russian olives, and lush lilacs. I nodded at the regal blue heron standing sentinel on a jutting boulder at the edge of the lake and giggled at court jesters — ebony coots sluicing the shoals, as endearing as wind-up toys. I measured the seasons and the years by comical goslings stumbling up rocky outcroppings, the annual roil of carp spawning in the spillway, and yawning ice holes drilled by hopeful fishermen.

Year after year, my speed-walking excursions kept me on track and in shape. Meanwhile, my kids raced out the door and on to college. Then, with an abruptness that shook me to my core, everything came to a halt.

My oldest child, a newly-minted college graduate, was critically injured by a drunk driver and on life support. Dazed, I sped to his side. I traded the wonders of the walking trail for the terrors of a trauma unit.

Distrustful of the rickety elevator system in Los Angeles' decrepit yet imposing County Hospital, I breached the battlements of dank stairwells to huff nine flights up — and counted each step that brought me closer to my comatose son. Day after day. Week after week. Then, one glorious day, I was sprinting up them to greet his re-entry to awareness.

A few months later, we returned home, my son and I, to face rehab and a hopeful future. Ready for some time alone, I slipped into my cross trainers and headed to the familiarity and comfort of the foot trail.

My own awareness sharpened in new appreciation. Had the lake always been so blue? The squirrels so frisky? The cottonwoods so towering? My steps quickened in eagerness — so quick, in fact, that

I found myself jogging.

Loping.

Running.

Toned by the hospital stairwells and with a newfound leanness honed from stress, my body insisted on more than my old walking pace. More speed. A longer stride. A steady gait.

Flushed with exhilaration, I emptied my mind of the worries I'd accrued over the past several months. I freed myself from the dungeon of despair to focus on my breathing. I listened to my heartbeat. I felt my hamstrings stretch and the muscles in my calves elongate.

My arms pumped in automatic rhythm. A rhythm sure and even. A rhythm that consumed all thought and demanded a delightful focus. A rhythm that belonged only to me.

And so it began. An instant love of running.

Oh, a kernel of recognition rankled: I knew I wasn't cut from the same cloth as the marathoners who clogged the streets at the annual Lake-to-Lake event. I couldn't compete with the high school team that pounded the pavement to shape up for track meets. Even so, I ran. A middle-aged housewife, legs pumping, pulse pounding, sweat beading my brow — having the time of my life. I discovered a new, joyous pace. I reveled in the novelty. I understood the possibilities and delighted in the potential.

I ran.

I ran towards a hopeful future and the promising kingdom that beckoned.

— Carol McAdoo Rehme —

98

The Birds and the Bees

Adopt the pace of nature. Her secret is patience.
~Ralph Waldo Emerson

T he timer was set for ten minutes. I sat down on a soft pillow and crossed my legs with hands resting on my knees, palms up, eyes closed. "Okay, time to center myself, inhale, exhale. Relax... Re-lax... RELAX!"

I cracked an eye to check the timer. Thirty seconds had passed. Oh boy, this "me time" was going to be difficult!

As a working mother, my years passed in a blur of family-oriented activity without time for relaxing. When the kids were finally out of the nest and I was able to retire from my full-time career, I thought, *Now I can take some time for ME!*

Of course, as a lifelong list maker, I did my research. There were many possibilities. There were relaxation activities like yoga, meditation, getting pampered at a spa, exercise, socializing... I was determined to find the one thing that truly filled my soul. And so began my not-so-smooth journey to finding myself.

Meditation was the first to come and go. I never fully understood how to shut my mind off for any length of time. I always felt like I was just waiting for it to end.

Next, I tried "Teatime as Me Time." At first, I was very enthusiastic about this dainty endeavor. I envisioned sitting across from a dear friend, sipping from delicate cups and nibbling tiny sandwiches, but that is as far as it ever went. I have the fancy tea set (never used) and a pantry shelf full of tea packages that I will never consume. (I prefer the electric jolt of coffee in the morning.)

The pampering stuff isn't for me either. I like being productive. Sitting around feeling special doesn't feel special to me. So, I immediately scratched the spa ideas off my list.

Exercise is a highly recommended me-time activity. I liked to exercise, so why not double up my workouts and plan some exciting fitness goals? But after a week or so of training, exercise time felt more like torture time.

Many other me-time experiments left me wanting less of them, not more. I felt like a failure at this relaxation thing, especially when I found myself procrastinating to begin a me-time routine. I would chastise myself for "wasting" precious hours daydreaming on my front porch with my two dogs, watching the big, fuzzy bumblebees buzz about my garden. In those moments, time stood still. I could while away the morning watching the bugs, birds, and critters do their thing. I would delight in the seasons — Mother Nature birthing and dying in her perennial cycle.

A profound perspective is gained when noticing the small details of this miraculous world. My self-absorbed human concerns were really nothing in the grand scale of things. Taking the focus off myself was a relief. I realized that all the shoulda-woulda-couldas of living my best life placed more expectations on me, my relaxation and my performance. Ironically, I discovered that I truly desired less emphasis on *me* altogether.

> *My self-absorbed human concerns were really nothing in the grand scale of things.*

Maybe the experts had this me-time thing all wrong, and it had little to do with "me" or "time" as I was defining it. Perhaps we are too concerned with how we spend our time instead of enjoying the nothing-ness of simply being. Instead of viewing it as a void, a hesitation between activities, we can shift our consciousness into embracing timelessness. Witnessing simple, humble moments of nature re-centered my soul better than anything else. Maybe a better version of "me time" is simply "be time"... or, better yet, "bee time!"

I just watched a young robin sunning its outstretched wings in the afternoon warmth. He closed his eyes as if to fully appreciate the moment, and I wondered if he was taking a little me time for himself. I watched until he flew away, and I am not sure how much time transpired. It could have been a minute or ten, but I enjoyed every second of it. However, I wonder, "Does it count as me time when I watch a bird enjoying his?"

I think back to all those busy years when I did not take a moment to appreciate our intricate natural world. Even when I rushed to make the 5:00 yoga class, to learn how to stretch and ground myself, the Earth's bounty was dancing outside the door. Now, I realize that me time is highly overrated if it makes me feel more pressure to fit one more thing into my schedule, especially if it takes away from the time I would have to simply… be.

—Kat Gottlieb—

99

Trail of Hope

The story ends up being a journey of self-discovery.
~Elijah Wood

My future glistened in the distance like a desert oasis. After twenty-two years raising three children, I was about to be introduced to an unfamiliar concept: the empty nest. Apparently, this was now my time. My time to dive into new experiences, develop new hobbies, and explore the world. It was time to reconnect with my husband and give my writing career a fresh jolt of energy. Why, then, was I not excited?

My oldest child had just begun life on her own; the other two were attending college 1,100 miles away. I missed them all terribly. My husband and I had sold our home and moved to a neighboring state for a job opportunity. Since we were living in temporary housing, I hadn't yet met neighbors or made new friends, and most of my colleagues were only accessible through an Internet connection. I began to feel isolated. I wasn't quite sure how to move forward.

"Why don't we go for a walk?" my husband suggested.

When I discovered a trail only a short drive from our apartment, I was thrilled. My husband and I began to use it regularly.

The paved trail meandered along a river lined with shrubs and towering trees. Mallard ducks lazed on the riverbanks. Robins perched in the treetops. Canada geese flew overhead. Often, a blue heron stood motionless on a rock in the center of the river. At dusk, small rabbits hopped across the pathway, then skittered into the brush.

One evening, a beaver diligently collected sticks, then disappeared with them downstream. These small snippets of nature provided me with a peaceful distraction, but only slightly lifted me out of my malaise.

Still, I continued to walk the path.

The trail was filled with fellow walkers, joggers, and bikers at all times of day.

"On your left," the bikers would shout as they zipped by us and continued up the trail. Some were single riders. Some rode in groups. Some toted children in attached seats or hauled them behind in trailers. They were young and old. They were thin and not so thin. On every walk, I spotted something new: unicycles, tandem bicycles, adult-sized tricycles.

One Saturday, I was astonished to see a homemade, automated race car speeding down the trail, and on another, a man with a prosthetic right leg sailing by me effortlessly.

I'd come home after a walk feeling vaguely different than when I left. Was it simply the fresh air and bright sunshine? Or was it the heart-pumping, endorphin-releasing exercise? I had a hunch it was something else entirely. But I didn't know what.

I began to take a longer look at my fellow trail users. A dad and two sons riding their scooters. A young husband and wife teaching their daughter how to ride her first two-wheeler. Couples, young and old, holding hands, chatting as they walked. Generations of families taking evening strolls together. Joggers, huffing and panting, as they raced toward that sixth, seventh, eighth mile. A woman doing Tai Chi on a platform next to the water. Not to mention the dogs. A plethora of breeds, sizes, and temperaments all took advantage of the trail.

These were just ordinary people doing the same thing I was doing: exercising and spending time with loved ones. That's what I thought. But I'd return home with a smile on my face, my excursion replenishing something I seemed to have lost. How could something so simple, so uncomplicated, alter my outlook on life?

I couldn't seem to get enough, so I returned to the trail again and again. Sometimes with my husband; sometimes alone.

As I walked, I'd peer into faces and listen for snippets of conversation, my eyes hidden behind my sunglasses. These people spoke French, Russian, Hindi, and numerous other languages I couldn't understand. They represented all races and cultures, and I became fascinated with the lives of these strangers: who they were, where they lived, how they were related. Most of all, I thought about their stories. Surely they had stories. What challenges did they face? Did any of them feel lost and empty? How were they moving forward?

One cloudy morning, I hiked up the trail, determined to find answers, or at the very least, inspiration. After thirty minutes, I turned to head back the way I had come, slightly disappointed that the trail held very little for me that day. Until I saw her. An elderly, gray-haired woman clasping the handles of her walker. She sprinted by me in the opposite direction like a marathon runner. I turned around to catch another glimpse of this one-woman wonder. She was definitely moving forward. She wasn't letting anything hold her back. Certainly not her age.

That's when it hit me. Nobody was.

Not the man with the prosthetic leg. Not the toddler taking his first steps. Not the two young boys casting their fishing lines into the river after the sun had already disappeared. Not even the group of four new mothers, tired though they may have been, standing in front of their strollers, counting aloud to their babies' delight. Everyone seemed to be rushing headlong into life. Rushing with optimism, clarity, and determinedness.

My fellow trail users were pushing past whatever challenges they were experiencing. Why, then, was I not doing the same? My nest may have been empty, but it didn't have to be joyless.

As I walked toward the car, remembering the elderly woman's energy and enthusiasm, I made a decision. I would rush home and fill my empty nest with abundance. Like the strangers-turned-allies on the trail, I wouldn't let anything hold me back. I was ready for the glittery future that stretched before me.

— Annette Gulati —

100

The Healing Garden

The glory of gardening: hands in the dirt, head in the sun,
heart with nature. To nurture a garden is to feed
not just the body, but the soul.
~Alfred Austin

When my husband Randy died in late fall, deciding what to do with his garden was way down on the list of necessary tasks. During the first few months, I cried with our daughters, ordered death certificates, planned a memorial, cried with my family, celebrated a quiet Thanksgiving, panicked over not having bought Christmas presents, cried with my friends, and diligently chipped away at stacks of paperwork.

As the calendar turned to a new year, the often rainy days and long nights compounded my grief. I found myself exhausted at the end of February, my mental and physical reserves depleted.

Then the daffodils bloomed.

Years before, Randy had planted dozens of these lemon-yellow bursts of color in strategic places around our yard. To him, they served as beacons of hope, a promise that light and warmth would soon replace cold and dark. Looking at those daffodils, I thought about how Randy had considered our garden a living work of art, strategically choosing plants so we'd see new blooms every month.

Then I noticed all the weeds. I needed to get to work.

At first, I felt overwhelmed. Randy's illness had lasted a couple of years, a time when he didn't have energy for yardwork the way he had before. The neglect showed.

Invasive species had taken root and spread. Shrubbery had gotten leggy. Weeds were sprouting everywhere. My daughters suggested I hire a service to clean everything up. But I wanted to do the work myself. In some way, I *needed* to do the work myself.

Randy had always found that working in the garden was a pleasure, an antidote to his structured corporate life. Many days he came home from work, changed into old clothes, and headed out the door to mow or prune or just "piddle around," as I called it. No matter how cold or wet it was, the fresh air and physical activity energized him.

I discovered that working outside helped me feel close to him, and I often asked him questions I wished he could answer: How much fertilizer should I use on the roses? Where do I clip the hydrangeas to get the same beautiful, huge flowers you did? Are these new shoots weeds or something we want to keep?

At times, I felt crushed by it all, certain my efforts could never be good enough. Somehow, every time I reached a low, the outdoors responded to lift my spirits. For several days, an orange dragonfly followed me around the yard as I worked, reminding me of Randy and his orange jacket. The buzz from honeybees and bumblebees gorging on pollen created a comforting thrum in my ears. Song sparrows trilled a mating call, squirrels chittered from high in the maples, and gentle breezes carried the scent of dirt teeming with earthworms and organisms too small to see. The work was quiet and comforting.

Spring turned to summer, and as the days grew warmer and lighter, my list of urgent garden chores got shorter. The vegetables were planted, the strawberries harvested, the weeds held at bay. I started to relax on the back deck without scanning the yard for areas needing attention. It felt good, this sense of accomplishment.

Yet, a touch of the bittersweet tinged my enjoyment. Working in the yard kept my hands busy and my mind focused on the task in front of me. Relaxing left me time to dwell on my loss. I still had questions for Randy, but now they turned more wistful: *Can you see how I've tended your garden? Do you know I picked the first ripened figs from the tree you planted? Have you noticed our prolific blueberry crop?*

Are you with me still?

As the weeks passed, though, I felt the seeds of healing begin to take root in my heart. My thoughts of Randy focused less on the sadness of his last months and my life without him, and more on the happy years of our early courtship and marriage, and the decades we raised our daughters. I noticed that I laughed more, cut flowers to bring inside, and paused after plucking a ripe tomato from the vine, breathing deeply of its warmth and grassy scent.

When neighbors and friends complimented the beauty in our yard, saying, "Randy would be so proud," I'd reply, "Yes, I believe he would." He always celebrated my success, always cheered the loudest when I worked hard to achieve something. Looking over his former domain, I felt gratified that my efforts this time helped preserve what he created and helped carry on the work he did before me.

When summer became fall and nearly a year separated me from Randy's passing, I turned my attention to "putting the garden to bed," as he used to say. It's necessary work, taking out the withered tomato vines, raking the leaves from the lawn, teasing sunflower seeds from spent flowers and leaving them for the squirrels to eat. But while a fall and winter garden may seem fallow, I now know it holds plenty of life. The lush abundance of spring and summer may be gone, but under the leaf piles and deep in the soil and down to the roots of every living thing rest the kernels of what is needed to emerge from a quiet repose, ready to thrive again.

— Cindy Hudson —

Walking Archer

Walk like a dog; it will lead you in the right direction.
~Author Unknown

'd never been one for walking. I'm married to a guy who loves to run, and he would always ask me if I'd take a walk with him. My response was always "I have a car" — until I became the caretaker of an eleven-pound furry ball of relentless enthusiasm.

I say "caretaker" because one can't really *own* a creature that has this much enthusiasm. Our latest addition, Archer, is a Terrier who believes with all his being that every day is AWESOME. Every. Single. Day.

And the most AWESOME thing is going for a walk.

Every. Single. Day.

It started when we were having trouble with housebreaking. I have a theory that before he got to the shelter, and during his formative years, Archer lived in a back yard. This meant he grew up with the philosophy that the whole world was his to mark with a seemingly endless supply of yellow fluid.

Since none of our usual housebreaking methods were working, I thought I'd try walking Archer in the morning to give him an opportunity to get it all out of his system. The goal was to let him mark up the whole neighborhood to satisfy that urge to shout to every other dog in the universe that ARCHER WAS HERE.

It started slowly, just a walk down the block. The entire time Archer would prance with joy from mailbox to clump of weeds like I had just set loose a person on a carb-free diet in a room full of French fries. Periodically, a particular bush would require the big-dog treatment: the extra step of pawing at the ground in long, proud strokes to show just how large a dog had marked that particular spot.

Then, after a week, I started to get a little organized. My walk progressed farther down the block. My husband asked me how far I was walking, so I downloaded an app for my phone to track it.

It's been three months of walking, and Archer is fully housebroken. But if I try to skip the walk on any given morning, he looks at me like I've announced that all the bacon in the world has disappeared.

Last Sunday, we walked three miles — this from a woman with a perfectly functioning car.

I'll admit it is nice to walk, and it's fun to see Archer practically leap into his orange walking harness. I even like seeing the bar graph on the app showing how much farther I walk every month.

But every now and then, I look at this little dog and think, *Who is walking who?*

— Winter Desiree Prosapio —

Meet Our Contributors

We are pleased to introduce you to the writers of the stories in this collection. Here are their bios at the time their stories were first published by us.

A graduate of the University of Maryland at College Park, **Tonya Abari** is a teacher turned freelance editor and writer. To supplement multi-passionate endeavors, she has also worked as a web moderator, Zumba instructor, and traveling set teacher. She enjoys reading and traveling with her husband and exuberant toddler.
Chicken Soup for the Soul: The Empowered Woman (2018)

Linda E. Allen is enjoying living happily ever after on the prairie of western Oklahoma. She writes about her family, pets and gardens, and volunteers her teaching experience to various groups. E-mail her at lindaeallen@pldi.net.
Chicken Soup for the Soul: Time to Thrive (2015)

Kathleen M. Basi is the quintessential jack-of-all trades writer: composer-songwriter, columnist, feature writer, essayist, novelist, and author of three short nonfiction books for families. In her "spare" time, Kate juggles disability advocacy, directing a church choir, and turning her four kids into foodies.
Chicken Soup for the Soul: The Power of Gratitude (2016)

Nancy Beach received her Bachelor of Science in Bible, with honors, and is working on a Master of Arts in counseling. She has been married

for twenty-six years and has two grown children. Nancy enjoys reading, sunsets, and sand between her toes. She writes devotionals and inspirational fiction. Learn more at www.filledtoempty.com.
Chicken Soup for the Soul: The Forgiveness Fix (2019)

Brenda Beattie is a retired letter carrier and chaplain. She writes for *The Mountaineer* and her church's devotional. She has published two books: *Finding Sacred Ground in the Daily Grind* and *The Case of the Missing Letter*. She's retired and living the dream in Florida. E-mail her at 1955beachbabe@gmail.com.
Chicken Soup for the Soul: Making Me Time (2021)

John Morris Benson graduated high school in Alexandria, MN, and spent nearly ten years in the Army. While teaching in Kelso, WA, he earned his M.S. degree. He authored *An Odyssey of Illusions* in 2012 and *Nescient Decoy* in 2018. He and his wife of nearly sixty years live in Vancouver, WA.
Chicken Soup for the Soul: The Best Advice I Ever Heard (2018)

Bonnie L. Beuth received her Bachelor of Science degree, with honors, in Computer Information Systems. She works in the legal industry as an Information Systems Trainer and Chair of an international nonprofit. Bonnie enjoys time at the beach with her two dogs, reading and writing short stories.
Chicken Soup for the Soul: Time to Thrive (2015)

Susan Boltz is a retired medical lab technician and basic logic assistant. She stays young by teaching Sunday school for high school students and baking muffins. Living in Cuyahoga Falls with her husband, writing and walking keep her busy.
Chicken Soup for the Soul: The Power of Gratitude (2016)

John P. Buentello is an author who has published essays, fiction, poetry and nonfiction for adults and children. He is the co-author of the novel *Reproduction Rights* and the short story collections *Binary Tales* and

The Night Rose of the Mountain. E-mail him at jakkhakk@yahoo.com.
Chicken Soup for the Soul: The Joy of Less (2016)

Sally Willard Burbank received her medical degree from the University of Vermont. She is a practicing internist. She is married and the mother of two college students. Sally enjoys writing, reading, gardening, and bicycling. To read other stories by Sally, visit her blog at patientswewillneverforget.wordpress.com.
Chicken Soup for the Soul: The Power of Positive (2012)

Jill Burns lives in the mountains of West Virginia with her wonderful family. She's a retired piano teacher and performer. She enjoys writing, music, gardening, nature, and spending time with her grandchildren.
Chicken Soup for the Soul: Time to Thrive (2015)

Kristine Byron retired from Tupperware Home Parties. Now she spends her time traveling with her husband and enjoying time with family and friends.
Chicken Soup for the Soul: Making Me Time (2021)

Brenda Cathcart-Kloke is a retired school district administrative assistant in Thornton, CO. She enjoys spending time with her family, oil painting, reading, and writing short inspirational stories.
Chicken Soup for the Soul: The Joy of Less (2016)

M. Scott Coffman lives in Central Illinois with his wife, daughter, dog, and two cats. He writes to fend off middle-age decrepitude and plays the piano for as long as his arthritis will allow. This is his fourth story published in the *Chicken Soup for the Soul* series.
Chicken Soup for the Soul: Think Positive, Live Happy (2019)

Allison Hermann Craigie earned her B.S. degree in Journalism from the University of Maryland. She credits her two children, Sam and Jillian, with helping her plan these parties and most importantly as the two people for whom she will always be grateful. Allison lives in

Florida and loves hockey, concerts, tennis, laughing and life.
Chicken Soup for the Soul: The Power of Gratitude (2016)

Barbara Davey is an adjunct professor at Caldwell University where she teaches the process of writing to undergraduate students. She is a graduate of Seton Hall University where she received her bachelor's and master's degrees in English and journalism. A yoga enthusiast, she and her husband live in Verona, NJ.
Chicken Soup for the Soul: Making Me Time (2021)

Laurie Davies is a twenty-five-year journalist and marketing professional whose passion is to inspire readers to see that their best days are ahead. When she's not writing for the corporate world, she blogs (and can be reached) at lauriedavies.life. She lives in Mesa, AZ with her husband, son and two very spoiled Puggles.
Chicken Soup for the Soul: The Best Advice I Ever Heard (2018)

A Cleveland native, **Joan Donnelly-Emery** graduated from Syracuse University with a musical theatre degree, then performed regionally and in national tours, even at various theme park shows in Orlando, FL. She now enjoys a quiet life with husband Alan in Franklin, TN, gardening and screaming for her beloved Cleveland Browns.
Chicken Soup for the Soul: Tough Times Won't Last But Tough People Will (2021)

Drema Sizemore Drudge received her Bachelor of Arts from Manchester College in 2008. She works for the Learn More Center. Drema is a graduate student in Spalding University's MFA program. She is working on her first novel. Drema is married to Barry and is the mother of two, Mia and Zack.
Chicken Soup for the Soul: Count Your Blessings (2009)

Tanya Estes spent most of her career as a librarian and bookseller. Now she is a writer who delights in experiencing her son's enchanted world each time he says "Fee Fi Fo Fum" while climbing a tree. You

can find her little family hiking through the woods of central Texas.
Chicken Soup for the Soul: Running for Good (2019)

Trisha Faye is happiest when she writes about life, now and then. She relishes honoring the memories of people of the past in her *Vintage Daze* stories. The only dilemma she faces is fighting a houseful of rescue cats for use of the keyboard.
Chicken Soup for the Soul: Be You (2021)
Chicken Soup for the Soul: The Power of Gratitude (2016)

Tanya Feke, MD is a board certified family physician and patient advocate. Her book *Medicare Essentials: A Physician Insider Explains the Fine Print* is a bestseller on Amazon. She is also a film critic for *Record Journal* and runs a health and entertainment website at www.diagnosislife.com. She enjoys time with her family.
Chicken Soup for the Soul: Reboot Your Life (2014)

Lisa Fowler lives in the Blue Ridge Mountains of Western North Carolina with her goofy American Bulldog, Hazel, and her loyal Pit Bull, Abby. Her writing interests are concentrated on middle-grade novels and early chapter books. When not penning stories, Lisa enjoys playing trumpet, reading, and flower gardening.
Chicken Soup for the Soul: Volunteering & Giving Back (2015)

Betsy Franz is an award-winning writer and photographer specializing in nature, wildlife, the environment, and human relationships. Her articles and photos reflecting the wonders of life have been published in numerous books and magazines. She lives in Florida with her husband Tom. Learn more at www.naturesdetails.net.
Chicken Soup for the Soul: Find Your Inner Strength (2014)

Victoria Otto Franzese has degrees from Smith College and New York University. She owned, operated, and wrote for an online travel guide for fifteen years before selling it to a major media outlet. Now she writes about a variety of topics and all of her travel is for fun. She lives

in New York City with her husband, two sons, and a Goldendoodle named Jenkins.
Chicken Soup for the Soul: The Power of Yes! (2018)

Jody Fuller was born and raised in Opelika, AL. He is a comedian, speaker, writer, and soldier with three tours of duty in Iraq. He currently holds the rank of Captain in the Alabama National Guard. Jody is also a lifetime stutterer. E-mail him at jody@jodyfuller.com.
Chicken Soup for the Soul: From Lemons to Lemonade (2013)

M. Elizabeth Gage, with her husband of thirty-five years, makes her home in the Deep South. On most days she can be located outdoors, working in her gardens. When the weather refuses to cooperate, she whiles away the day with her old friends (Chopin and Schumann) at the piano.
Chicken Soup for the Soul: Age Is Just a Number (2020)

Amber Garza lives in Folsom, CA with her husband Andrew and her children Eli and Kayleen. She writes Christian fiction and hopes one day to fulfill her dreams of publication. She works as the Administrative Assistant to Outreach at Lakeside Church.
Chicken Soup for the Soul: Tough Times, Tough People (2009)

Jennifer Kathleen Gibbons has been published in *Salon, Stereo Embers, Bird's Thumb* and *Hunger Mountain*. She lives in Central California and Vermont and will be getting her MFA in Writing and Publishing at Vermont College of Fine Arts in May 2018. She is currently working on a memoir about her involvement in the Suzanne Bombardier cold case.
Chicken Soup for the Soul: The Empowered Woman (2018)

Kat Gottlieb is a writer and artist whose stories and creativity encourage others to discover their most authentic, joyful, soulful existence. Gottlieb enjoys sharing life with her husband, six children, three horses and two dogs. See more of her work at KatGottlieb.com.
Chicken Soup for the Soul: Making Me Time (2021)

Award-winner **Melody S. Groves** is a full-time freelance writer living in Albuquerque, NM. She writes fiction and nonfiction Westerns and magazine articles. When not writing, she plays rhythm guitar, tambourine and backup vocals with the Jammy Time Band.
Chicken Soup for the Soul: Christmas Is in the Air (2020)

Nicole Guiltinan is a first-year college student in Northern California. She plans on entering the field of social work, and works on writing poetry in her spare time. Nicole enjoys reading, poetry, and art. E-mail her at nguiltinan@yahoo.com.
Chicken Soup for the Soul: Find Your Inner Strength (2014)

Annette Gulati is a freelance writer and children's author living in Seattle, WA. She's published stories, articles, essays, poems, crafts, and activities in numerous magazines, newspapers, and anthologies. She also writes books for children's educational publishers. Learn more at www.annettegulati.com.
Chicken Soup for the Soul: Making Me Time (2021)

On Mondays, **Rebecca Hill** can often be found "socializing" (i.e., playing with) the cats at the Lange Foundation, searching thrift stores for a new dress or roaming the candy aisle of CVS looking for a special treat. She probably won't answer her phone on a Monday, but you can try e-mailing her at bohoembassy@verizon.net.
Chicken Soup for the Soul: Time to Thrive (2015)

Amelia Hollingsworth wishes everyone could have a friend like Lois Thompson Bartholomew. When Amelia told Lois that she was interested in writing, Lois encouraged her. She mentored Amelia, and even sent her the submission guidelines that led to Amelia's first publication in *Chicken Soup for the Soul: Just for Preteens*.
Chicken Soup for the Soul: The Joy of Less (2016)

Cindy Hudson lives in Portland, OR with her two daughters and a cat named Zipper. The author of *Book by Book: The Complete Guide*

to *Creating Mother-Daughter Book Clubs*, she enjoys writing about the things that inspire her: family life, her community, reading, and family literacy. Learn more at CindyHudson.com.
Chicken Soup for the Soul: Tough Times Won't Last But Tough People Will (2021)

Debby Johnson — Wife. Mother. Karate instructor. Just a few of the labels she proudly wears. As the mother of five she has plenty of tales to tell. Debby has been writing for as long as she can remember and has published several children's books. She loves to hear from her readers so e-mail her at debby@debbyjohnson.com.
Chicken Soup for the Soul: Making Me Time (2021)

Val Jones, a professional freelance writer, has taught English for twenty years. A breast cancer survivor, she founded the Facebook community, Victorious Val & the Breast Cancer Crusaders, to encourage survivors, co-survivors and supporters. When she's not writing, Val volunteers in the breast cancer community.
Chicken Soup for the Soul: Reboot Your Life (2014)

Nancy B. Kennedy is the author of seven books, including four titles in the *Miracles & Moments of Grace* series, a collection of inspiring true-life stories. Her eighth book will tell the dramatic story of the American women suffragists. To learn more about her writing, visit her website at www.nancybkennedy.com.
Chicken Soup for the Soul: The Best Advice I Ever Heard (2018)

Kate Lemery worked for the National Gallery of Art and Smithsonian Institution for fifteen years before becoming a stay-at-home mom. Her writing has appeared in *The Washington Post*, *Motherwell* magazine, and *Fiction Writers Review*. She's finishing her first novel, which combines her love of art history and literature.
Chicken Soup for the Soul: The Power of Yes! (2018)

L. Y. Levand is a fantasy author who occasionally writes nonfiction. She

lives with her husband and their two cats — Frodo and Rosie — who remain convinced that they are, in fact, supreme rulers of the world.
Chicken Soup for the Soul: The Forgiveness Fix (2019)

Patricia Lorenz is the author of fourteen books and hundreds of stories, articles and essays. She has written devotionals for the annual *Daily Guideposts* books for thirty-one years and has been published in sixty *Chicken Soup for the Soul* books. To hire Patricia as a professional speaker contact her at patricialorenz4@gmail.com.
Chicken Soup for the Soul: Age Is Just a Number (2020)

Michelle Mach is a freelance writer in Colorado. Her stories have appeared in several anthologies, including *Chicken Soup for the Shopper's Soul* and *Chicken Soup for the Coffee Lover's Soul*. Visit her website at www.michellemach.com.
Chicken Soup for the Soul: Count Your Blessings (2009)

Lauren Magliaro lives in Northern New Jersey with her husband, twelve-year-old son, and lots of fish and other saltwater creatures. She enjoys reading, Springsteen, and the New York Yankees. This is her second story in the *Chicken Soup for the Soul* series and she dreams of writing a tween book someday. E-mail her at LaurenMags19@aol.com.
Chicken Soup for the Soul: The Forgiveness Fix (2019)

James C. Magruder is the author of *The Glimpse*, an inspirational novel, as well as many reflective essays. He has been published in nine *Chicken Soup for the Soul* books and many national publications. Visit his website at jamescmagruder.com to read his blog and sign up for his inspiring newsletter, *Pause More. Rush Less.*
Chicken Soup for the Soul: Making Me Time (2021)

Kathryn Malnight has been published several times before, and this is her second story in a *Chicken Soup for the Soul* book. As of right now, she lives with her four awesome siblings and parents. She enjoys film, reading, writing (obviously), Broadway musicals, and working

with kids with special needs.
Chicken Soup for the Soul: The Power of Forgiveness (2014)

Scott Martin and Coryanne Hicks are co-authors of the inspirational memoir *Moving Forward In Reverse*, available exclusively on Amazon in late 2012 and various other retail outlets in 2013. This story has been adapted for the good folks at Chicken Soup for the Soul and you, the reader. Visit scomartin.com to learn more.
Chicken Soup for the Soul: The Power of Positive (2012)

Nancy Martinz is a retired federal law enforcement officer. Her thirty-one year career was completed at Jewel Cave National Monument as the Chief Park Ranger. She lives in Custer, SD with her husband Duane and raises two boys. Her passion for protecting America's national treasures was evident wherever she worked.
Chicken Soup for the Soul: Be You (2021)

Ian McCammon is an outgoing guy from Sugar Land, TX. This story is for him as well as the many people who will be inspired to be themselves and not let anyone get in their way.
Chicken Soup for the Soul: Find Your Inner Strength (2014)

Audrey McLaughlin lives in Pittsburgh, PA, with her husband Tom, spending her winters in Florida. She retired after working twenty-seven years in early childhood education. She enjoys writing and sharing what she has learned from working with young children, their families, and her personal life experiences. E-mail her at audreylengyel@comcast.net.
Chicken Soup for the Soul: The Power of Positive (2012)

Brianna Mears is a high school student from Austin, TX. She feels the most herself on the court with her tennis team and enjoys spending time with friends. Brianna has always enjoyed her academic courses, but has recently discovered her passion for English and writing.
Chicken Soup for the Soul: Time to Thrive (2015)

Mary Anne Molcan is currently a fine arts student at North Island College on Vancouver Island. She has published poetry in a local magazine and plans to continue sharing her words and artwork so that others can learn about themselves. Mary Anne can be contacted via at faerie.artiste@gmail.com.
Chicken Soup for the Soul: The Power of Positive (2012)

Ann Morrow is a writer, photographer and frequent contributor to the *Chicken Soup for the Soul* series. She lives in the Black Hills of South Dakota, where she consults the trail often. Read more of Ann's work, and see her trail photos at annmorrow.net.
Chicken Soup for the Soul: Running for Good (2019)

A recent, self-described escapee of the corporate world, **Lauren Mosher** now enjoys a career with a dog-walking company. She is devoted to her volunteer work with animal-rescue nonprofits and human-welfare organizations. She believes that living life in service to others is paramount. Her favorite color is pink.
Chicken Soup for the Soul: Think Positive, Live Happy (2019)

Courtney Lynn Mroch is the Ambassador of Dark and Paranormal Tourism for Haunt Jaunts, a travel site for restless spirits. When she's not exploring haunted places or writing, it's a safe bet you'll find her on a tennis court or yoga mat somewhere. She lives in Nashville, TN with her husband.
Chicken Soup for the Soul: Curvy & Confident (2016)

Rachel Dunstan Muller is a professional storyteller and the author of four children's novels. She is married to her best friend of thirty years, and they have five children and three grandchildren. They call Vancouver Island, on the west coast of Canada, home. Learn more at www.racheldunstanmuller.com.
Chicken Soup for the Soul: Be You (2021)

Trudie Nash, a retired educator, has worked for over forty years with the Greenville County School District. She received her Bachelor of Arts degree from Winston-Salem State University and her Master's of Education from Columbia College. She is the grandmother of three of the world's most adorable children.
Chicken Soup for the Soul: Best Mom Ever! (2017)

Catina Noble received her Bachelor of Arts in psychology from Carleton University in 2009. She lives in Ottawa, Ontario with her four children. Catina enjoys reading, writing and taking photos. Catina plans on writing a novel at some point. E-mail her at catina.noble@yahoo.ca.
Chicken Soup for the Soul: Reader's Choice (2013)

Alli Page is a special needs tutor and founder of exhilaratedliving. org, an inspirational website designed to help readers lead fulfilled, healthy lives daily. When she is not writing or tutoring, you can find Alli playing her cello or ukulele and dreaming of further travel adventures.
Chicken Soup for the Soul: Reboot Your Life (2014)

Ava Pennington is a writer, speaker, and Bible teacher. She writes for nationally circulated magazines and is published in thirty-two anthologies, including twenty-five *Chicken Soup for the Soul* books. She also authored *Daily Reflections on the Names of God: A Devotional*, endorsed by Kay Arthur. Learn more at AvaWrites.com.
Chicken Soup for the Soul: Step Outside Your Comfort Zone (2017)

Stuart M. Perkins enjoys relating observations of everyday life and sharing recollections of growing up in a large Southern family. He believes that layers of ordinary reality can be peeled back to reveal humorous or poignant themes. Stuart blogs his observations at storyshucker.wordpress.com.
Chicken Soup for the Soul: Volunteering & Giving Back (2015)

Lori Phillips has a B.A. in communications and Master's of Education. She is an editor for BellaOnline.com and writes about living simply,

Japanese food, marriage, self-help and spirituality. E-mail her at hope037@ hotmail.com.
Chicken Soup for the Soul: Inspiration for the Young at Heart (2011)

Pam Phree retired from Social Service in 2017 to become a full-time writer. She is nearing completion on her latest novel about life in heaven. She lives in Ellensburg, WA with her dog, Bella.
Chicken Soup for the Soul: Think Positive, Live Happy (2019)

Winter Desiree Prosapio is a humor columnist and novelist in the Texas Hill Country. She has written trivia books, mysteries, and a few truly hilarious e-mails. She is a mom, a rabble-rouser, and enthusiastic dog person. You can read more about her writing life at wdprosapio.com.
Chicken Soup for the Soul: Life Lessons from the Dog (2019)

Jennifer Quasha has been a freelance writer and editor since 1998, and she loves to write for the *Chicken Soup for the Soul* series. When she's not writing, editing, or reading, you'll find her chasing after her human and canine family members, or asleep. Learn more at www.jenniferquasha.com and www.smallpawsbarefeet.com.
Chicken Soup for the Soul: Find Your Inner Strength (2014)

Jennifer Reed received her MFA in Writing from Vermont College of Fine Arts in 2013. She has published over thirty books for children, with a focus on educational nonfiction books. Jennifer enjoys traveling, gardening and paper quilling. She lives in Maryland with her husband and two dogs.
Chicken Soup for the Soul: The Power of Gratitude (2016)

When she isn't writing or editing, **Carol McAdoo Rehme** runs errands, runs after grandkids, runs the household — and might even run for office. Anything is possible! Coauthor of five gift books, she has compiled several others, most recently *Chicken Soup for the Soul: Empty Nesters*. Visit her at: www.rehme.com.
Chicken Soup for the Soul: Runners (2010)

Jayna Richardson graduated from the University of Central Arkansas with a double major in English and Writing. She loves reading, writing, and exploring the world with her husband and kids.
Chicken Soup for the Soul: The Best Advice I Ever Heard (2018)

Mark Rickerby is a writer, screenwriter, singer, voice artist and multiple Chicken Soup for the Soul contributor. His proudest achievements are his daughters, Marli and Emma. He released a CD of fifteen original songs for them, and co-wrote his father's memoir. For info on these and other projects, visit www.markrickerby.com.
Chicken Soup for the Soul: The Power of Forgiveness (2014)

Kimberly Ross, M.Div. is a spiritual teacher and writer living in the Kansas City, MO metro area. She is the mother of three wonderful adults and grandmother to two feisty grandchildren. "Three Choices" is her fourth essay to be published in the *Chicken Soup for the Soul* series.
Chicken Soup for the Soul: The Best Advice I Ever Heard (2018)

Nicole K. Ross is a corporate marketer, freelance copywriter, aspiring novelist, recovering blogger, and chronic hobbyist who is equally at home on the back of a horse, inside the boxing ring, pounding away at her keyboard, or perched in downward dog atop her yoga mat. Learn more at nicolekristineross.com.
Chicken Soup for the Soul: Reboot Your Life (2014)

Larry Schardt, PhD, is a motivational speaker, facilitator, professor at Penn State and Pitt, and writer. Larry enjoys writing, reading, speaking, walking, community, skiing, football, and friends. His current projects are *The Magic in Every Moment* (non-fiction) and *The Angel of the Mountain* (fiction). Visit themagicineverymoment.com or e-mail him at larryschardt@gmail.com.
Chicken Soup for the Soul: Find Your Inner Strength (2014)

Deborah Shouse is a speaker, writer, and editor. She loves helping people write and edit books and she enjoys facilitating creativity and

storytelling workshops. Deborah donates all proceeds from her book *Love in the Land of Dementia: Finding Hope in the Caregiver's Journey to Alzheimer's*. Visit www.thecreativityconnection.com and read http://deborahshousewrites.wordpress.com.
Chicken Soup for the Soul: Find Your Inner Strength (2014)

Billie Holladay Skelley received her bachelor's and master's degrees from the University of Wisconsin–Madison. A retired clinical nurse specialist, she is the mother of four and grandmother of two. Billie enjoys writing, and her work crosses several genres. She spends her non-writing time reading, gardening, and traveling.
Chicken Soup for the Soul: The Best Advice I Ever Heard (2018)

Doug Sletten taught in the public schools for a number of years before going into business for himself. He wrote a humor column in a weekly newspaper for twenty-five years. He has two children, Mitch and Sara, and currently lives in Mesa, AZ with his fiancée Kathi.
Chicken Soup for the Soul: The Power of Yes! (2018)

Aleksandra Slijepcevic has been writing about yoga, health, and mental wellness since 2015. She is a yoga teacher and energy healer, and lives in Delaware. Aleksandra enjoys traveling the world and hiking the world's most beautiful mountains. She is currently writing a book about living your most authentic, wholesome life.
Chicken Soup for the Soul: Be You (2021)

Michael T. Smith lives in Caldwell, ID with his lovely wife Ginny. He works as a project manager and writes inspiration in his spare time. Sign up for a weekly story at visitor.constantcontact.com/d.jsp?m=1101828445578&p=oi or read more stories at ourecho.com/biography-353-Michael-Timothy-Smith.shtml#stories.
Chicken Soup for the Soul: The Power of Forgiveness (2014)

Deborah Starling is a graduate of Carlow University with a master's in creative writing and a bachelor's in social work. She utilizes her

education, experience and skills to help students achieve academic excellence. Debbie gives all honor and glory to the Lord and dedicates her story to her mother, father and Aunt Ruby.
Chicken Soup for the Soul: Navigating Eldercare & Dementia (2021)

James Strickland moved to NYC after graduating from the University of Texas at Austin with degrees in sociology and psychology. James worked as a case manager in the homeless shelter system until 2004 and has volunteered at God's Love We Deliver since 1987. James also participates in his church and spends time with his Yorkie, Zeke.
Chicken Soup for the Soul: Volunteering & Giving Back (2015)

Still a beach girl, **JC Sullivan** tries to make me time and often meets friends for walks. She feels that by encouraging others, we can keep each other on a healthy track, which is more important than ever. Small steps day after day add up to make a big difference, so please walk or (favorite exercise) on! E-mail her at poetrybyjc@yahoo.com.
Chicken Soup for the Soul: Making Me Time (2021)

Lynn Sunday is an artist, writer, and animal advocate who lives near San Francisco, CA. Her stories have appeared in eleven *Chicken Soup for the Soul* books and numerous other publications. E-mail her at sunday11@aol.com.
Chicken Soup for the Soul: The Forgiveness Fix (2019)

Lisa Swan is a University of Texas at Austin graduate who lives in New York City. She has written for a variety of publications, including *Guideposts*, the *New York Daily News*, and *The Washington Post*. Lisa is also a back-of-the-pack runner, triathlete, and eight-time marathoner whose goal is to run marathons in all fifty states.
Chicken Soup for the Soul: Think Positive, Live Happy (2019)

Annmarie B. Tait resides in Conshohocken, PA, with her husband Joe Beck. Annmarie has stories published in several *Chicken Soup for the Soul* volumes, *Reminisce* magazine, *Patchwork Path*, and many other

anthologies. Annmarie is a current nominee for the 2011 Pushcart Prize. E-mail Annmarie at irishbloom@aol.com.
Chicken Soup for the Soul: The Power of Positive (2012)

Tsgoyna Tanzman's career spans from belly dancer to speech patholo- gist to fitness trainer to memoir teacher. Writing is her "therapy" for raising her adolescent daughter. Published in nine *Chicken Soup for the Soul* books, her essays and poems can be read at More.com, mothering. com and in *The Orange County Register*. E-mail her at tnzmn@cox.net.
Chicken Soup for the Soul: The Power of Positive (2012)

Cassandra L. Tavaras is an aspiring writer from Lynn, MA. She is pas- sionate about all things natural hair, empowerment, positive affirmations, education, music, dancing and living her best life. She is currently a youth development program evaluator and Zumba instructor.
Chicken Soup for the Soul: I'm Speaking Now (2021)

Kamia Taylor is a real estate paralegal who changed her life by mov- ing from Los Angeles, CA to a small organic farm in the Midwest. She began writing professionally and doing large black dog rescue after becoming disabled because a drunk driver hit her truck head-on at 70 mph. E-mail her at bigblackdogrescue@gmail.com.
Chicken Soup for the Soul: The Joy of Less (2016)

Jayne Thurber-Smith is an international award-winning freelance writer for various outlets including *Faith & Friends* magazine, *Sports Spectrum* and writersweekly.com. She loves tennis, swimming, horseback riding and being included in whatever her husband and/or their four adult children have going on.
Chicken Soup for the Soul: Making Me Time (2021)

Miriam Van Scott is an author and photographer who works in a variety of media, including print, television and online content. Her books include *Song of Old*, *Encyclopedia of Hell*, *Candy Canes in Bethlehem* and the *Shakespeare Goes Pop!* series. For clips, photos and to learn

more visit miriamvanscott.com.
Chicken Soup for the Soul: The Best Advice I Ever Heard (2018)

Jessie Wagoner is the laughing lady behind the www.thenilaughed.com. She is mom to one wonderful son and is a full-time reporter. In her little free time she enjoys traveling, reading and going on adventures with her son.
Chicken Soup for the Soul: Reboot Your Life (2014)

Nick Walker is an on-camera meteorologist on *The Weather Channel*, a voice over narrator, speaker, writer and The Weather Dude®, educating young people about weather through music. He writes the "Tales from a Weathered Man" blog and podcast at nickwalkerblog.com.
Chicken Soup for the Soul: Think Positive, Live Happy (2019)

Susan Walker has the free-spirited soul of a gypsy, and the heart of a warrior. An Air Force veteran, she loves telling a story that will touch her readers. She lives in central Texas with a muse who demands lots of time off to play between books and snacks. Lots of snacks.
Chicken Soup for the Soul: The Best Advice I Ever Heard (2018)

Joan Wasson received her Bachelor of Arts degree, with an emphasis in Accounting, from California State University, Fullerton in 1979. She lives with her husband Charlie in Orange, CA and enjoys teaching children.
Chicken Soup for the Soul: The Joy of Less (2016)

Fred Webber holds the British Columbia Provincial Instructors Diploma and still teaches part-time for the Laborers' Union. He plays bass in a popular classic rock band and writes and records original music. He lives with his beautiful wife of forty years and a black Lab named Becky, in Harrison Hot Springs, BC.
Chicken Soup for the Soul: Age Is Just a Number (2020)

Aimee Mae Wiley is a wife, mother, writer, and editor living in historic Cedarburg, WI. She recently started her own writing and editing business, and for fun she also blogs about faith, family, and simple living. In her free time, Aimee enjoys frequenting local libraries and parks with her five children.
Chicken Soup for the Soul: Random Acts of Kindness (2017)

Robin Howard Will lives in rural Pennsylvania with her husband of almost forty years. She is the mother of two beautiful daughters, and Gigi to the sweetest granddaughter ever. She loves writing, reading, sewing, crafting, baking, and upcycling things that other people throw away. She is currently writing an inspirational memoir.
Chicken Soup for the Soul: Age Is Just a Number (2020)

Ferida Wolff is author of seventeen children's books and three essay books, her latest being the award-winning picture book *The Story Blanket* and *Missed Perceptions: Challenge Your Thoughts Change Your Thinking*. Her work appears in anthologies, newspapers, magazines, and in her nature blog feridasbackyard.blogspot.com. E-mail her at feridawolff@msn.com.
Chicken Soup for the Soul: The Power of Positive (2012)

Deborah K. Wood is a writer, consultant, life coach, and adventurer on the journey of Life. She has been writing (and rewriting) forever, and believes in the healing power of telling one's story.
Chicken Soup for the Soul: Reboot Your Life (2014)

Maxine Young is a writer based in New York City. She is an avid listener of audiobooks, a passionate lover of tea and an enduring fighter of multiple sclerosis. She is a big fan of planting seeds of encouragement. E-mail her at maxiney7@gmail.com.
Chicken Soup for the Soul: Curvy & Confident (2016)

Meet Amy Newmark

Amy Newmark is the bestselling author, editor-in-chief, and publisher of the *Chicken Soup for the Soul* book series. Since 2008, she has published 182 new books, most of them national bestsellers in the U.S. and Canada, more than doubling the number of Chicken Soup for the Soul titles in print today. She is also the author of *Simply Happy*, a crash course in Chicken Soup for the Soul advice and wisdom that is filled with easy-to-implement, practical tips for enjoying a better life.

Amy is credited with revitalizing the Chicken Soup for the Soul brand, which has been a publishing industry phenomenon since the first book came out in 1993. By compiling inspirational and aspirational true stories curated from ordinary people who have had extraordinary experiences, Amy has kept the twenty-nine-year-old Chicken Soup for the Soul brand fresh and relevant.

Amy graduated *magna cum laude* from Harvard University where she majored in Portuguese and minored in French. She then embarked on a three-decade career as a Wall Street analyst, a hedge fund manager, and a corporate executive in the technology field. She is a Chartered Financial Analyst.

Her return to literary pursuits was inevitable, as her honors thesis in college involved traveling throughout Brazil's impoverished northeast region, collecting stories from regular people. She is delighted to have come full circle in her writing career — from collecting stories "from the people" in Brazil as a twenty-year-old to, three decades later, collecting stories "from the people" for Chicken Soup for the Soul.

When Amy and her husband Bill, the CEO of Chicken Soup for the Soul, are not working, they are visiting their four grown children and their spouses, and their four grandchildren.

Follow Amy on Twitter @amynewmark. Listen to her free podcast — Chicken Soup for the Soul with Amy Newmark — on Apple, Google, or by using your favorite podcast app on your phone.

Sharing Happiness, Inspiration, and Hope

Real people sharing real stories, every day, all over the world. In 2007, *USA Today* named *Chicken Soup for the Soul* one of the five most memorable books in the last quarter-century. With over 110 million books sold to date in the U.S. and Canada alone, more than 300 titles in print, and translations into nearly fifty languages, "chicken soup for the soul®" is one of the world's best-known phrases.

Today, twenty-nine years after we first began sharing happiness, inspiration and hope through our books, we continue to delight our readers with new titles, but have also evolved beyond the bookshelves with super premium pet food, television shows, a podcast, video journalism from aplus.com, licensed products, and free movies and TV shows on our Popcornflix and Crackle apps. We are busy "changing your world one story at a time®." Thanks for reading!

Share with Us

We all have had Chicken Soup for the Soul moments in our lives. If you would like to share your story or poem with millions of people around the world, go to chickensoup.com and click on Submit Your Story. You may be able to help another reader and become a published author at the same time. Some of our past contributors have launched writing and speaking careers from the publication of their stories in our books!

We only accept story submissions via our website. They are no longer accepted via mail or fax. Visit our website, www.chickensoup.com, and click on Submit Your Story for our writing guidelines and a list of topics we are working on.

To contact us regarding other matters, please send us an e-mail through webmaster@chickensoupforthesoul.com, or fax or write us at:

Chicken Soup for the Soul
P.O. Box 700
Cos Cob, CT 06807-0700
Fax: 203-861-7194

One more note from your friends at Chicken Soup for the Soul: Occasionally, we receive an unsolicited book manuscript from one of our readers, and we would like to respectfully inform you that we do not accept unsolicited manuscripts, and we must discard the ones that appear.

Paperback: 978-1-61159-093-7

eBook: 978-1-61159-331-0

More feel-good stories

Chicken Soup for the Soul

Kindness Matters

101 Feel-Good Stories of Compassion & Paying It Forward

Amy Newmark

Paperback: 978-1-61159-088-3
eBook: 978-1-61159-325-9

with a positive perspective

Chicken Soup for the Soul

Think Positive, Live Happy

101 Stories about Creating Your Best Life

Amy Newmark
& Deborah Norville
Journalist and Anchor of *Inside Edition*

Paperback: 978-1-61159-992-3
eBook: 978-1-61159-293-1

More great tips and advice

Changing your life one story at a time®
www.chickensoup.com